Aging in America

c

Aging in America:

AN INTRODUCTION TO GERONTOLOGY

SANDRA ZINS

Hutchinson Area Vocational-Technical Institute

 Delmar Publishers Inc.®

NOTICE TO THE READER

Publisher does not warrant or guarantee any of the products described herein or perform any independent analysis in connection with any of the product information contained herein. Publisher does not assume, and expressly disclaims, any obligation to obtain and include information other than that provided to it by the manufacturer.

The reader is expressly warned to consider and adopt all safety precautions that might be indicated by the activities described herein and to avoid all potential hazards. By following the instructions contained herein, the reader willingly assumes all risks in connection with such instructions.

The publisher makes no representations or warranties of any kind, including but not limited to, the warranties of fitness for particular purpose or merchantability, nor are any such representations implied with respect to the material set forth herein, and the publisher takes no responsibility with respect to such material. The publisher shall not be liable for any special, consequential or exemplary damages resulting, in whole or in part, from the readers' use of, or reliance upon, this material.

Text Prepared by
 Scharff Associates, Ltd.

Delmar Staff
 Administrative Editor: Leslie Boyer
 Associate Editor: Karen Lavroff

For information, address Delmar Publishers Inc.
2 Computer Drive West, Box 15-015
Albany, New York 12212

Printed in the United States of America
Published simultaneously in Canada
by Nelson Canada
A Division of International Thomson Limited

10 9 8 7 6 5 4 3 2

Library of Congress Cataloging in Publication Data

Zins, Sandra.
 Aging in America.

 Bibliography: p.
 1. Gerontology—United States.   I. Title.
HQ1064.U5Z56   1987   305.2'6'0973   87-5304
ISBN 0-8273-2825-7 (pbk.)

CONTENTS

Chapter 9   *PRERETIREMENT-RETIREMENT*

Chapter 10   *MYTHS*

Chapter 11   *REALITY OF OUR AGING*

Chapter 12   CAREERS IN GERONTOLOGY

PREFACE

For everything and everyone, there is a time and a place. For the dispelling of myths and stereotypes faced by an aging generation of peole who have no reason to deserve them, the time is now and the place is the United States.

The author's attitude toward aging has made its way into *Aging in America* somewhere between the lines. That attitude can be summed up in the phrase, "A sunset can be as beautiful as a sunrise." In fact, when seeing a picture depicting either event, the viewer could not distinguish which it is, and perhaps the choice of sunset or sunrise would be only in the mind of the beholder. When all is read, believed or denied, and lived, is not how well we have aged in the attitude of the ager?

Aging in America: An Introduction to Gerontology meets two major goals. First, it introduces the multidisciplinary study of aging to readers of all ages—the student, the professional, and other interested people. It is done in a manner that has the statistics demanded by the scholar, the facts desired by the professional, and the readability appreciated by the general public. Second, it assists the reader by containing definitions within the text, plus exercises, reviews, and extended reading suggestions to aid anyone who wishes to pursue any topic in depth. Without the author's deliberate intent, the readers will not get very far before they hear a laugh or feel a smile; and who is to say whether that laugh or smile may be the fountain of youth or the Shangri La that will keep us all young at heart.

What causes aging? If *Aging in America* contained the answer to this question, it would be on the best seller list because an answer to that question would also provide the much sought-after method to stop or reverse aging. Instead, this book is about how to slow down the process of aging. It presents the sociological, psychological, and physiological aspects of aging. The student, the health care worker, and the interested reader, young or old, can see the impact all facets of aging have on the total person. Lest the readers apply the information only to other people who they believe are aging, Chapter 11 is a reminder that when it comes to the passage of time, the calendar plays no favorites. This textbook presents aging as it *can* be: full of potential, rewarding relationships, and joy. Can we ask more of any age?

ACKNOWLEDGMENTS

For the statistics and theories in *Aging in America,* the author has called on the great champions in the field of gerontology. To the following distinguished textbook authors, I credit this text: Lewis Aiken, Barbara G. Anderson, Robert C. Atchley, James E. Birren, Robert N. Butler, David H. Fischer, Elizabeth J. Forbes/Virginia M. Fitzsimons, Diana K. Harris/ William E. Cole, Margaret H. Huyck, Richard A. Kalish, Marguerite D. Kermis, Maggie Kuhn, Sheila McKenzie, Ashley Montagu, John W. Santrock, Arthur N. Schwartz/Cherie L. Snyder/James A. Peterson, Diana S. Woodruff, and other authors whom such a listing always inadvertently misses.

No one person writes a book. Many people contribute their knowledge, skills, patience, and encouragement in countless ways to make it all happen. Individuals whose skills are most visible in the book are photographer Dawn Stamness, cartoonist Bill Haas, and proofreader Barb Peterson. Not as visible but present nonetheless were:

Carol Adams	Mary Anderson	Julie Fischer Becker
Leslie Boyer	Pat and Marty Ernst	Joyce Evenski
Mary Brown	David and Marilyn Gleisner	Linda Lorenzen-Groth
Paul Ginkel	Karen Lavroff	Chris Marsh
Vern Hartfield	Kris Swanson	Wallace Zins
Doris Smith		

and Hutchinson A.V.T.I. for their support of the gerontology program.

Special gratitude goes to my mother, whose daily life demonstrates the most successful way to age; to my brother Bryan and sister Linda, who never seem to age; and to my beautiful son Brent, who still has all the joys of aging to experience.

S.Z.W.

Aging in America
Need not mean falling from place,
But rising to new and different experiences,
Not closing but opening,
Not shrinking but growing,
Not becoming less
But becoming more.

(Text taken from Beverly Enterprises 1985 Annual Report. Used with permission.)

CHAPTER
1
Introduction to Aging

Learning Objectives

After studying this chapter, the reader should be able to:

- Define *aging* and *old age* as they were defined historically and as they are presently defined by society.
- List three theories societies used to explain how people reached unusually old ages.
- Realize that all individuals grow older, mature, and develop at different rates and in different ways.
- Understand the psychological, social, and biological factors that affect aging.

Preview

Before reading this book, select the correct answer to each of the following "True or False" statements.

1. All the needs of the elderly can be met by the services of a nursing home.   T   F
2. All older people are neglected or ignored by family.   T   F
3. Most elderly people feel that it is their children's responsibility to care for them in old age.   T   F
4. Grandparenting is universally enjoyed.   T   F
5. As people grow older they become more alike.   T   F
6. Elderly people, as individuals or as workers, are less creative, productive, and efficient than younger people.   T   F
7. Older people tend to be inflexible and obstinate.   T   F
8. The performance of elderly persons in IQ tests is lower than that of young adults.   T   F
9. As people become older, they are likely to become more religious.   T   F
10. Most older people are lonely and isolated.   T   F
11. Old age is generally a period of serenity.   T   F
12. Retirement has a negative effect on health and in some instances can lead to premature death.   T   F
13. Medical problems in the elderly are assumed to be the inevitable consequences of aging.   T   F
14. Old age is sexless.   T   F
15. If people live long enough, they will become senile.   T   F
16. Older people complain the most about their health.   T   F

There are people who believe that some of these statements are TRUE. This reflects a way of thinking that is untrue or overly negative. To some extent, older people themselves may believe some of these statements to be factual. The impact of society's or elderly people's erroneous beliefs about aging is great in terms of psychological and social stress. This book attempts to dispel these myths and misunderstandings so aging can be fully appreciated by society and anticipated and enjoyed by the individual.

This chapter introduces the multidisciplinary field of gerontology and defines aging and other common terms related to aging. It examines the effects of ageist philosophies on society and how they have become part of America's social fabric.

Our first goal is to define *aging* and *old age*. We can start the easy way, by consulting *Webster's New World Dictionary:*

[Aging or Ageing], to grow old or mature; show signs of growing old. [Old], 1. having lived or been in existence for a long time; aged. 2. of a characteristic of aged people; mature in judgment, etc.; wise. 3. of a certain age.

Communication from a Flying Saucer

"The trouble with earthlings is their early adulthood. As long as they are young, they are lovable, open-hearted, tolerant, eager to learn and to collaborate. They can even be induced to play with one another. The only educational problem earth has is how to keep them young."

(Montagu 1983, xi)

WHAT IS AGING?

Aging is what happens to you as you read this paragraph. You will be older when you reach the period at the end of this sentence than when you began reading it. Every human being shares this common experience with

FIGURE 1.1

every other human being regardless of age, sex, or race. Denial of this aging process will not stop it or reverse it. Aging is a natural, progressive process that begins at the moment of conception and continues until it is ended by death.

Age is a central topic in human thought. When young we tend to view aging as something exciting, eagerly anticipating growing up, and when old—facing physical decline—as something depressing. With typical human perversity, we nearly always want to be an age we are not (*Reader's Digest,* June 1984, 27).

No age is inherently miserable or inherently sublime. Every stage in life, including old age, has problems to be solved, joys to be experienced, fears to be reckoned with, and potential still to be experienced.

WHEN WILL YOU BE OLD?

It depends on the age of the person you ask. A poll of 1,007 people conducted by Cadwell Davis Partners asked the question, "What's old age?" As can be seen in Table 1.1, the results showed that the younger the respondent, the younger the age chosen as old. Likewise, the older the respondent, the older the age chosen as old.

> "To be seventy years young is sometimes more hopeful than to be forty years old."
>
> Oliver Wendell Holmes

TABLE 1.1
What's old age?

Age of respondent	Age cited as "getting older"
Under 30	62.7
30-39	66.5
40-49	69.6
50-59	71.0
60-64	72.5
65 and older	75.2

Cadwell Davis Partners poll, reported in *USA Today.* "USA Snapshots," January 14, 1986.

Even George Burns, in his humorous manner, tackles this question. He states, "Old is when you stoop to tie your shoelaces and ask yourself, 'What else can I do while I'm down here?' (Burns 1983, 23)." Although this is a tongue-in-cheek answer, it may, in fact, have a theoretical basis. Age can best be defined as an attitude. Therefore, when we believe we are old, then perhaps we are.

The question of what is old age requires a more complicated explanation than the definition of aging. Aging is a process, whereas the aged are people! Oldness may not be the mere passage of time. For example, some individuals may appear old at forty-five years of age and some may appear young at sixty-five years of age. Perhaps age is in the eye of the beholder!

On admission to the nursing home, each new resident was interviewed by a social worker. During one session, an alert, twinkling-eyed, ninety-six-year-old man was asked, "Did you have a happy childhood?" "So far, so good!" he replied.

Answers to the question "When will you be old?" as well as to other questions concerning aging appear ambiguous because the human stages of birth, maturation, and death may have received equal curiosity but not equal attention and research. Many library shelves overflow with prenatal and child development books. Adequate volumes are available on the teen-age years, but fewer volumes occupy space on the topic of middle age and sparse are the number of books found on old age. In fact, some libraries may not have a shelf labeled "gerontology."

IS "OLD" MYSTICAL OR MAGICAL?

During some periods in history, life spans did not exceed twenty years. This may be one reason few or no studies were done on aging. Perhaps this is the reason old age was associated with myths, mysticism, and superstition. People who survived to later years were given special status or titles accompanied by authority because to have reached old age was to have survived hardships other people did not. Such survival took magical power bestowed by Someone greater than man or woman.

The desire for a longer life has been the subject of search and research for centuries. Curiosity and philosophy about aging and the secrets of long life are as old as history. Four basic theories emerged to explain why some people experienced longer lives than others or how they intend to do so. These theories are:

1. Rejuvenescent theory
2. Hyperborean theory
3. Antediluvian theory
4. Cryonian theory

Rejuvenescent Theory

This theory is best explained by the legend of Ponce de Leon, a Spanish explorer, who went in search of the fountain of youth as early as 1512. It

FIGURE 1.2

was believed that a fountain of special water existed that if drunk or bathed in would rejuvenate or refresh the individual and prevent or reverse aging.

> Ponce de Leon searched for the magical fountain in the territories now called Florida. He died at the age of forty-seven.

Today, the modern fountain of youth stories come from Romania where shots of Gerovital are given or from Switzerland where doctors inject live cells from unborn sheep into high-paying clients. This procedure stems from the belief that certain hormones not present in adult animals are believed to be in the embryo. When rat embryos were injected into old rats, these rats lived slightly longer than normal. Rats were also treated with megadoses of various antioxidants. They have also been given Vitamin E and lecithin, two more examples that are believed to be longevity potions. Such procedures capture the imagination of people. However, an old and often used saying is appropriate here: "It's a rat race and the rats are ahead," for there is no scientific proof that any of these methods have retarded or reversed the aging process in humans.

Hyperborean Theory

This was a Greek belief that somewhere (**hyper,** meaning *beyond* and **Boreas** meaning *northwind*) was a culture where people enjoyed unusually long life. This society was also free of all natural ills. In modern times, the concept was resurrected in the form of a Shangri-La. The location most often notated as a contemporary Shangri-La is the Caucasus region of the USSR, where the Abkhazians are reputed to live to be 115 and older. (There are some claims of a 168-year-old Russian peasant, but the average life-expectancy in Russia is barely 75 years.) Two lesser known regions are Hunza in Pakistan and Vilcabamba in Ecuador, where many elderly people claim to be well past the age of 100.

Antediluvian Theory

The antediluvian theory was the belief that people of the past lived to be much older than any present standards of old. To live to be 900 years of age or more was thought to be common. Some tribes of Northern Japan believed this long life was achieved by people who shed their skins like snakes.

Cryonian Theory

This twentieth-century theory involves a small but growing number of individuals who have arranged to have their bodies or brains frozen at death and stored—for centuries if needed—in the belief that technology will find a way to rebuild, revive, or clone them. To date, a Fullerton, California, cryonics group has six members "in suspension" (Elias, October 25, 1985).

Scientific Research

Not until 1835 did serious scientific research on aging begin. A Belgian scientist and perhaps the first gerontologist, Lambert A. Quitelet, published his findings on age and productivity. He introduced the concept that aging varies in each person and that this variation results from natural causes. He concluded that decline due to age began between fifty to fifty-five years of age. Interest in aging continued to focus on longevity—great span of time—and on the physical factors involved in deterioration. In the 1900s, scientists also began to investigate the effects of environmental, social, and psychological elements of aging. Even then, the emphasis continued to be on decline, illness, and pathology—all negative facets of biological aging.

The researchers' conclusions were varied. One biologist stated that eating large quantities of yogurt-like milk accounted for the long life of the Soviet elders. This conclusion has been picked up commercially in the last decade by American yogurt companies. Other biologists supported the theory that heredity is an important factor in reaching old age. Gerontologists in the late 1940s combined earlier studies to declare that both heredity and environment were instrumental in determining longevity.

> Francis Bacon, Francis Galton, and Benjamin Franklin were among the early researchers and writers in the field of aging. They hoped that science would be able to discover the laws governing the aging process, with the goal of rejuvenating people.

Even present-day research does not match in intensity the growing size of the over-sixty-five population. In 1985, one-fourth of the federal government's budget was directly related to the population over age sixty-five. But these dollars were aimed at providing sympathetic relief. Less than a tiny fraction of 1 percent of those allocated dollars were designated for research (Cranston, August 1985). Dr. Robert Butler, chairman of the department of geriatrics at Mt. Sinai Medical Center in New York, believes that amount must triple just to expand research into Alzheimer's disease (*U.S. News & World Report,* July 2, 1984, 52). It would appear that research in the area of aging is still far from reaching its proper position on the priority list. Dr. Edward Schneider of the National Institute on Aging states, "If solving aging were like doing a jigsaw puzzle we've got maybe a 10th of the puzzle done, or less. We're where cancer research was in the 1950s" (Elias, October 25, 1985).

OLD AGE: A DEFINITION

> "Old age is hard to understand for me because I don't really feel old at sixty-nine. But I would say old age is when you like to do something but aren't able to do it."
> (Hilmar Hlavka, personal interview, Dec. 30, 1984)

A common definition of **gerontology**—*Geronto-* a Greek word meaning old man or old age; *–ology* meaning the study of—*is an organized study of the causes and consequences of aging and old age.*

That definition may appear oversimplified. The truth is that there is no adequate definition of aging or old age. What we do know is that each person experiences the process of aging in a very personal and unique manner. We also know that when we talk about old age, we are talking about our own future.

WHAT DO WE CALL THEM?

Many names are adequate, some are accurate, and others are stereotypes. *Older Americans, senior citizens, older adults, old, elderly, aged, aging, golden agers,* and *retirees* are just a few terms used to refer to those

FIGURE 1.3
(From Geriatrics: A Study of Maturity *by Esther*
Caldwell and Barbara R. Hegner, copyright © 1986
by Delmar Publishers Inc.)

golden years, sunset years, retirement years, and the autumn of their lives. Different terms have different meanings. For the purpose of this book, the most accurate term to describe the attitude or meaning we are attempting to convey will be used. We leave it to the reader's discretion to select the one most meaningful to him or her.

> Ed Wynn, the late comedian, had a formula for staying young. He said that instead of worrying about his actual age and feeling old, he picked some important event in his life and figured his age from that point. In his particular case, the event was his marriage. Therefore, he quoted his age twenty to thirty years younger . . . and felt the same.

OLD AGE: A STUDY

> Gerontology differs from geriatrics, which is a special branch of medicine that studies the diseases of old age.

TABLE 1.2
Gerontology is a multidisciplinary study.

Psychology Deals With:	Sociology Deals With:	Biology Deals With:
Intellectual changes	Family relationships	Physiological changes
Patterns of adjustment	Retirement	Anatomical changes
Learning	Social expectations	Disabilities

Gerontology is not a branch of knowledge in and of itself. It is a broad study concerned with every aspect of human activity during the later years of life. Gerontology is thus a multidisciplinary study that must call on the sciences of psychology, sociology, and biology for the answers to such gerontological questions as (see Table 1.2):

1. What is it like to be old?
2. What causes aging?
3. What happens to people as they grow old?

Every field of study that involves people can have a subspecialty in gerontology. There are biologists, economists, psychiatrists, psychologists, architects, sociologists, theologians, and philosophers who specialize in the study of aging.

OLD AGE: A NUMBER

> "We do not count a man's years until he has nothing else to count."
>
> Ralph Waldo Emerson

Chronological age—calendar age—is but a number. Throughout the course of life, we attach number labels to each of life's stages. (See Figure 1.4.)

Along with those number labels goes a set of social, psychological, and physical patterns common to each stage.

Not all gerontologists agree on the number of candles that signify old age. The majority of tax legislation, retirement policies, and, to some degree, popular acceptance seems to set the number at sixty-five. It is important to emphasize that a person will seldom display every social,

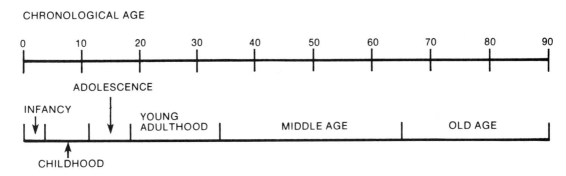

FIGURE 1.4
Life cycle

psychological, or physical characteristic given as a description of a particular stage. It is also interesting to note that everyone is old to someone else.

IS SIXTY-FIVE REALLY OLD?

For the purpose of this textbook, we use the widely accepted age of 65 as old. In literature, however, characters were portrayed to have lived much longer than today's concept of old. To be "as old as Methuselah" meant living to be 969 years old. That age was accepted because it was believed that Noah lived to be 950 years old and that Adam was 930 years old when he died. They were all very young compared to mythological characters. Larek, a god-king of ancient Sumeria, lived to the ripe old age of 28,800 years. Mythology made achievable in the mind what could not be achieved in the body.

TO AGE OR TO ADVANCE IN AGE?

The difference between *aging* and *advancing in age*—to develop or improve—is very important. Aging is the accumulation of calendar time. People age, cars age, and furniture ages. Aging is a universal characteristic. However, cars and furniture do not advance in age. A living or animate organism advances through stages that represent growth and development. It is interesting to note, however, that even with inanimate objects, calendar aging can have positive results. The value of furniture may increase as it takes on the label of antique. Wine reaches its stage of perfection by aging. Add to those positive aspects of calendar time the accumulation effects of *advancing in age,* and suddenly the label *old* takes on positive features we may not have considered before.

The life stages referred to in the life cycle chart (Figure 1.4) were given definite time periods. This is necessary for a convenient frame of reference for specific ages, even though we know that time in a human being's life is an accumulation of knowledge and experience. Therefore, an individual does not automatically become an adult at the age of twenty-one. Some states in which legislation made eighteen years of age adulthood changed their minds and by a stroke of the legislative pen made it age nineteen. Obviously, if the calendar does not make one an adult, neither does it make a person old. Thus, the concept of *advancing in age* has practical value. The knowledge and experience living brings with it shape the uniqueness of every individual. The study of gerontology helps us view the advancement of age from a positive, practical point of view rather than from a mythical, prejudiced point of view.

FIGURE 1.5

It is important to study the advancement of age through all of life's stages because for each stage, including old age, the following statements apply:

1. Each stage has unique challenges to be met.
2. Society has different expectations and demands for individuals in each stage.
3. Some fairly accurate predictions can be made about the psychological, sociological, and physical characteristics of people in each stage.

TYPES OF AGING

The three major areas of aging are:

1. Psychological
2. Sociological
3. Biological

Any one of these three categories would fill a book. Gerontologists cannot address the topic of aging without identifying what category of aging they are dealing with and then calling on that science for information. Since all of these sciences affect a person at the same time, such intertwining causes an overlap of information from science to science. However, each science approaches aging from a different viewpoint.

Psychological Aging

Geropsychology is the branch of psychology that studies the behavior of individuals we refer to as "old." How individuals cope with the experience of aging is as unique as the individuals themselves. For that reason, geropsychology can claim only a limited understanding of the dynamics of behavior in old age. What is normal aging is just as complicated as determining what is normal teen-age behavior. The answer turns out to be another question—"Which old person and which teen-ager are you asking about?" The effect of lifelong experiences, intelligence, motivation, and personality are all determining factors that come under the study of the psychology of aging.

Sociological Aging

This field of study offers insights into the effects of society on the aging person and the effects of the aging person on society. The all-encompassing term society includes close relationships, such as family, friends, clubs, and religious groups, as well as far-reaching aspects of society, including state and national organizations, economics, and politics. When life expectancy was shorter and fewer people survived into later adult years, these people experienced a different status and lived under different role expectations than older people do today. Membership in their family, position in the community, and responsibilities in the work force are sociological changes that have taken place since the beginning of the century. The effects of urbanization, modernization, and the increasing older population comprise major issues for study. Of equal importance is the evolution of intergenerational conflict and stereotyping. Myths concerning the aging process, believed by the old as well as the young, may lead to self-fulfilling prophecies, with an end result of lowering self-esteem, creating poor self-concepts and finally lowering what could have been realistic and achievable expectations and goals for old age.

> "Old people are people who have lived a certain number of years, and that is all. . . . Once an older person comes to be seen, not as old first and provisionally a person second, but as a person who happens also to be old, and who is still as he or she always was, plus experience and minus the consequences of certain physical accidents of time—only then will social gerontology have made its point."
> (Comfort "Age Prejudice in America," 1976, 4)

Biological Aging

Biological aging gives evidence of gradual physical losses. Science's inability to reverse or stop aging means that the continuous use of the body over a long period of time will cause it to act and react more slowly and/or less efficiently than in younger years. Old age brings with it the gradual loss of the body's ability to renew itself. How the individual approaches aging must include the physical and health factors relevant to the process of aging. The changes that occur are, most often, a gradual process. These changes have an accumulative effect rather than an instantaneous effect. Many biological aging changes can be slowed down and, in some cases, reversed when corrective measures as simple as eyewear and hearing aids or in the form of corrective surgery are taken. The most predictable fact is that changes will occur. Many of these changes are in the loss category, not unique to aging but associated with aging. The answer to the question, "What does physical change mean to the older person?" comes under the scope of study called the biology or physiology of aging.

AGING: ON WHAT DO GERONTOLOGISTS DISAGREE/AGREE?

1. *Disagree* — On a single definition of aging.
   Agree — That aging is complex in nature.

Aging involves psychological, sociological, and biological changes which, in turn, affect all facets of everyday life. There is internal as well as external aging. These changes are very gradual and, therefore, nearly imperceptible. Whether or not the signs of aging are noticeable, the passage of time cannot be denied. Neither has the phenomenon of reversal ever taken place. People who were forty years of age never became twenty-nine again except in their conversation!

2. *Disagree* — On how old the body is actually capable of aging.
   Agree — That the biological limit is older than the now 79.5 for males and the 83.9 years for females.

Medical science believes the biological time clock is set somewhere between the 110 and 120 year range. Some doctors even go so far as to set the upper limits of that range at 140. The oldest person on earth whose age has been authenticated is a 120-year-old Japanese man whose name can be found in *Guinness Book of World Records*.

3. *Disagree* — On whether the effects of aging is genetic or environmental.
   Agree — That every person ages at a personal rate and there has to be an explanation for this.

Just as in youth there are early and late bloomers, so in the later stage of life there are early and late agers. We also know that a person may be old physically, young mentally, and middle-aged socially.

It appears that this rate and type of aging is both genetic and environmentally influenced. The "How Old Will You Get To Be" tests, however accurate or inaccurate, are based on family history and environmental factors. The fact that your grandparents lived to be in their nineties may be a plus in your aging favor. However, there may be the added fact that your grandparents did not smoke and consumed alcohol only moderately. Your pack-a-day smoking habit and/or excessive social drinking are environmental factors that may negate your genetic advantage.

4. *Disagree* — On what causes a person to be old.
   Agree — That genetic and environmental factors *affect* aging but it cannot be certain that they *cause* one to age.

It is agreed, however, that when there is an answer to that question, science will have the ability to slow down or stop aging.

OLD AGE: WHY A SUBJECT OF STUDY?

"Why focus attention on people whose lives are nearly over? Why not spend that time on people whose lives have just begun?"

"It is difficult to relate to old age. It is too far away to be realistic to me!"

"Elderly people operate from a different set of values than mine. I can't really identify with them."

Valid arguments? Gerontologists would say, "No!" In order to preserve the dignity of all human beings, we must understand the entire life cycle. We cannot isolate segments of life and still come to understand other members of life's community or ourselves. In fact, the recurring human cycle has always been a source of fascination and interest. Human curiosity in the unfolding drama of human existence is as old as human history itself.

Here are five basic reasons for studying aging:

1. By understanding the concerns of today's elderly people and working toward positive solutions, we prepare an accepting climate when we become the elderly.
2. By understanding and relating to the aging process, we will cease to fear that portion of our life cycle and instead will prepare to enjoy it.

3. By understanding that aging is a developing process, we can use those years to an even greater fulfillment of our life's goals.
4. By understanding the people of all age groups, we can enjoy, as a total community, what every person has to contribute.
5. By understanding that life is a continuum—something whose parts cannot be separated—beginning at conception and ending at death, we can approach later life, not as a problem but as a completion of earlier stages.

HOW AGING AFFECTS THE SOCIAL SYSTEM

Society must respond to the impact aging has on it. Ignoring it only magnifies the problem. Modern science has extended the quantity of life. It is up to society to help extend the quality of life. However, society is poorly prepared to deal with the increasing number of the elderly.

Society's usual response in dealing with a dilemma is to react through:

1. Cultural ideas.
2. Media.
3. Education.

What society learns through these avenues forms the attitudes and actions that result. Americans appear to be confused. Thoughts on aging range from a slight attraction to retirement to total repulsion. On the surface, people appear to be positive about aging—particularly about other people's aging. But for the most part, the thought of getting old is threatening. It endangers some of the basic social values. Four of those fundamental social values are:

1. Family security.
2. Freedom of choice.
3. Independence.
4. General happiness.

These values are vulnerable to the aging process because aging presents uncertainty. For example:

1. Will there be a family member who will be responsible for my care, should it be needed?

2. Will I be economically secure enough to be able to determine my own environment?
3. Will I maintain my independent role, or will I be forced to return to a dependent role?
4. Will I be prepared to accept the changes old age will bring, so that I can still enjoy life?

Society's confused responses through cultural ideas, the media, and education have not quieted individual's fears and apprehensions. Cultural ideas have given rise to many general beliefs as well as to many stereotypes. **Ageism**—the dislike of aging and older people based on the belief that aging makes people unattractive, unintelligent, and unemployable—gives strength to **age discrimination**—the treating of people unjustly simply because of their age—and keeps alive negative and inaccurate beliefs about people simply because they are old, just as racism and sexism accomplished this based on skin color and sex.

This negative attitude causes people not only to dislike the idea of aging, but also to dislike the people who are aging. An example of how extreme negative attitudes toward the old can go is the following boxed quotation:

> August 29, 1970
> "Mr. Douglas J. Stewart in *The New Republic* (Vol. 163, No. 8-9) advocated that all persons should lose their vote after retirement, or at the age of 70, or at 55 when moving to another state."
> (Butler 1975, 12)

People who associate aging with illness, wrinkles, and memory loss find it a very unpleasant prospect. But for people who equate aging with wisdom, freedom from the rat race, and gentleness, aging takes on a positive image. Such is America's confusion.

THE AGED: A NATURAL RESOURCE

Ageism and/or age discrimination is a waste of our natural resources. We can read about people wasted by society's neglect of the handicapped. We can question the lives wasted in society's crowded prisons, and we can wonder about our street people. But society's neglect of its elderly people is, in many respects, the greatest waste of all. They have lived the longest. They are our richest resource in terms of experience in dealing with life and life's challenges. Have we not taken people who have gone through kindergarten, grammar school, junior high school, high school, junior college, college, postgraduate school, and perhaps obtained doctorates or who have gone through the school of hard work and then told them they must quit and be unproductive the rest of their days? Can America afford such waste?

Perhaps research by the industrial psychologist Bruce Avolio will reverse this human wastefulness. His research analyzed thirteen studies of workers of all ages done between 1940 and 1983. Job performance among professionals (scientists, academicians and managers) and nonprofessionals (skilled and semi-skilled workers and technicians) was measured by productivity and ratings by supervisors and co-workers. Productivity increased with age among workers in both groups: academicians published more papers as they aged; salesmen wrote more contracts. "If you work hard early in life," says Avolio, "you will work hard later" (*USA Today,* March 19, 1986).

AGING: HOW IT IS PORTRAYED

Television is one of the most influential forms of communication in America. With Americans watching an average of three hours a day, there can be no question that glamorous and exciting life-styles are associated mostly with the young. Television programs as a whole choose to use elderly characters sparingly. Only between 12 to 15 percent of the characters used are over the age of fifty-five. When age is portrayed, it is done with the Walton effect; that is, the older adults supply the wisdom and experience, a very stereotypic portrayal. But television, too, is showing telltale signs of gray. There is a new awareness and a new appreciation of older people. News programs, however, search out the sensational. As a result, elderly people, for the most part, are ignored except for when they are victimized or involved in a May-December wedding.

Television commercials add to the confusion Americans experience. Elderly people are often shown as having health problems and thus are found in remedy ads selling denture cream, pain killers, and laxatives, or they are portrayed as feisty, as in the "Where's the beef?" commercials. Change is on the way, however, because today's television is being largely produced and programmed by men and women in their thirties and forties. They have gray hair. The viewing public is also getting a bit grayer. Their viewing demands must be met if the networks are to financially survive. As a result, program selection seems to be carving a safer path toward those golden years for future generations.

Schools are instrumental in shaping the attitudes and values of America's young people. Education is a subtle but real influence on the beliefs children have of aging. Most characters in children's literature are attractive, athletic, and young. These images provide the young readers with youthful role models with which they can identify. The old characters, who are less often portrayed, are left to story roles that are more boring and less eventful than those for youthful characters. Older people are generally excluded from the central action of the books. That is not to say that old is negatively portrayed. Age is given the role of respect and authority; however, these are not the more popular of images among youth. A study of literature (Monk, 1979, p. 40) concluded that writers treated older people very much as contemporary America does:

1. They are only partial people.
2. They are not developed.
3. They are not essential to the real plot.
4. They are useful only as they relate to important people.
5. They are there but can easily go unnoticed.

This media approach may be a thing of the past. In May 1985, *People* magazine set a record of sorts, making Bette Davis, seventy-seven, the oldest person ever featured on its cover. The previous age record had been set just a few weeks earlier by fifty-six-year-old sex counselor Dr. Ruth Westheimer. One of the top movies of the summer of 1985 was *Cocoon,* a science-fiction tale set in a Florida retirement community. Television also seems increasingly willing to tackle the less pleasant issues of aging, such as on a 1985 CBS movie special about Alzheimer's disease. No television network would have aired such a special fifteen years ago.

After years of glorifying the young, popular culture is no longer synonymous with the youth culture. In advertising, television, and other areas, Americans have shown a waning devotion to all that is young and a growing fascination for the possibilities of the old and middle-aged.

Part of the reason for this fascination is money. Many people over fifty have plenty of it—more than popularly believed—and business has begun to pay more attention. Another part of the reason is the march of time. It appears "the Pepsi generation" is getting smaller and the postwar

FIGURE 1.6

baby-boom generation—and its crop of image-making publishers, advertising executives, television executives, and television programmers—is getting older. So are the generation's pop music stars, once a clear symbol of youth. Tina Turner, Willie Nelson, Mick Jagger, Paul McCartney, and Eric Clapton are all over forty—and still popular.

Some older people are considered among the nation's most beautiful. When *People* magazine queried readers in 1985 on who was the best-looking woman in America, the winner was forty-two-year-old Linda Evans. Runners-up included Joan Collins, fifty-two and Elizabeth Taylor, fifty-three. The first time *People* magazine asked the question in 1979, the winner was Jaclyn Smith, then thirty-two. In 1980, the winner was twenty-three-year-old Bo Derek.

THE "NO DEPOSIT–NO RETURN" GENERATION

Society often has an unrealistic way of dealing with any group that creates a dilemma. They ignore the people in that group. The sociological term is **societal disengagement**—*when society withdraws support from the individual or group and prevents the individual or group from becoming involved* (an example is forced retirement).

Society's withdrawal of support is not a deliberate shunning of elderly people, but it is real just the same. This withdrawal of opportunities forces a tremendous number of changes in the life-styles of elderly people. Age discrimination, as shown by societal disengagement, is due to prejudice not to the inability of elderly people to continue to make positive contributions to society. The truth is that America has fostered a throw-away culture. Cartons, leftovers, and out-of-date objects all get thrown away. No need to think twice about it or reconsider our decision. Still useful items ranging from cars to clothes that are no longer in fashion are also discarded. If they are kept out of necessity, it is done so grudgingly and tolerated only until they can be conveniently thrown out. "Planned obsolescence—the idea that what is not new is not desirable—is the belief of the industrial world. It is a way of life many have grown up taking for granted over the last few decades" (Steep 1984, 31). According to this reasoning, it would follow that when people wear out, when they become old fashioned, they also become part of our throw-away mentality. We label them *aged* and assign them the role of spectator. They should be content to watch our supercharged society pass them by. We then fail to understand why they experience feelings of uselessness, loneliness, depression, and fear. How did we let this happen?

HOW AGING AFFECTS THE INDIVIDUAL

Since the time in history when old was thirty-five years of age, we have populated, integrated, urbanized, mechanized, computerized, and robotized. Either because of, or in spite of, all this progress, aging seems to frighten little children, offend the young, and terrify middle-aged people. How does it affect the elderly people themselves? Do they see themselves as others see them? Or, do they see themselves as the unique individuals they have been for sixty-four years and still are at sixty-five?

Louis Harris & Associates, Inc., (Monk 1979, 45) have conducted polls to answer these questions. Generally, the American public view elderly people as contributing members of society. However, the public's view differs from the views of the elderly people themselves.

Qualities as seen by ages:	18–64	65+
Elderly as bright and alert	29%	58%
Elderly as open-minded and adaptable	21%	63%
Elderly very good at getting things done	35%	55%

The general public seem to question the alertness, flexibility, and efficiency of the older population, but people sixty-five years of age and over seem more positive about their own qualities. The large percentage differences pose the question of whether we have a realistic view of aging.

The Best Years of My Life

How the addition of years affects a person after sixty-five is not different than how the accumulation of years affects a person before sixty-five. Researchers asked individuals to identify the best year of their life throughout eight-year intervals. It was found that the best year increased with age until age sixty-five. Young people in the study believed that their future lives would not be as happy as older people actually said their lives were. However, what is perceived by a twenty-five-year-old as essential to happiness (Monk 1979, 47) is not so perceived by a person sixty years of age. But the young person putting so much emphasis on that essential ingredient (whatever it may be) is almost certain it will be missing at age sixty. Therefore, the twenty-five-year-old sees age sixty as a definite comedown from a content age of twenty-five. As the age of the respondents increased, they indicated that life was better than those who were younger thought it would be. Optimism appears to increase with age.

Perhaps society's negative attitudes of aging do not fully affect the aging. Or perhaps as age increases, expectations decrease. A more positive conclusion may be that one's lust for life exists at all ages, but the young do not have the opportunity to perceive it in those who are old aged. The segregation of elderly people has taken from them the opportunity of being role models for younger people. Studies have shown (Monk 1979, 47) that older role models do influence the attitudes of younger people toward those aged sixty-five and over. Viewing the positive, well-adjusted elderly person can help youths feel favorable toward

FIGURE 1.7
(From Geriatrics: A Study of Maturity *by Esther Caldwell and Barbara R. Hegner, copyright © 1986 by Delmar Publishers Inc.)*

their own eventual aging. Helping younger people to view their aging in a positive light is no small contribution elderly people could make as integrated members of society. Problems can be solved and pleasures can be enjoyed. Happiness does not favor one age over another.

Accepting Our Own Aging

Our optimism must also be realistic. Some people experience a social illness called **gerontophobia**—*the fear of aging and the refusal to*

FIGURE 1.8

accept the aged into what they believe is a youth-oriented society. Aging does bring limitations and adjustments, which must be acknowledged. However, to focus on limitations in aging is like focusing on teething in babyhood or acne in teen years. These aspects are part of the process of getting older, but they are not the total process itself.

> Robert Browning stated this feeling with poetic skill when he wrote:
> Grow old along with me!
> The best is yet to be,
> The last of life, for which
>   the first was made:
> Our times are in His hand
> Who saith "A whole I planned,
> Youth shows but half; trust God:
>   see all, nor be afraid!"
>   ("Rabbi Ben Ezra")

The personality qualities that are you will always be there. Life at forty may be but a preview if you hang in there. If you are basically a curious, involved person, age will not change that. Old people do not become indifferent and passive. However, indifferent and passive people do become old.

The Self-fulfilling Prophecy

The grave danger of negative attitudes toward aging or the untruths about aging that persist is the strength they give to the self-fulfilling prophecy. If individuals make these negative expectations their own, the end result may, in fact, be the living out of those negativisms. We have only to recall when being black in America made people unemployable, and expendable "unpeople" (Comfort, "Age Prejudice in America," 1976, 10). Then came the time when being female meant being too emotional to be assigned professional roles. When society made victims of blacks and women, the victims were forced to live with prejudice from the day of their birth.

But we are not born old. Only after the human clock strikes old at the appropriate age does being old suddenly make one unintelligent, unemployable, and asexual. Modern research confirms that most of these changes are not the effects of aging but the effects of role playing. This role is a destructive one. We cannot ignore the oppressed minority of old because we are inevitably going to join them. To change things, a society must ultimately cry, "Stop! The prejudices will be no more." Instead, the attitudes of all people must focus on the fact that all people of all ages remain people. This is illustrated well by the following story:

A well-meaning young senator was showing a party of seniors around the Senate Chamber. He treated them a little like school children, explaining the legislative process in words of one syllable and shouting in case they were deaf. Finally, turning to one of the group, the senator asked, "And what did you used to be?" The old man fixed a beady eye on him and replied, "I still am."
(Comfort, "Age Prejudice in America," 1976, 23)

SUMMARY

Everything ages, including human beings if they are lucky. Aging is an inevitable, natural process. Although sixty-five is often thought of as the age when someone is considered old, it is an arbitrary number used merely as a reference. Gerontology is the multidisciplinary study that focuses on aging and old age.

Old was historically thought of as magical or mystical because so few people survived to become old. There has always been the hope that a fountain of youth existed and that it would be found within each person's lifetime. Search turned to research on aging, but the main goal was and still is the extension of life.

The sciences of sociology, psychology, and biology all contribute information to the field of gerontology. Their combined efforts attempt to answer the all-important question, What causes aging? Without that answer, the human life span cannot be significantly lengthened.

Advancing in age and aging differ markedly. To advance in age is to change and to improve the quality of life as it is experienced. To age chronologically is but to experience the quantity of life.

The study of aging is vital to everyone's own aging. Only by understanding the concerns of today's elderly people will the solutions reduce or eliminate the concerns of the future. Today, we are the aging. Tomorrow, we will be the old.

Society does not always respond to aging or portray aging in a positive manner. Society's customs, media, and education reflect social attitudes concerning elderly people. Modern society's negative feelings can be seen in the ageist treatment of its older population. This negativism often forces individuals to withdraw from society as society withdraws from them. The accumulated wisdom and experience of the aged generation are viewed as obsolete rather than valuable resources.

People who are old view their lives in a much more satisfying way than does the younger generation who is observing them. However, neither age group would choose the golden age of sixty-five over the contented age of twenty-five as the ideal age. The danger lies in the fact that if society's negative description of aging becomes a part of the elderly generation's attitude, then the self-fulfilling prophecy can do more destruction to the mind and body of the old than age itself could.

EXERCISES

1. Poll a number of individuals from varied age groups and ask them to give you their definition of *old* in:
   a. An age number.
   b. A definition.

2. Using the same individuals as in exercise 1, or another varied age group, poll them as to the qualities referred to in the Harris Poll figures. Calculate the percentage of the two age groups and compare them to poll's percentages.
3. Find an article or ad that guarantees the buyers that they will "look younger," "feel younger," or "slow aging" as a result of its purchase and use.
4. Record for a specified period of time when and where you come in contact with individuals age sixty-five and over. During that record-keeping period, record how many minutes or hours of conversational contact you actually spend with an older person. How did it influence your image of old age?

REVIEW

1. List and explain the three theories historically used to account for the reason some cultures and/or individuals reached old age.
2. List some of the first scientists who studied the causes of aging in hopes of extending longevity.
3. Define *gerontology*. How does gerontology differ from geriatrics?
4. List the three sciences that contribute to the multidisciplinary science of gerontology. What information does each science contribute?
5. Do people age or advance in age? What is the difference?
6. List four concepts of aging with which gerontologists agree. List four concepts of aging with which gerontologists disagree.
7. What are the five basic reasons gerontology is an important area of study?
8. List three ways in which society reveals its attitude toward aging to the public.
9. What is ageism/age discrimination?
10. What has society to lose by engaging in age-discriminatory practices?
11. Does the media portray aging in a positive or a negative way? How do they achieve this?
12. How do elderly people see themselves? Is this the same view younger people have of them?
13. What is gerontophobia?
14. What is one of the gravest dangers of society's negative attitude toward aging?

RECOMMENDED READINGS
AND REFERENCES

Baltimore Longitudinal Study of the National Institute on Aging. Washington, D.C.: U.S. Dept. of Health and Human Services, 1980.

Brody, Jane. "Researchers Progress in Delaying Effects of Aging." *Minneapolis Star and Tribune,* December 9, 1984.

Burns, George. *How to Live to Be 100.* New York: New American Library, 1983.

Butler, Robert N. *Why Survive? Being Old in America.* New York: Harper Colophon Books, 1975.

Comfort, Alexander. "Age Prejudice in America." *Social Policy,* Nov./Dec. 1976, 3-8.

———. *A Good Age.* New York: Crown Publishers, 1976.

Cranston, Alan. "We *Can* Do Something About Aging." *50 Plus,* August 1985, 32.

Elias, Marilyn. "The Search For Life Without End." *USA Today,* October 25, 1985.

Elliot, Gordon, and Mary Elliot. *The Ideal Life: 50 and Over.* Madison, Wis.: Ideals Publishing Corp., 1980.

Freese, Arthur S. *The Brain and Aging: The Myths the Facts.* Public Affairs Pamphlet No. 591. New York: Public Affairs Committee, 1981.

Hallegan, Tom. "Social Security's Reform Package." *Gray Panther Network,* March/April 1983, 1-3.

Jerome, John. "The Gerontology Puzzle." *50 Plus,* August 1985, 24.

Monk, Abraham. *The Age of Aging.* New York: Prometheus Books, 1979.

Montagu, Ashley. *Growing Young.* New York: McGraw-Hill Book Company, 1983.

National Institute on Aging. DHEW Pamphlet No. 78-1129. Washington, D.C.: U.S. Government Printing Office.

People Weekly. "The Best Years Ever," May 5, 1985, 88-89.

Reader's Digest. "Quotations," June 1984, 27.

Satier, Virginia. *Peoplemaking.* Palo Alto, Calif.: Science and Behavior Books, Inc., 1972.

Steep, Clayton. "Life Can Get Better With Age." *Plain Truth,* September 1984, 31.

U.S. News & World Report. "Dynamic Elderly Busier, Healthier, Happier." July 2, 1984, 48-53.

USA Today. "USA Snapshots." January 14, 1986.

———. "Your Work May Improve with Age." March 19, 1986.

CHAPTER
2
History
of Aging

Learning Objectives

After studying this chapter, the reader should be able to:

- Outline the hopes and apprehensions of the elderly people from century to century as historical events brought about change in their treatment.
- List the social factors that brought about the changes in the attitudes toward the old.
- Realize that customs are strong evolutionary forces that affect extended family structures.
- Demonstrate how race, religion, sex, and economic forces determined the status of the elderly people.

Preview

Historically, in cultures that did not change quickly, life had a sense of continuity. The wisdom of the older generation had value to the younger generations because it still applied to the experiences in life. Significant inventions and discoveries were infrequent. Life followed a fairly predictable pattern. Most people were generally content to maintain ties to the family circle, which, in turn, was tied to the land.

The explosion of technology has brought rapid economic changes, including a shift from a rural to an urban society. Industry and money-making opportunities have attracted young people to the cities. Members of the extended family unit—babies, children, parents, grandparents, and other relatives—who once were anchored to one geographical area were now great distances apart. The plight of the elders was finding their place in this new social environment.

AGING: DO WE UNDERSTAND IT?

Riddle: What animal walks on four feet in the morning, two feet at noon, and three feet in the evening?

Answer: The human being—crawling in the morning, walking erect at noontime, and walking with the assistance of a cane in old age.

For too long, we have ignored the three-footed segments of humanity. We forget that for each one of us, the two feet at noon will, with time, become three feet in the evening.

We all grow older faster than we think. Old age, when it comes, is apt to take us by surprise. Nothing in life is so inevitable and yet so unexpected. At the same time, the experience of aging has also changed faster than our understanding of it. Growing old in America today is an experience greatly different from what it was two or three centuries ago. If we wish to understand aging in these modern times, we must understand the attitudes and experiences of aging in the past.

FIGURE 2.1
(From Geriatrics: A Study of Maturity, 4th ed., by Esther Caldwell and Barbara R. Hegner, copyright © 1986 by Delmar Publishers Inc.)

ATTITUDES TOWARD OLD AGE— HISTORY REPEATS ITSELF

Throughout time, both the young and the old have greatly changed their attitudes toward each other both in the direction of esteem and indifference. Historical research can follow the path from past gerontocracy— rule of the elders—to their descendents, who have made youth their god. Fischer writes:

> The people of early America exalted old age; their descendents have made a cult of youth. In the Constitutional Convention of 1787, Benjamin Franklin

had enormous influence, partly because his fellow delegates knew him to be shrewd and wise, but also because he was very old—an octogenarian—and old men were held in high esteem. In the twentieth century, the prevailing attitude is the reverse. In one of the most popular motion pictures of the 1960's—the Beatles' *A Hard Day's Night*—an old man is treated throughout the film with sovereign contempt, punctuated only by occasional expressions of pity. "Poor thing," one Beatle says to another. "He can't help being old." That film was made as recently as 1964, and yet the Beatles themselves have already become faded historical figures. A new set of attitudes toward old age is presently in the making.*

These major changes have affected the self-image of the elderly, their expectations of old age, as well as their economic and social status. These changes cleared the path for dangerous forms of ageism and age discrimination. There has never been a golden age for the elderly. "There were periods, however ironic, when old people received respect without affection, honor without devotion, veneration without love" (Fischer 1978, 224).

WHEN OLD WAS TWENTY-FIVE YEARS OF AGE

Not everything about aging has changed with time. One thing that has always remained the same is the existence of old age itself. Recorded history shows us that all human societies divided people into age categories. However, the strictness of those age divisions differed from society to society. In addition to assigning the category *old age* was assigning a set of social rules. "Act your age" seems to have been spoken centuries ago. How each specific age should act changed according to geographical location and the passage of time.

PREHISTORIC CULTURES

Information on primitive and prehistoric cultures is sketchy at best because aging was a topic almost totally ignored by historians. However, the events that were recorded provide some fascinating insights. The treatment of elderly people from culture to culture was as varied as one might imagine.

The ancient Greek historian Herodotus reported of tribes who worshipped their elders and of other tribes who deserted them (Figure 2.2).

---

*Growing Old in America, David Hackett Fischer. New York: Oxford University Press, 1978, p. 4. Used with permission.

> The Issedones gilded the heads of their aged parents and offered
> sacrifices before them. (Asia Minor, 700 B.C.)
>
> In West Irian they put the old person in a pit by the side of a busy track
> so that passersby could throw in a stone, eventually burying the old
> person alive. (South America, 400 B.C.)
>
> Herodotus (as quoted in Fischer 1978, 6)

Respect of the Old: The Law

To conclude that primitive or prehistoric tribes had no respect for their
elders is to come to a wrong conclusion. Custom dictated behavior. When
looking at the customs of another culture, one culture often labels some
of their behaviors *bizarre* or even *brutal*. Tribal customs are seldom
instituted or carried out for either of these reasons, however. In fact, each
tribe believed its custom was a respectful way to deal with elders with one
exception: fear of and misunderstanding of the senile.

It would be correct to go so far as to say: Respect for the elders was
a common element of the primitive and prehistoric tribes.

A positive contribution of respect for the elders was that as a social
practice, it created continuity, stability, permanence, and order in society. Respect for age was more than an economic or social idea. It was
sacred in its nature. As in many of the ancient and primitive societies, age
relations were closely interwoven with religion. Why did some people
live to be older than others? Since there was no other answer, many
people believed that age was endowed with supernatural properties. A
person survived to old age because God, or the Devil, had lengthened
their days. This attitude often appeared in primitive societies. The elders
were often thought to possess important magical powers—not always for

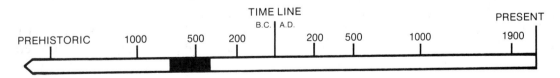

FIGURE 2.2
Time line

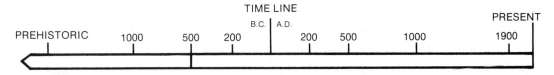

FIGURE 2.3
Time line

good. Witchcraft was commonly associated with old age. In particular, it was associated with old women. Did sex discrimination occur in primitive societies?

Respect for elderly people was not always a matter of choice. The ancient Chinese (Figure 2.3) provided an example of what could happen if proper respect was not shown (Fischer 1978, 14):

A Chinese, aided by his wife, flogged his mother. When it was discovered, the two were put to death. In addition, the head of the clan was put to death. The immediate neighbors each received 80 blows and were sent into exile. All in the clan that had a bachelor's degree (B.A.), as did the son who flogged his mother, were to be flogged and exiled. The granduncle, uncle and two elder brothers were put to death. All other rulers of the clan were deprived of their rank. The mother of the female offender was tattooed with symbols of "neglect of duty" and sent into exile. The father of the offender was not allowed to receive any higher educational degree than a B.A.; he was also flogged and exiled. The sons of the offenders were given another name and they denied any inheritance. (500 B.C.)

Respect for an elderly person, however, lasted only as long as that person could make a positive contribution to society. The useful role of the elder most often was that of passing on the wisdom of experience from generation to generation. Primitive tribes had no other way to pass on ancient customs except by word of mouth.

Because of this vitally important service, respect and authority were given to the elders when it came to tribal wisdom. One can then understand why tribes feared and violently destroyed the senile elder. An elder was either of use to the tribe or, if unable to contribute, a burden. Senility was a threat to a society whose only source of survival methods and ancestoral customs was the elders.

When Young Was Actually Old

Why did the treatment of the elderly range from the bizarre, to the brutal, to that of worship? This question has no one answer. There is, however, a pattern that fits most prehistoric cultures and most primitive societies. The following generalizations give some insight into the behaviors of primitive peoples:

1. *People were considered old at a much earlier age.*

Not a lot of individuals reached old age as we define it today. The old of prehistoric or primitive times were twenty-five years of age on the average. Of prehistoric skeletons found, 95 percent showed they had died before they reached the age of 40. Of that percentage, 75 percent did not reach 30 years of age. Aging, as we know it today, did not exist (Fischer 1978, 7).

FIGURE 2.4

Population: Neanderthal	Percent dead by age 30 = 80%
	40 = 95%
	50 = 100%
Population: Cro-Magnon	Percent dead by age 30 = 62%
	40 = 88%
	50 = 90%
	(Cook 1972, 595)

2. *Bodies aged more quickly because of living conditions.*

No matter how many people reached fifty years of age, there were always some people who were thought of as old. Aging was accelerated so maturity had to come quickly. In the life of primitive persons, twenty-five years of living made them old. To be thought of as decrepit at forty years of age was not unusual. The hard times and constant fighting against the elements for survival aged the body quickly.

3. *Custom determined how the elderly were treated.*

As noted, treatment of the old differed with each society; but in these societies, the elders were treated in ways the society determined were moral and even religious in nature. The elderly played a major role in the tribe's customs and were supporters of the customs with which they would be treated when old. Another example of different treatment of the elderly by different cultures is found in the writing of Herodotus (Figure 2.5):

> King Darius of Persia asked the Greeks in his court how much money they would want to eat their parents' bodies instead of burning them as was their custom. The Greeks replied in horror and stated that there was not enough money in all of the world to make them change their custom.
>
> Then Darius asked the Callatiae who ate their dead parents, how much money they would want to burn them instead. The Callatiae were as shocked as the Greeks had been and pleaded with Darius not even to request such a thing. (522-486 B.C.)
>
> Herodotus (as quoted in Fischer 1978, 8)

Herodotus, on hearing this story, concluded that not Darius but custom was truly the king! (Fischer 1978, 8). Each of these customs reflected the high respect each society held for its elders.

Fear of the Senile Old

In a world in which literacy was limited, elders were keepers of their culture and agents of its communication from one generation to the next. Because mental impairment of elderly people was not understood, it was feared. Prehistoric and primitive people set aside the group of old people who caused them fear. These people were the senile old—*senile* being a nonmedical term used to refer to mental impairment.

The senile old or already dead elders, as they were referred to, were treated with brutality. These aged who could make no contribution were shown no mercy. Because of the merciless manner in which they were treated, some took their own lives. History paints a barbaric picture of treatment of the already dead elders. Some primitive tribes killed them outright. In other tribes, they were disposed of in horrible ways, often with the planning and help of the victim. Writings tell us the Samoans buried their elders alive. Other tribes were known to do away with their elders by abandoning them or deliberately neglecting them until they died of starvation or exposure.

One pathetic story tells of an Eskimo woman who carried out her aged father's wishes and pushed him into the icy ocean to drown. But he did not sink because of his bulky clothing. "Put your head down, Papa, it will be quicker," she cried with tears in her eyes.

The Indians of the Bolivian jungles, like other groups living under severe climatic conditions, had to keep moving all the time in search of rare and elusive game. If they had stopped every time grandfather faltered, the whole family might have starved to death.

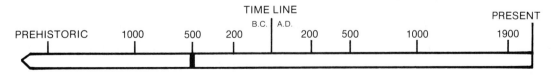

FIGURE 2.5
Time line

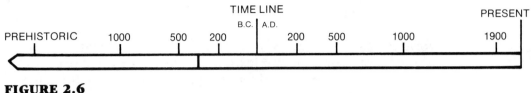

FIGURE 2.6
Time line

AGING IN THE ROMAN EMPIRE

With advanced cultures came dramatic changes in aging. One of the more dramatic changes was the increase in life expectancy. Most ancient civilizations were similar to that of the late Roman Empire. It is believed that about one-fifth of the population lived to be fifty-five years of age.

Of course, by today's standards that is still a short life; it means that four-fifths of that civilization died before reaching middle age.

> When the ancient Romans were still a primitive tribe (Figure 2.6), they disposed of their decrepit elders by drowning them in the Tiber River. (350 B.C.)

Chronological Aging

> Grecian ladies counted their age from their marriage, not their birth.
>
> Homer

The significance of the age increase, however, is our historical indication that the aging process, by definition, had begun. It was also at this time in history that the concept of chronological age began and numerical birthdays were kept, but only for personal reasons. World census taking did not begin until the 1800s (1790 in the United States). The questions asked did not focus on determining the number of people in age categories but rather the number of free persons, slaves, and free white males under and over sixteen years of age.

Population:	Greece (300 B.C.)	Percent dead by age	30 = 61%
			40 = 66%
			50 = 71%
			60 = 77%
			70 = 79%
Population:	Rome (200 B.C.)	Percent dead by age	30 = 65%
			40 = 70%
			50 = 75%
			60 = 80%
			70 = 83%
			(Russell 1958, 132)

Economic Security

The advancement of these civilizations saw other significant changes in the treatment of the elderly, both material and spiritual. More secure economics were a result of increased, even abundant, supplies of life's necessities. Food, shelter, and the security that abundance brings brought about social changes. The elderly no longer had to be abandoned because of insufficient food supply; they could assist in the fields until they were physically unable, then they could work at less strenuous tasks or assume purely religious roles. Economics no longer established custom.

FIGURE 2.7

AGING: THE FORGOTTEN CENTURIES
(400 B.C.–1600 A.D.)

A large historical gap exists in the history of old age. For nearly 2,000 years (Figure 2.8), there is an astonishing absence of information. Studies have been published on old age in primitive societies and the ancient world, but nothing has appeared in modern history before 1600 A.D. The main reason is that little or no attention was paid to aging during this long period of time.

We do know that the invention of writing (about 5,000 years ago; the oldest writings that have come down to present day were written in 3100 B.C.) had its impact on the treatment of the elderly. Social ethics changed because society no longer depended solely on its elders to pass on cultural customs. One might conclude that this would result in greater destruction of the elders. The opposite became true, however. Senility was no longer a threat, and so the deliberate destruction of the elderly person was no longer a custom of any major ancient civilization.

The Romans established old age homes—called *gerocomeia*—for the elderly rich, but the lot of the elderly poor changed little. For the slaves and servants, old age could be so cruel that early death could have been a blessing. The elderly rich received both improved care and power. The power went to the first-born male who had absolute power, even of life and death, over other family members.

This establishment of eldest male supremacy, in a sense, set some rules that were followed for centuries.

Old age was honored when and if:
1. It could defend itself.
2. It could maintain its power.
3. It could be subservient or inferior to no one.
4. If, to its last breath, it could rule over its domain.

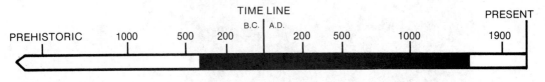

FIGURE 2.8
Time line

FIGURE 2.9

AGRARIAN POWER AND CONTROL (1000 B.C.–400 A.D.)

During the time of the Roman Empire (Figure 2.10), treatment of the elderly person was bound to societal factors:

1. Agrarian-agricultural—in economy.
2. Extended in its family structure.
3. Rural in its residence.

Although the elders were few in number, they:

1. Controlled the land.
2. Controlled the power.
3. Remained uninfluenced by outside changes or pressure to update.

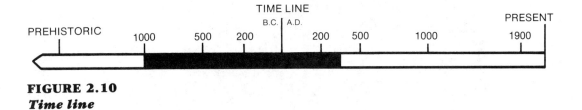

FIGURE 2.10
Time line

AGING AND MODERN TECHNOLOGY

From the middle 1800s to the 1900s, significant social changes brought about another set of dramatic changes.

Useful or income-generating power is a thread woven through all of history to indicate an individual's worth!

First: Modern technology was a major influence. High tech contributed to the aging of the population and thus the elderly population multiplied. This created new concepts, one of which was retirement!

Modern technology forced the aged out of valued and prestigious roles. They were no longer needed in the work force. This in turn lowered their income and, as a direct result, their status.

Second: Modern technology created new jobs that demanded new and greater skills. The direct result was again:

1. Loss of jobs.
2. Loss of income.
3. Loss of status.

Third: Modern technology created the city. Young people were attracted to this job market, breaking up the extended family. As education of youth was required to meet the demands of the more technical skills, the concept of the wisdom of the old was no longer regarded with respect. In fact, as it involved the new technical advancements, it was no longer true.

> The three factors that gave the elderly power took a dramatic change:
>
> From...   To...
>
> 1. Agrarian economy $\longrightarrow$ Urban industrialization
> 2. Extended family $\longrightarrow$ Individual conjugal family
> 3. Rural residence $\longrightarrow$ Urban in residence

The foundations of elderly power and respect were weakened, but they did not entirely crumble. They would not, however, recover their original position of influence in modern society.

The percentage of elders who held the power historically was low. When studying aging in the past, we come to a common illusion. We see yesterday's population as primarily elderly. The fact is that two hundred years ago, the population of America was actually younger than it is today.

In the 1790s, the median age was barely 16.
In the 1970s, the median age was nearly 30.

America's Youthful Population

This statistic means that in the 1790s, half the population was below sixteen years of age! Few people were very old. Fewer than 2 percent were sixty-five years of age or older, compared with 11 percent today. This young median age changed little from the years 1790 to 1890 (Figure 2.11). Even Oscar Wilde (1854-1900) wrote, "The youth of America is their oldest tradition."

The astonishing youthfulness of the American population was caused more by high fertility than high death rates. Large families were the rule rather than the exception. However, high mortality was also a factor.

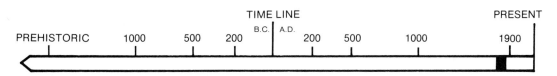

FIGURE 2.11
Time line

> In the Chesapeake colonies during the 1600s, life expectancy at birth was twenty-five years of age for both black slaves and their white masters.
>
> In Massachusetts during the 1600s, the life expectancy from birth was the highest. It was 38 years of age.

Old age was highly respected in early America, perhaps, in part, because it was comparatively rare. Literature of the times also taught people how they were expected to behave toward their elders. Without exception, it prescribed the ancient ideals of submission and respect for old age. The attitude the young were expected to assume before their elders was unlike that of any other social relationships. The ideal social order was gerontocratic—the young were to serve, the elderly were to rule.

> a. Respect,
> b. honor,
> c. obligation, and
> d. submission were all involved.
> But there was something deeper than submission. It was summarized in a word not often used today: "veneration." Veneration—a feeling of reverence—was more than just a form of respect. It was also a form of worship. It was an emotion closer to awe than affection. *Veneration* had nothing to do with love.
>
> (Fischer 1978, 30)

However, veneration may have had a lot to do with material need. The not-so-visible but ever-present economic needs of youth were forceful factors, perhaps more so in America than in Europe. In an agrarian society, land wealth was the basis for power. Parents kept possession and control over their land usually until their death. Sons would remain economically dependent on their fathers long after they were physically mature. Parents, however, could not keep their children from marrying. Some states went so far as to protect the children's right to marry. But because of the need for economic security before marriage, marriage was often delayed. The reluctance of fathers to release their land was motivated in part by a concern for their own security in old age. This concern may have gone beyond material needs. Wealthy fathers could have turned over some of their assets and still have been economically secure, but they were reluctant to set their children free. Land was a tool by which the father preserved both his power and authority. Sons were bound to their fathers by ties of economic dependency. Youth was the hostage of age.

Ranking of the Elders

The power and privileges of old age were not enjoyed by all the old. Old age had social boundaries. It is generally true that people were ranked according to their years. Older meant better and oldest meant best. People were also ranked by:

1. Economic worth.
2. Knowledge.
3. Sex.
4. Race.

Respect Was not Prejudice-Free

Without question, social inequalities existed. Respect for age was strongest for people who were old, rich, and male. Old age brought greater contempt for people who were old and poor. These people were despised. Elderly poor males in early America were treated so badly that it was fortunate there were so few. The unattached poor often met with brutality.

Old women did not receive the veneration of old age, either. The idea of the rich widow was rare. Old women were dependent on what their children chose to give them. Often, they were reduced to dependency and degradation. Seldom did old widows remarry. They were more often abandoned by family members and died of neglect.

SUFFERING AMONG THE OLD: PHYSICAL AND MENTAL

To be old in early America was also often to be wracked by illness. We often think of the surviving old as being hale and hardy, but this was not the case. Old age usually meant living in physical misery, with pain as a constant companion. There were many diseases and illnesses for which medicine knew no remedy. Very few people experienced a serene old age.

> It was fully documented that Benjamin Franklin suffered terribly in his last years. As he lay in misery upon his deathbed his daughter, it is said, tried to console him with the hope that he would live many years longer. Franklin was to have replied, "I hope not!"
>
> (Van Doren 1938, 779)

Emotional suffering was no less a reality. Because old age was so rare, the aged suffered from isolation, loneliness, and emptiness. Nevertheless, the aged were endlessly instructed to be up and doing. They were expected, even required, to live with dignity and to provide a good example to youth. They were to be religious and to be active in public affairs.

The aged were forbidden to lay their burden down, and the young were not allowed to take it up. An undercurrent of resentment and hostility existed, but it was a quiet mental rebellion.

AGE: SELF-ACCEPTANCE

Growing old had another dimension. Beyond the physical infirmities and social stress were the mental sufferings. Old people in early America found it difficult to deal with their own oldness. Although they had the power, they did not have the affection, love, or sympathy of the young. The elders were kept at an emotional distance from the young. There were no outward hostilities between generations, but there was no outward affection, either. Veneration was a cold emotion. The elderly people often complained that they had lived to become strangers to their own society. They felt like aliens in their own time.

For nearly 200 years, this pattern persisted in America. As the colonies in the 1760s found themselves increasing in opposition to En-

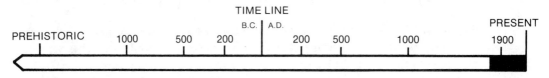

FIGURE 2.12
Time line

gland, the mother country, so, too, was there the growing trouble between the generations in American families. Both conflicts developed out of the issues of authority and independence. A new set of social ideas had found a sudden release in the American air. A political and generational revolution was in the making.

FROM AGE RESPECT TO AGE EQUALITY
(1800 A.D. to Present)

Late in the eighteenth century (Figure 2.12), the western world experienced a social revolution. It brought about a fundamental change in world culture. This social upheaval began in the western nations and spread swiftly to every human society on earth.

This revolution introduced a spirit of
AGE EQUALITY!

This new equality first took form in France in a new type of ritual. Harmony between age and youth was symbolized in public rituals in which old men gave gifts of figs and raisins to the young, and young women presented baskets of bread and fruit to the elders (Fischer 1978, 78).

A graphic example of this social revolution was that in 1701 in Northhampton, Massachusetts, people were seated in church or town meeting by:
a. Age.
b. Money.
c. Usefulness.
In the 1830s, the meeting-house benches were auctioned and sold to the highest bidder. Thereafter, seating was based solely on money! There was *no* regard for age.

Such ceremonial change was a forerunner of many other changes. One innovation was forced retirement. Due to a problem in New York with a presiding judge who was senile, that state passed a law in 1777 stating that judges must retire at seventy years of age (Thorpe 1909, 889). Other states adopted similar laws, some using the age requirement of sixty years.

A unique place in which to find further evidence of this social revolution is in the census reports. **Demographers**—*social scientists who describe human behavior on the basis of statistics for a given population*—use the interesting term *age heaping*—adding years to one's age—that indicates people's attitude toward their age.

In the late 1700s, people tended to round off their ages and to report them around 30, 40, 50, and so on, instead of the exact years. Age heaping was common because:

a. Some people were not sure of their age.
b. Some people really did not care what their age was. (Williams 1976, 174)

As people become more calendar conscious, this type of age heaping stopped and another form took its place. Age heaping changed to deliberate age cheating as people pretended to be younger than they really were.

> Contrary to popular belief, men are more vain about their age than women.
>
> The age 39 syndrome is a masculine weakness, not a feminine one.

In each subsequent census, more individuals age cheated by representing themselves as younger than they actually were. The percentage of age cheating coincided with each decade's bias toward youth.

Dress Styles

A more visible and perhaps predictable change occurring as the result of the social revolution was dress style. In the seventeenth century, there was one dress style for all age groups. It was a style designed to flatter the old. Hair was hidden under a powdered wig made to look white with age. Clothes were tailored to narrow the shoulders and round them; hips and waists were made to look broader than they were, and body posture within the coat design was made to appear stooped with age. Only the lower part of the legs were revealed as they are not age identifiable.

A clergyman in 1765 was advised not to wear his own hair "till age had made it venerable."

(Thomas 1976, 8)

In the early 1800s, men's dress revolutionized. The fashions favored and flattered youth.

Wigs	→ replaced by →	hairpieces; toupees	→ made old look young
White powder	→ replaced by →	hair dyes; tints	→ made old look young
Coat	→ replaced by →	narrowing hips; puffed shoulders; straight back	→ made old look young
Knee breeches	→ replaced by →	trousers	→ made old look young

Fashion definitely had an impact on emphasizing youth and accelerating the dethroning of old age from its status of veneration.

Trousers were trimmed tightly. Corsets were designed and worn by both males and females.

Titles

The terms or titles used to address the elderly people gave evidence of changing attitudes. As the elders lost their social status, they became more vulnerable to verbal abuse. In the late 1800s and early 1900s, such terms as *old gaffer, fogy, codger, old goat,* and *geezer* were coined. Obviously, these terms are not titles of respect. The words were meant to be rude and vulgar when used by the young to describe the old. These terms were used for old men since men, not women, had been among the venerated.

Old women also had degrading titles. Such terms as *hag, crone, old maid,* and *old trot* had been used as far back as the 1400s. These terms were not a direct result of this new wave of social equality. They were just a continued practice.

There never was an abundance of slang used for the youth because the concept of *youth* was not a negative one; just some of the behaviors youth engaged in were seen as unacceptable. One example is the term *young punk.* The term shows displeasure because the people were punks, not because they were young.

Family Portraits

Another indication of age-attitude change was in family portraits. In the early 1700s, portraits showed the father standing above his wife and family. By the late 1700s, the family portraits had all members of the family on an equal plane. This horizontal style picture remained throughout the following centuries.

First Born

The advantages of being the first born did not remain unchanged, either. Both the custom of how wills were drawn up and the laws of inheritance within states were changed. First born sons lost their advantage by the late 1800s, never to regain it again. Laws and customs made it such that the wealth of the oldest and youngest were virtually equal.

ATTITUDES TOWARD AGE: A GRADUAL SOCIAL CHANGE

All these evidences of custom changes leave no doubt that a revolution occurred in the attitudes toward age. However, this does not mean that at a given moment one unchanging system suddenly gave way to another unchanging system. Change is constant, but the pace and direction of change vary. There were now two social settings: one of age veneration overcome by another of age equality. These two cultural forces engaged in complicated and intense battles. Concepts of *age-respect* were strengthened while an undercurrent of increasing inner hostility set out to weaken it. Age equality won and lost battles for many decades. The victims of the battle for equality were:

1. The hierarchy of age.
2. The hierarchy of social rights (legal status, political rights, etc.).

This battle set up as future battles to be won:

1. The hierarchy of sex.
2. The hierarchy of race.

HISTORY OF AGING: A LESSON FOR THE FUTURE?

When studying the history of aging, two facts concerning the future are apparent:

1. What will happen in the future is closely linked to what has happened in the past.

Futurology—the dream or fad that we can predict the future on the basis of our knowldge of the past—is unrealistic. No book on the history of aging will end with a Book of Revelation. However, even though history does not spell out the future by identical replication, it has us better prepared when it comes. It provides a plot for the story although the characters and setting may differ. The future is always different from the past but not so unrelated that we do not recognize it.

2. What the future holds closely resembles what we wished it held.

The future is not written without its authors. Not all our hopes and dreams for it come true, but the positive attitudes for what we hope the future to be are influential. The history of aging was not without its disappointments and failures. It also taught us that positive changes could and were made because people worked toward that goal. History has demonstrated the kinds of obstacles that got in the way of success as well as the opportunities that were present if they were recognized.

SUMMARY

The study of primitive and preindustrial societies and the relationship of the elders in the family structure are difficult at best. We tend to view customs from a contemporary frame of mind. This view can distort the intentions of cultures centuries ago.

In all societies before the industrial revolution, the aged enjoyed a favorable position. Their economic security and their social status were assured by their role and place in the extended family. This golden age of living for older people was disturbed and undermined by the industrial revolution. Urbanization weakened family relations and undermined the extended family as an economic unit. In preindustrial society, parenthood had been a lifelong career. The growing segregation of different stages of life brought with it a growth of new institutions, especially for the old. It became the work of society to determine the new role for the elders. Future gerontologists studying later cultures would judge whether society provided a golden age or one of ageism.

EXERCISES

1. Interview several elderly people and have them talk about major discoveries, inventions, and so on that they lived through. Have them relate the impact these changes had on society.
2. Select any ancient society and research its customs that affected the treatment of its elders.
3. While reading about the industrial revolution, list the major influences of that era and how it changed family roles in society for the rest of history.
4. Look through your family's photo albums and see if you can find changes in dress, seating arrangement, and so on that point out the hierarchy of age.

REVIEW

1. Has age categorizing always been a part of human societies?
2. List the three generalizations that applied to most primitive societies and provide insight into their behavior toward their elders.
3. Why was senility such a threat to primitive societies?

4. During which advanced culture did significant changes in life expectancy take place?
5. What treatment changes of the elderly did the advancement of civilizations bring?
6. In order for the elders to maintain their power in the Roman Empire and in the centuries to come, what four abilities must they have and maintain?
7. How did the invention of writing have a direct impact on the respect of the elders?
8. Which society was the first to construct old homes for its elders?
9. What significant social changes took place from 1850 to 1900?
10. List the dramatic changes of the following:
    a. Agrarian economy
    b. Extended family
    c. Rural residence
11. Explain the social revolution of age equality.
12. What profession was the first to experience forced retirement? Why?
13. How did age heaping and age cheating reflect the time in which they were practiced?
14. Explain how dress styles, use of titles, and family portraits were signs of society's attitude toward aging.

RECOMMENDED READINGS AND REFERENCES

Cook, Sherburne. "Aging of and in Populations." *Developmental Physiology and Aging,* edited by P. S. Timiras. New York: Macmillan Publishing Co., 1972.

Fischer, David Hackett. *Growing Old in America.* New York: Oxford University Press, 1978.

Mathews, Mitford M., ed. *Americanisms: A Dictionary of Selected Americanisms on Historical Principles.* Chicago: University of Chicago Press, 1966.

Russell, J. C. "Late Ancient and Medieval Populations." *Trans American Philosophy and Sociology* 48 (1958): 1-152.

Thomas, Keith. *Age and Authority In Early Modern England.* New York: Edwards, 1976.

Thorpe, Francis N. *Federal and State Constitutions.* 7 vols. Washington, D.C.: Government Printing Office, 1909.

Van Doren, Carl. *Benjamin Franklin.* New York: Gazette, 1938.

Williams, Raymond. *Keywords: A Vocabulary of Culture and Society.* New York: Oxford University Press, 1976.

CHAPTER
3
Demography of Aging

Learning Objectives

After studying this chapter, the reader should be able to:

- Understand the contributions demographers make to the field of gerontology.
- State how demographers, through statistics, can tell "what were," "what are," and "what could be" the social effects of the aging population.
- Be aware of the political, legal, and educational impact of the ever-increasing graying population.
- Comprehend the economic implications of the dependency ratio on the young and middle-aged worker.

Preview

Demographics provide an important tool for gerontologists—statistics. This chapter uses those statistics, in terms of percentages, to consider the impact of the increasing numbers of the group aged sixty-five and over on society. We show how demographers account for human behavior on the basis of analyses of the numbers of elderly people in a society. The chapter also contains projections for the future based on present statistics. Interestingly enough, the demographics of this chapter show how demographers have, without intent, defined old age as a social problem.

FACTS AND FIGURES ABOUT AGING

Aging indicates the relentless running out of every individual's biological time clock. To gerontologists, this means the psychological, sociological, and biological changes that result from aging. To demographers, aging is dealt with in terms of chronological (calendar) age. Demographers take advantage of all the figures gathered by census bureaus and population surveys.

Demography, *the statistical study of human populations (births, marriages, deaths, etc.),* can paint a picture of the gerontic population by showing percentages, averages, and future projections. Statistics do not provide for individual differences nor are their projections intended to be predictions. Forecasting social trends depends on society's remaining basically the same in the future as it is in the present. Such social forecasting is, at best, risky. However, such attempts are necessary if we are to plan effectively for the future. Demographers thus make us aware of what could be, not what will be (Schwartz 1984, 138).

WHO ARE THE AGING?

The *Minneapolis Star and Tribune* in October 1984 ran this headline:

Report: Elderly outnumber teens for 1st time in U.S.

In 1776, when Americans declared their independence, every fiftieth American was sixty-five years or older. By 1900, because the older population had increased at a greater rate than the younger population, every twenty-fifth American was sixty-five years or older. By 1982, every ninth American was sixty-five and over. Demographic projections show that by the year 2010, every seventh American, and by 2030, every fifth American will be sixty-five years or over. The increase of this gerontic population is reflected in the table below.

Year	Percentage of population 65+
1900	4.0
1920	4.7
1950	8.1
1980	11.3
2000*	13.1
2010*	13.9
2030*	21.1
2050*	21.7

*estimates

(U.S. Senate 1984, 5)

Since 1900, technological changes have resulted in longer life spans and lower mortality rates. In the year 1900, only two-fifths of the babies born were expected to reach the age of sixty-five. By 1984, however, four-fifths of all babies born were expected to reach the age of sixty-five years of age. The death rates fell more sharply from 1969 to 1984 than in any other fifteen-year period in United States history. The sharp reductions of deaths from heart disease and strokes are credited for the improved life expectancy of the elderly.

When looking at the third diagram in Figure 3.1, you can ignore the percentages and simply note the graphic changes of the past, present, and future population distributions according to age. In 1900, when the fertility and mortality rates were quite high, they produced a pyramid or triangular effect. By the year 2050, the population age shift will create a nearly square form.

CAUSES OF POPULATION SHIFTS

Three factors influence the changes in age composition and the growth of the older population in the United States:

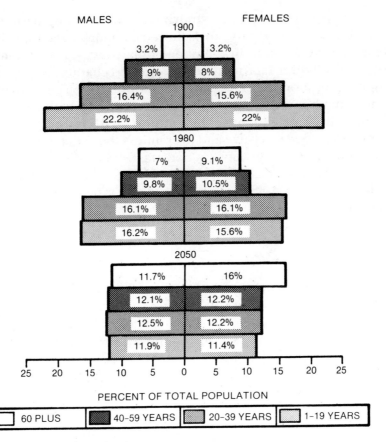

FIGURE 3.1
Actual and projected change in population distribution: 1900-2050 (U.S. Senate Special Committee on Aging, Aging America: Trends and Projections, *1984.)*

1. Fertility rates = refers to the number of births in society. This affects the population by adding new individuals each year.
2. Mortality rate = refers to the number and distribution of deaths. This subtracts members from society.
3. Migration rate = can provide either gains or losses in a population, depending whether people are moving in or out of the population area.

At first glance, when studying the elderly population, one might assume that the mortality rate is the most important factor bringing about demographic changes in the population. However, that is not the case. Although all three factors affect the size and characteristics of the elderly population, mortality rates and migration rates are relatively unimportant. A number of demographic analyses have shown that general declines in mortality rates do not contribute to a rise in the proportion of the population aged sixty-five and over unless those declines are concentrated in the older age groups (Woodruff 1983). Likewise, migration rates have a relatively small role in the changes in the elderly population. Elderly population generally has the lowest rates of migration of any other age group.

Fertility Rates

The primary factor affecting the size of the elderly population is fertility rate. Fertility rates determine the size of each cohort in the population. Each *cohort—a group of persons born at the same time; approximately the same age*—becomes elderly approximately sixty-five years after the time of birth. Thus, the higher the birth rates, the larger the future elderly population will be. Likewise, the lower the birth rates, the smaller the elderly population (Figure 3.2).

Example

In the 1930s, the birth rates were very low. In the 1990s, the people born during the 1930s will reach age 65. The result is that we will see a decrease in the growth of elderly people in the 1990s. Similarly, in the 1950s, the birth rates were very high, resulting from a baby boom. The result is that in the 2010s, when this cohort reaches 65, there will be a high growth in the elderly population, or a gerontic boom. We are, in fact, about to see the population of the post-World War II baby boom turn gray.

Mortality Rates

The decline in death rates has contributed to the increase in the number of aged persons. However, its effects on such increases are less than the effects of the rise in the number of births. Deaths, which are fewer than

PERCENT

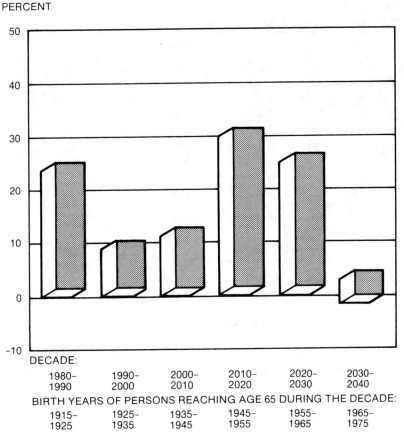

SOURCE: U.S. Bureau of the Census, Demographic and Socioeconomic Aspects of Aging in the United States, Series P-23, No. 138, August, 1984.

FIGURE 3.2
Percent increase of the population sixty-five years and over: 1920-2040 (U.S. Bureau of the Census, Demographic and Socioeconomic Aspects of Aging in the United States, Series P-23, No. 138, August 1984.)

births, are distributed over all the ages of the life span. Deaths are subject to less fluctuation over a period of a century than are births. Thus, the potential role of fertility in changing the size of the elderly population over certain periods of time exceeds the potential role of mortality. Mortality rates have fallen rather regularly through most years of this century. As a result, the initial cohorts of births have a better survival rate. Mortality, at the other end of the life span, has also been reduced. Such a

TABLE 3.1
Mortality rates: 1920–2050

Year (July 1)	Percent	Year (July 1)	Percent
Estimates:		Projections:	
1920	4.6	1990	12.7
1930	5.4	2000	13.1
1940	6.8	2010	13.9
1950	8.1	2020	17.3
1960	9.3	2030	21.1
1970	9.9	2040	21.6
1980	11.3	2050	21.7

Source: U.S. Bureau of the Census, Current Population Reports, August 1984, p. 9.

trend could mean a somewhat larger elderly population than originally estimated by the Census Bureau (see Table 3.1).

Immigration Rates

Immigration, movement into a country, and emigration, movement away from a country, have only a minimal effect on demographic figures. Whether immigration contributes to the growth of the older population depends on its volume. The fluctuation in immigration has sometimes resulted in an acceleration of population growth rates for the elderly and at other times in a deceleration. The large and increasing volume of immigration before World War I, particularly of youth, contributed greatly to the increase in the number of persons aged sixty-five and over in about 1960. Since 1960, immigration has decreased and thus has been much less important in the growth of the elderly population. Immigration is expected to play only a minor role in the future.

Population Growth among the Old Groups

The effects on an increased elderly population due to these three factors, fertility, mortality and migration, are reflected not only in the future estimates of the sixty-five-year age group (young-old) but also of the seventy-five years and over age group (middle-old). There are also dramatic increases in the eighty-five years and older age group (old-old). Statistics show that the group aged eighty-five years and over is expanding faster than the general population.

Years	Percentage of population 75+
1920	1.4
1950	2.6
1980	4.4
2000*	6.5
2010*	6.7
2030*	9.8

Year	Number of 85+
1940	365,000
1984	2,600,000
2000*	5,400,000

*estimates

An overall effect of the increased number of elderly people is the increase in the median age of all Americans:

- 1790 median age was 16.0
- 1980 median age was 30.2
- 2000 median age will probably be 36.3

AGING POPULATIONS: A WORLD PHENOMENON

The United States, although having a high percentage of elderly population as a country, does not rank highest in the world. For the year 1980, the chart below gives some comparisons with other countries. Note that although 65 is used in this demographic comparison, it does not mean that other countries consider ages sixty-five and over old. Individual cultures determine such factors.

Country	Percentage of population 65+
Russia	27.4
Poland	19.2
England	17.9
Ireland	16.3
United States	11.3

The aging of populations is an international phenomenon. All world regions are witnessing an increase in the size of their elderly population. The number of elderly people in the world is expected to increase from 376 million in 1980 to 1,121 million in 2025, and the proportion of older persons in the total world population is expected to increase from 8.5 percent to 13.7 percent during that period. This increase will result in a world population in which one out of every seven individuals will be sixty years of age or older by the year 2025 (U.S. Senate 1984, 19).

Developed Versus Developing Populations

A substantial difference exists among the rates of aging of the populations in developed (industrialized) and developing (nonindustrialized) countries. In fact, the 1980s mark a turning point in which the numbers of people aged sixty and over are about evenly divided between developed countries (e.g., United States, USSR, Canada, Japan, and France) and developing countries (e.g., South Africa, Uganda, Kenya, and Ethiopia). However, by the year 2025, the group aged sixty years and over is expected to equal 315 million in the developed regions and 806 million in the developing regions. This will mean that only 28 percent of the world's elderly people will reside in currently industrialized countries, and 72 percent will reside in developing countries (U.S. Senate 1984, 19).

Reasons for Elderly Population Increases

The world's increase in elderly populations is primarily due to two factors:

1. A slowing down of the birth rate, creating large numbers in the cohort that will be elderly during the next century.
2. An increase in longevity due to improvements in health care and nutrition.

However, differences in longevity rates remain for developed and developing countries. Differences in the average life span of men and women in developing countries is as much as twenty years less (fifty-four to fifty-six years) than for women in developed countries (sixty-eight to seventy-six). The differences in longevity rates for men and women is less great in developing countries (two years) than in developed countries (eight years).

Although historically, the life expectancy of human beings has undergone a dramatic change (as shown in the following chart), the majority of the increase has taken place in the last eighty years.

Year	Country	Life Expectancy
1000 B.C.	Greece	20
100 A.D.	Rome	25
1200 A.D.	England	35
1900 A.D.	U.S.	47.8
1980 A.D.	U.S.	73.7

Since 1900, we have gained nearly 50 percent of the age increase. To avoid the false conclusion that this percentage of increase will continue, it must be stated that between:

1. 1900 to 1940, there was a 15.6-year increase;
2. 1940 to 1980, there was a 9.6-year increase.

The rate of life expectancy has slowed down and will continue to do so unless major medical findings greatly reduce the major causes of death—heart disease, stroke, and cancer.

WHERE ARE THE AGING?

Although elderly people live in every geographic location in our country, persons aged sixty-five and over made up 13 percent or more of the total population in twelve states in 1983, as shown in the following chart, and in the map in Figure 3.3.

Rank	State	Percentage of 65+
1.	Florida	17.6
2.	Rhode Island	14.4
3.	Arkansas	14.3
4.	Iowa	14.1
5.	Pennsylvania	14.1
6.	Missouri	13.6
7.	South Dakota	13.6
8.	Nebraska	13.5
9.	Massachusetts	13.4
10.	Kansas	13.3
11.	Maine	13.2
12.	West Virginia	13.1

STATES IN WHICH 13 PERCENT OR MORE OF THE TOTAL POPULATION WERE PERSONS AGED SIXTY-FIVE AND OVER IN 1983

SOURCE: U.S. Senate Special Committee on Aging, Aging America: Trends and Projections, 1984.

FIGURE 3.3
Where are the aging?

Table 3.2 ranks each state, shows the percentage increase in population age sixty-five and over from 1974 to 1984, and the percentage of the total residents age sixty-five and over in each state for the year 1984.

At the time of the 1980 census, seven states had more than 1 million people sixty-five years of age and older: California, New York, Florida, Pennsylvania, Texas, Illinois, and Ohio. Michigan's elderly population was close to 1 million. Almost one-half of the total elderly population resided in these eight states. Alaska had the smallest number of elderly people, with only 12,000, which was 3 percent of its total population.

One-half of states with the highest percentage of elderly populations are located in the North Central region of the United States. These states are mainly rural and agricultural. Presently, people aged sixty-five and over are less likely to live in metropolitan areas than are young people, although the percentage difference is less than one might expect.

TABLE 3.2
Population increase: 1974–1984

Rank	State	Percent Increase in Population Age 65 and Older, 1974 to 1984	Population Age 65 and Older As Percent of Total Resident Population, 1984
1.	Nevada	112.2%	9.6%
2.	Alaska	87.5	3.0
3.	Arizona	77.7	12.3
4.	Hawaii	77.4	9.1
5.	New Mexico	57.0	9.5
6.	Florida	52.4	17.6
7.	South Carolina	51.1	10.0
8.	North Carolina	45.5	11.2
9.	Utah	45.5	7.8
10.	Idaho	42.1	10.8
11.	Georgia	39.7	9.9
12.	Delaware	39.6	10.9
13.	Virginia	39.5	10.2
14.	Washington	39.0	11.3
15.	Colorado	37.3	8.8
16.	Oregon	37.1	12.9
17.	California	35.6	10.5
18.	Texas	35.2	9.5
19.	Maryland	34.2	10.3
20.	New Hampshire	32.6	11.7
21.	Tennessee	32.6	12.0
22.	Montana	31.5	11.7
23.	Wyoming	31.3	8.2
24.	Alabama	30.4	11.9
25.	Connecticut	29.6	12.9
26.	Louisiana	29.1	9.8
	UNITED STATES	28.5	11.9
27.	Arkansas	27.3	14.3
28.	Michigan	26.2	11.1
29.	New Jersey	25.8	12.6
30.	Maine	24.6	13.2
31.	Mississippi	24.4	11.8
32.	Pennsylvania	24.3	14.1
33.	Rhode Island	24.3	14.4
34.	West Virginia	23.8	13.1
35.	Vermont	23.5	11.9

(continued)

TABLE 3.2 (continued)
Population increase: 1974–1984

Rank	State	Percent Increase in Population Age 65 and Older, 1974 to 1984	Population Age 65 and Older As Percent of Total Resident Population, 1984
36.	Oklahoma	22.3	12.2
37.	Indiana	22.2	11.6
38.	Ohio	21.9	11.9
39.	Wisconsin	21.0	12.8
40.	North Dakota	20.8	12.7
41.	Kentucky	20.3	11.8
42.	Minnesota	19.7	12.4
43.	Illinois	19.6	11.8
44.	Massachusetts	17.6	13.4
45.	Missouri	15.4	13.6
46.	Kansas	15.0	13.3
47.	South Dakota	14.3	13.6
48.	Iowa	13.9	14.1
49.	Nebraska	13.1	13.5
50.	New York	12.5	12.7
51.	Dist. of Col.	5.6	12.0

Source: NEA Research and U.S. Bureau of the Census

However, the profile of the average elderly person is expected to change from rural to urban by the year 2000. Urbanization among elderly people is expected to increase from 46 percent in 1975 to 55 percent in the year 2000. Elderly women are becoming more urbanized as they become more professionally active. It is forecast that 60 percent of the women aged seventy and over will be living in urban areas by the year 2000.

Age	Percent in Metro Areas
Under 65	68%
65+	64%

FIGURE 3.4

Living Arrangements: Institutionalization versus Independence

The majority of elderly people live in their own home in a family setting. Sixty-eight percent of these elderly living in their own home live independently, and another 27 percent have made some other noninstitutionalized living arrangements. A very small percentage of the population aged sixty-five and over (5 to 7 percent) is confined to an institution. At about 75 years of age, the percentage of people institutionalized begins to rise sharply. For people aged 85 and over, the percentage increases to 25 percent.

Living Arrangements: Sex Differences

Living arrangements, family setting versus living alone or with relatives, are affected by the sex ratio. Because women live longer and usually marry

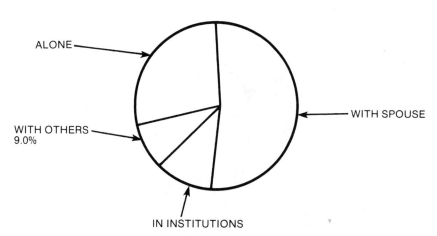

FIGURE 3.5
Living arrangements of the elderly in Minnesota:
1980 (Courtesy of University of Minnesota)

older men, a greater number of women will find it necessary to live with a relative, nonrelative, or alone. Such living arrangements affected 40 percent of the women sixty-five years old and over in 1981 as compared to 15 percent of men sixty-five years old and over (Figure 3.5).

LIFE EXPECTANCY: SEX DIFFERENCES

Three demographic facts have not changed over the past century:

1. The proportion of the aged population continues to increase.
2. The average life expectancy of human beings continues to increase.
3. The amount of time that women live longer than men continues to increase.

Women have a lower mortality rate than men at all ages. More males than females are born, but females have a higher survival rate from birth on. Researchers can only speculate as to the reasons for the higher survival rate of females. There are two popularly accepted reasons—one is physical and the other social.

Physical Causes

The extra X chromosome in the female provides more immunity to disease; for example, the hormone estrogen would seem to protect women against coronary heart disease. Males suffer more from the major killers—such as heart disease, stroke and cancer—than do females.

Social Causes

Males find it difficult to make the transition from working to nonworking. Females have had numerous roles, many of which retirement does not change. Males lose their work and sometimes provider role and have no previous roles to resume. Assistant housewife is not an attractive one for them to take on. This occurrence creates a stressful time in their lives. War-related deaths also contribute, but they are not the major reason for the difference in the sex ratio.

Year	Life Expectancy in Years for Females beyond Males:
1900	2.0
1940	4.4
1950	5.5
1960	6.5
1970	7.5
1980	7.7
2000*	15.0

*estimate

The physical and social reasons for the female's longer life not only appear as though they will not change, but the life expectancy gap between males and females also continues to widen. In 1980, even after a person had reached sixty-five years of age, he or she could expect an average of 16.4 more years of life. But a difference exists between males and females. Females could expect an additional 18.4 years; males could expect only another 14.1 years.

Sex Ratio

The difference in life expectancy between males and females creates a sex ratio. The following chart shows the proportion of males aged sixty-five and over to the females for the same age group. When the sex ratio is determined for old people aged seventy-five and over, the differences in the statistical findings are not unique to the United States. This life expectancy difference is worldwide. Many psychological and social adjustments must be made as a result of the sex ratio.

Year	Males per 100 Females
1980	68
2000*	64
*estimates	

Year	Ages	Number of Widowed Females to Males
1978	65-74	41.0% females widowed
		9.3% males widowed
	75+	69.7% females widowed
		24.3% males widowed

FIGURE 3.6
(From **Homemaker-Home Health Aide,** *2nd ed., by* **Helen Huber, Audree Spatz, and Carole Coviello,** *copyright © 1985 by Delmar Publishers Inc.)*

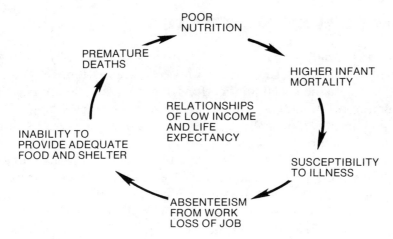

FIGURE 3.7
Low income and life expectancy

Racial Differences

Life expectancies differ not only with sex but also with race. The race age difference may be due to socioeconomic reasons (Figure 3.7). Lower income affects medical care and living conditions. These, in turn, create factors that shorten the life expectancy of black Americans, Mexican Americans, and Indians.

Year	*Life Expectancy at Birth*
1976	69.7 years—white males
	64.1 years—black males
	77.3 years—white females
	72.6 years—black females

The sex ratio gap also exists among the minorities. It appears that for males, the effects of employment, retirement, and unemployment are the same regardless of skin color. To be old is to lose one's friends in the work force and thus lose one's support group. Forced retirement does not have a favorite color. Ageism is color blind.

AGING NUMBERS EFFECT CHANGE

All the demographic charts demonstrate how demography can be used as a tool to describe the age composition of our population. They can also be a tool to assess the social implications of these aging numbers. The older population is not a homogeneous group nor is it unchanging. Every day, approximately 5,200 Americans celebrate their sixty-fifth birthday, but only 1,000 celebrate their twenty-first birthday. About 3,000 people aged sixty-five and over die each day. There thus is a net gain of about 438,000 elderly people a year. These seniors are unique and have brought with them their individual life histories and expectations. People who live longer plan differently. This graying population will create striking changes in the structure and values of our society. These demographic changes will affect the economic, political, legal, and educational systems of our nation.

AGING AND ECONOMICS

A few elderly people are financially well off. A few are rich. But in 1982, about 1 out of every 7 (14.6% of the elderly population or 3.751 billion) elderly Americans were considered to be living in poverty. The official definition for poverty in 1980 was an annual income of $4,954 for an older couple household or $3,941 for an older individual living alone. Another 10 percent of the elderly population can be described as nearly poor. Together, these figures mean that one-fourth of the older population is poor or nearly poor. These statistics do not include the many older people

1980 Annual Income Distribution of U.S. Elderly by Age		
	65-79	80+
Less than $3,000	6%	9%
$3,000- 4,999	16%	25%
5,000- 6,999	13%	14%
7,000- 9,999	16%	15%
10,000-14,999	18%	14%
15,000-19,999	11%	7%
20,000+	21%	16%
Median Income	$9,901	$7,390
		(Galle 1985, 29)

who experience financial difficulty. The economic position of people aged sixty-five and over, in general, is considerably lower and much less secure than that of the younger population. The lower incomes in the elderly population are associated with factors over which they themselves have little control: their sex, their race, their spouses' survival, their own health, fixed incomes, and their ability to continue to work at acceptable wages.

Demographers predict there will be more affluent elderly householders in the future as the baby boom generation ages. The following projections are by income categories (in millions of people):

Income Category	Numbers in Millions of Age 65+	
$50,000 and over	1985 = 0.8	1995 = 1.2
40,000-49,999	1985 = 0.6	1995 = 0.8
30,000-39,999	1985 = 1.1	1995 = 1.6
20,000-29,999	1985 = 2.4	1995 = 3.2
10,000-19,999	1985 = 5.7	1995 = 7.1
Less than 10,000	1985 = 8.2	1995 = 8.3
		(*USA Today,* February 4, 1985)

Sources of Income

Retirement reduces income and may thus reduce the level of living one is accustomed to. People who experience this economic change can suffer as great or greater an emotional impact than those who have always been poor. Families with a head of household aged sixty-five years or older have traditionally relied on wages and earnings for the greater portion of their incomes. That portion of income contributed by wages has steadily diminished over the years to the point at which Social Security is presently of at least equal significance. This trend is due in part to the decline in labor force participation rates and the trend toward the earlier retirement of elderly men. The importance of Social Security income is evident when compared to the relative contributions of other sources of income. However, the extent to which individuals receive income from these sources depends in a large part on their income level. At the lowest levels of income, Social Security plays a major part in their economic welfare. As income from sources other than Social Security increases, the reliance of older people on Social Security itself decreases and their reliance on earnings increases dramatically. See Figure 3.8.

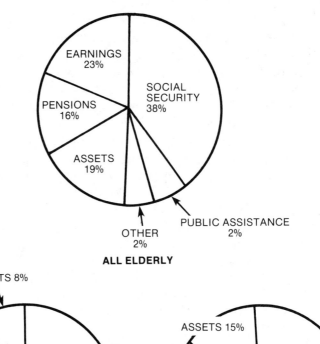

ALL ELDERLY

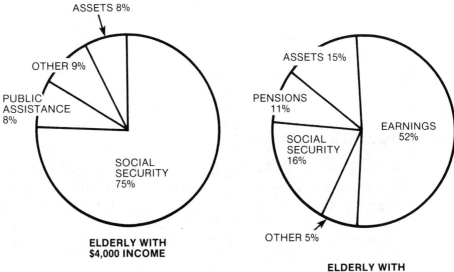

ELDERLY WITH $4,000 INCOME

ELDERLY WITH $20,000 INCOME

FIGURE 3.8
1980 income sources of the elderly in the United States

Income Differs with Sex of Elderly People

Elderly widowed women have lower retirement incomes than do elderly widowed men. Contrary to the stereotype of the older rich widow, in 1981 only 86,000 women of all marital statuses had incomes over

$50,000. Males were much more likely to be included in the small portion of wealthy older people. Almost 9 percent of elderly white males had incomes greater than $30,000 in 1981 compared with 1 percent of females.

Elderly people who live alone receive much less income than do those who live as part of a family or as members of multiperson households.

1980 Income Distribution of U.S. Elderly People by Marital Status		
	Married Couples	Unmarried Couples
Less than $3,000	2%	18%
$3,000-4,999	7%	35%
5,000-6,999	11%	17%
7,000-9,999	18%	14%
10,000-14,999	24%	9%
15,000-19,999	13%	3%
20,000+	23%	4%
Median Income	$12,020	$4,780
		(Galle 1985, 26)

Some of the percentage difference shown on this chart may be attributed to the following three factors:

1. The average older age of people living alone.
2. Income is decreased with the loss of a spouse.
3. Due to age, there will be a loss of income from work.

Fixed incomes become increasingly more inadequate as inflation and cost of living increases affect goods and services. Even with Medicare and Medicaid, the increased costs of medical care and medicines force many elderly people to go without adequate medical aids or help.

As a rule, it is more difficult for older people to save money than for younger people. They are without opportunities to get additional, or perhaps any, employment. They may need to take public transportation because they cannot walk even short distances. Heating costs may be greater because poor circulation forces them to keep their homes at warmer temperatures. They cannot purchase groceries in large quantities on special sale because large amounts may spoil; they may not have the money to purchase larger amounts for future use; or they may not be able to carry numerous items due to weight or stairways. Borrowing money is also very difficult for the elderly person.

FIGURE 3.9

These and many other financial difficulties do not always meet the definition of poverty, but they do create financial hardships. Many people face poverty for the first time in their lives after they retire. Psychologists confirm that severe, or perceived severe, economic limitations can affect physical and mental health. Poor economic conditions affect the overall quality of life for one-fourth of the elderly population.

DEPENDENCY RATIO

$$\text{Dependency ratio} = \frac{\text{Population 65+}}{\text{Population 18-64}} \times 100$$

The dependency ratio is arrived at by taking the number of the dependent retired population and dividing it by the number of wage earners in the eighteen to sixty-four age group (per 100) (Schwartz 1979, 48-49). The reason this concept is vital to the economics of elderly people is that demographic composition of the population gives the number of economic supporters and the corresponding number of recipients for any given year. As the elderly group aged sixty-five and over grows larger in comparison to the eighteen to sixty-four age group, the

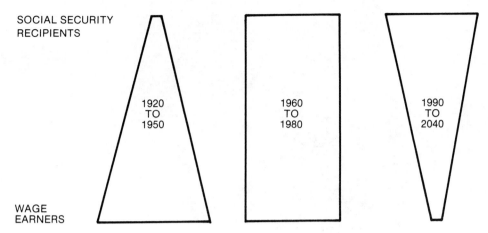

FIGURE 3.10
Wage earners and Social Security recipients:
1920-2040

amount of money to be exchanged is less per individual. It must be remembered that the Social Security deducted from every wage earner's check is immediately paid out. Social Security money is not an account reserved for the depositor. The flow of money comes from an increasingly smaller number of wage earners and is being distributed to an ever increasing number of retirees. See Figure 3.10.

	Age Dependency Ratio		
1920	8.0	1990*	20.7
1930	9.1	2000*	21.2
1940	10.9	2010*	21.9
1950	13.4	2020*	28.7
1960	16.8	2030*	36.9
1970	17.6	2040*	37.7
1980	18.6		
*estimates			
			(U.S. Senate 1984, 124)

AGE AND POLITICS

On November 6, 1984, the oldest president in United States history swept the electoral and popular votes to be reelected for four more years.

FIGURE 3.11
Maggie Kuhn, founder of the Gray Panthers (From
Geriatrics: A Study of Maturity, 4th ed., by Esther
Caldwell and Barbara R. Hegner, copyright© 1986
by Delmar Publishers Inc.)

President Ronald Reagan was described in news reports as having displayed strength and stamina throughout the long campaign. Even though his age was presented as an issue during the campaign, the American voters obviously did not feel that age was a negative factor.

Providing the necessary services for the growing population age sixty-five and over has become a legislative obligation. Elderly people are a vocal population using organizations to make their needs known. The American Association of Retired Persons (AARP) is the nation's largest organization of older Americans. Its membership exceeds 14 million. This number represents more than half (55 percent) of Americans aged sixty-five and over. Other active organizations include the National Council of Aging (NCOA), the National Council of Senior Citizens, and the popular Gray Panthers. No politician or political force can ignore the impact these numbers can exert. The future changes this aging population will bring about will be in the major areas of health services, mandatory retirement, private pensions, and Social Security.

AGING AND THE LEGAL SYSTEM

The legal system also has felt the impact of demographic changes in the aging population. The 11.3 percent of the American population sixty-five years of age and over need legal support, consumer protection, legal counseling, and assistance in dealing with the effects of crime that affect elderly people. Muggings, rape, and fraud are devastating crimes at any age and no less so for the targeted elderly people (Figure 3.12).

Attempts have been made over the years to establish in all fifty states legal service centers offering free services or a sliding fee scale based on need. By 1970 there were 850 Legal Service Program offices operating in forty-nine states, staffed by nearly 2,200 lawyers. Fifty-three million dollars for this program was provided by the Office of Economic Opportunity. In November of 1970, a 75% to 25% federal state financial match was mandated for inclusion in *all* state plans. This certainly reflects the impact of 25,544,000 elderly Americans.

AGING AND EDUCATION

The increases in older people and in more older people interested in additional learning are affecting the educational system. A growing need also exists for training in gerontology itself. Classes in every kind of school, including colleges, for people aged 65 and over only are gearing their curriculum, hours, and goals to meet the needs of their new student population.

The decline of the youthful, traditional, school-age person means that educational institutions must be creative and flexible in hopes that they can tempt the elderly person to return to school. They need to change the overall administration policies and also need knowledge of and a sensitivity to the special needs and discomfort that returning to school after a long (thirty to fifty years or more) absence can bring. These

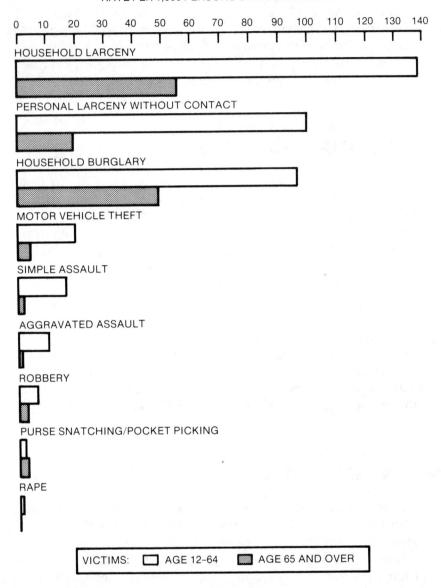

RATE PER 1,000 PERSONS OR HOUSEHOLDS

HOUSEHOLD LARCENY

PERSONAL LARCENY WITHOUT CONTACT

HOUSEHOLD BURGLARY

MOTOR VEHICLE THEFT

SIMPLE ASSAULT

AGGRAVATED ASSAULT

ROBBERY

PURSE SNATCHING/POCKET PICKING

RAPE

VICTIMS: ☐ AGE 12-64   ▨ AGE 65 AND OVER

SOURCE: U.S. Department of Justice, Bureau of Justice Statistics, December 1981.

FIGURE 3.12
Criminal victimization rates—persons twelve to sixty-four years and older: 1973-1980 (U.S. Senate Special Committee on Aging, Aging America: Trends and Projections, *1984.)*

different physical, emotional, and intellectual needs must be met if school is to be a pleasant and fulfilling experience for the gray student.

The educational institutions must also consider the amount of formal education the group aged sixty-five and over actually achieved. Educational attainment declines with increasing age in any year, but this inverse relationship cannot apply to an actual birth cohort. Educational attainment is cumulative and would rise for an actual cohort. As the number of school years completed increases, it reflects the increasing educational opportunities available to each new cohort. It is also associated with the rising socioeconomic status of the population in the United States.

During the last decades, the level of education has increased for every age segment of the population, as seen in the following boxed table.

Both Sexes	Education Median School Years Completed	Percentage of High School Graduates
1959	8.3	19.4
1965	8.5	23.5
1970	8.7	28.3
1975	9.0	35.2
1981	10.3	41.8
1985	11.3	46.2
1990	12.1	53.3
1995	12.2	58.4
2000	12.4	63.7

(U.S. Bureau of the Census 1984, 99)

The younger population with more years of education completed will move into the adult age group. They will be more articulate, have more diverse interests, and will participate more actively in public issues.

AMERICA'S CENTENARIANS

"What is the secret of your longevity?" This is the question most often asked of people who have remained vigorous and healthy to an extreme old age. Most *centenarians, people over 100 years of age,* say they have a theory to explain their longevity. "I never drink"; "I have a drink every

FIGURE 3.13

day"; "I have a yearly checkup"; "I never went to a doctor." These opposing thoughts, plus many others, including exercise, hard work, vitamins, and belief in God, have all been proposed as reasons centenarians sustained the health to celebrate their 100 years of age or over birthday.

The actual number of centenarians in the United States is unknown. Two main reasons account for the lack of demographic information:

1. Census gathering does not break down age categories beyond 85 years of age. Thus, all people aged 85 and over are grouped together. The 1990 census will gather more specific numbers, including the number of centenarians.
2. People usually reduce their age when reporting it during their middle-age years, but people tend to exaggerate their age in their later years. As a result, the number of individuals who claim to be 100 years of age or over tends to be very inaccurate.

Demographers now estimate that there are only 2 or 3 centenarians for every 100,000 persons, only 1 person in 1,000,000 at the age of 105 or over, and only 1 person in every 40,000,000 at the age of 110 or over.

The Soviet Union has reported certain regions to have concentrations of between 39 to 63 centenarians per 100,000 persons. No demographic proof exists of such claims. Even Russian gerontologists question the existence of such centenarian numbers.

Centenarians, as a result of their unusual accomplishment, experience:

1. Social status.
2. Family and community attention.
3. Publicity.

The very old thus tend to exaggerate their age to make the 100-year mark and as far beyond as they dare to stretch it!

FIGURE 3.14

SUMMARY

Demographers provide a statistical portrait of the elderly population. About one out of every nine United States citizens falls within the sixty-five years or over category. Birth rates, death rates, and immigration have contributed to this proportional increase in the aged population.

The average life expectancy of all human beings has constantly increased since 1900. However, it has increased more for some groups than for others. To be white and female is to expect to live the greatest number of years.

The increasing numbers of elderly people create new social problems. Major problems include the economic impact of a large, nonworking class dependent on a smaller working class. This dependency ratio imbalance has serious implications for present and future generations.

It is the work of demographers, who assist gerontologists, sociologists, psychologists, biologists, economists, and politicians, to anticipate the needs of the future. The numbers tell them what could be. Without all segments of society actively seeking solutions, demographers may unintentionally have painted a portrait of what will be!

EXERCISES

1. Watch the daily newspaper or monthly magazines for a period of time and cut out any and all statistics dealing with people aged sixty-five and over. Compare these statistics to those found in this chapter.
2. List two to four names of people for each of the three years you have chosen. The three-year periods chosen should be ten years apart.

	Year:		*Year:*		*Year:*
1.		1.		1.	
2.		2.		2.	
3.		3.		3.	
4.		4.		4.	

Compare the experiences of each year's cohorts as to what they decided was among the greatest event in their lifetime. How did these events affect each group? How did it make each group different?

3. Read about the well-known elderly populations of Russia, especially of Abkhasia. In that reading, did you learn any reasons Russia should have the largest percentage of elderly people, not only 65 years of age and over, but also 100 years of age and over?
4. Write a paragraph explaining how this chapter's chart on life expectancy at birth can provide a possible explanation of life expectancy differences for minority groups.
5. Ask several people aged sixty-five or over what opportunities they had for economic retirement planning during their working days. What types of opportunities exist now in comparison?
6. Determine your year of retirement. By reading the chart on the ratio of Social Security recipients to wage earners, determine how the dependency ratio of that decade will affect your retirement income security. Do future decades anticipate better or worse ratios?

REVIEW

1. Why is knowledge of demographics vital to a student of gerontology?
2. Demographers are interested in aging only in terms of _____ .
3. Population statistics affects what other disciplines of study?
4. Which discipline is the most important in relation to the elderly population?
5. What are the three primary forces that affect the size and composition of the population?
6. Define *cohort*.
7. What has happened to life expectancy rates since 1900? Can we anticipate that the same increase will continue in the future?
8. List the three states with the largest percentage of elderly population. List the three states with the largest numbers of elderly in their state.
9. Why do women outlive men? Will this change in the future?
10. Do life expectancy figures differ only with sex?
11. What is the formula to calculate the dependency ratio?
12. How are the statuses and trends of the elderly population related to the following characteristics?
    1. Size
    2. Age distribution
    3. Sex
    4. Living arrangements
    5. Educational attainment
    6. Economic status
13. Why are these changes important for policymakers?

RECOMMENDED READINGS
AND REFERENCES

Cutler, Neal E. "The Aging Population and Social Policy." *In Aging: Prospects and Issues* (rev. ed.), edited by Richard H. Davis. San Francisco: Andrus Gerontology Center, 1977.

Galle, Bart W., Jr. *Multidisciplinary Perspectives on Aging: Independent Study Guide.* Minneapolis: University of Minnesota, Continuing Education and Extension Department, 1985.

Kermis, Marguerite D. *The Psychology of Human Aging.* Boston: Allyn and Bacon, Inc., 1984.

Minneapolis Star and Tribune. "Report: Elderly Outnumber Teens for 1st Time in U.S.," October 13, 1984.

Schwartz, Arthur N. *et al. Aging and Life.* New York: Holt, Rinehart and Winston, 1984.

Schwartz, Arthur N., and James A. Peterson. *Introduction to Gerontology.* New York: Holt, Rinehart and Winston, 1979.

U.S. Bureau of the Census. *Demographic and Socioeconomic Aspects of Aging in the United States.* Series P-23, No. 138. Washington, D.C.: U.S. Government Printing Office, 1984.

U.S. Senate Special Committee on Aging. *Aging America: Trends and Projections.* Washington, D.C., 1984.

USA Today. "Aging of the Affluent," February 4, 1985.

Woodruff, Diana S., and James E. Birren. *Aging Scientific Perspectives and Social Issues.* Monterey, Calif.: Brooks/Cole Publishing Co., 1983.

CHAPTER
4
Sociology of Aging

Learning Objectives

After studying this chapter, the reader should be able to:

- Realize the adjustment elderly people must make to feel comfortable in society and the adjustment society must make to feel comfortable with the growing population of elderly people.
- Understand that life expectancy affects the way people live and plan.
- Outline historically how contributions once made toward extended family survival later became energy spent in personal, competitive job survival.
- List and define the theories by which aging individuals try to adjust to new roles and expectations in order to find self-fulfillment during that stage in their lives.

Preview

"**Sociology** *is the scientific (or systematic) study of society, social institutions, and social relationships—of the development, structure, interaction, and collective behavior of organized groups of people.* So- ciological gerontology focuses on changes in social structure that accompany the aging of people. The sociology of aging examines how people (groups and whole populations) adjust, change, develop, or remain the same over time. This chapter explores the social conse- quences of individual and group aging as well as the implications for generations that follow and the effects of such factors as income, gender, ethnicity, and health on the aging process.

SOCIOLOGY OF AGING: A DEFINITION

Advanced aging has the potential to alter life in countless ways. It also poses new questions. Is the large number of elderly people in the United States causing a social problem? Are the prejudices, myths, and jokes about old age making it difficult for elderly people to live in our society?

The sociology of aging is the scientific study of older people in society. It studies the behavior patterns of elderly people trying to adjust to society's expectations and of society trying to adjust to elderly people's needs. These recorded observations can help solve existing conflicts and also can show a future pattern from which problems can be anticipated. Aging seems to be receiving more attention as a social issue than as a scientific question.

On the one hand, modern society has taken pride in enabling more people to reach an older age. Many people who are the recipients of that achievement face their added years with hesitancy and fear.

The social problems arise from the fact that the energy spent to ensure a longer life has not been equalled in preparing society to receive that enlarged group of longer-life individuals. Who is to blame? Where do we turn for the answer?

WHAT CAN HISTORY TELL US?

Social aging consists of passage from one socially defined position to another in the course of growing up and growing old. Life expectancies affect the way people plan and live. Shortly before the 1900s, the average person planned for a lifetime of forty-five years. The family setting was mainly rural. Family members, regardless of age, contributed whatever abilities they had. Chronological age meant little. Tasks were assigned by ability and talents possessed, not age.

Contributions of Experience and Age

Authority went to the people with the most experience. Everyone affected the amount of money earned and spent. As years advanced, so did experience and knowledge, which were valuable contributions. Sometimes these qualities were more valuable than physical energy. An older person's wisdom also served as a model for younger members of the family unit. Indeed, the status of the entire family, economic as well as social, was dependent on the valuable contributions of older members.

FIGURE 4.1

Obsolescence

Industrialization, technology, and medicine, however, brought about drastic changes in that traditional family system:

1. An increased life span added quantity to life without providing a paralleling increase in the quality of life.
2. Family-centered work settings were exchanged for individualized employment settings.
3. Valuable experience gained over many years of work had to be replaced by constant upgrading of skills, because the way a job used to be done was now obsolete.

The extended family was broken up by the individual family member's need to relocate, seek higher education, or follow individual professions. The elderly members of the family were no longer needed for their wisdom and experience. Their contributions were outdated. The goal was no longer extended family survival, but individual competition to survive in a competitive job market.

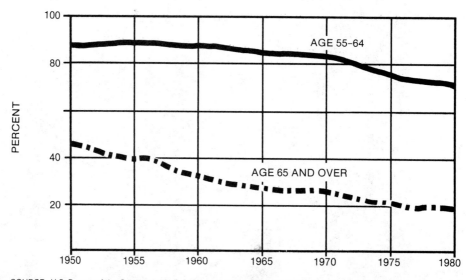

SOURCE: U.S. Bureau of the Census and U.S. Bureau of Labor Statistics reported in U.S. Senate Special Committee on Aging, Developments in Aging: 1982, Volume One.

FIGURE 4.2
Labor force participation of men aged 55-64 and 65 and over: 1950-1980 (U.S. Senate Special Committee on Aging, Aging America: Trends and Projections, 1984.)

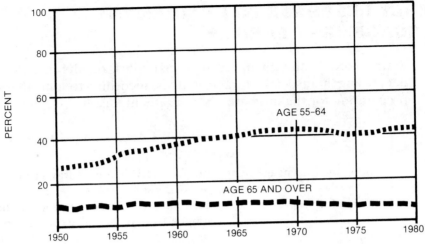

SOURCE: U.S. Bureau of the Census and U.S. Bureau of Labor Statistics reported in U.S. Senate Special Committee on Aging, Developments in Aging: 1982, Volume One.

FIGURE 4.3
Labor force participation of women aged 55-64 and 65 and over: 1950-1980 (U.S. Senate Special Committee on Aging, Aging America: Trends and Projections, 1984.)

One new role that emerged for older workers was retirement. The labor-force participation of elderly men has dropped rapidly during the last thirty years. In 1950, almost half of all elderly men were in the labor force; by 1960, only one-third were working or looking for work; by 1970, only one-fourth; and, by 1980, less than one-fifth (Figure 4.2).

The labor-force participation of elderly women has not varied as greatly as that of men. In 1950, about 10 percent of elderly women worked, and, by 1980, the percentage had dropped to only 8 percent. Women between the ages of fifty-five and sixty-four have increasingly joined the labor force. In 1950, only 27 percent of these women worked, but by 1981 the proportion had risen to 41 percent (Figure 4.3).

Therefore, years of leisure, do-nothing roles were forced on elderly people in a society in which a lack of productivity was frowned on. Noncontributing members of society had no status. Needless to say, older people found their retirement years a most difficult transition. They had to make two major adjustments:

1. Elderly individuals had to accept retirement as an acceptable alternative.
2. Society had to acknowledge a nonworking lifestyle as an acceptable way of life.

ELDERLY RESPONSE TO RETIREMENT: DISENGAGEMENT THEORY

Retirement, or the giving up of social roles, results in elderly people decreasing their social interaction. This, according to some theorists, is in preparation for the ultimate disengagement, death.

Note the difference:

Individual disengagement = how an individual withdraws from his or her many social roles.

Societal disengagement = how society withdraws support and no longer has any social expectations for the person.

Society, in turn, permits and even encourages such behavior so that an individual's eventual death will not be disruptive when transferring power from older members to younger members. Disengagements are thus a two-way street: the individual withdraws from society and society withdraws from the individual. Individuals can fully choose to begin this process; if they refuse, society can break their resistance with forced retirement.

Arguments rage on as to whether disengagement is beneficial to an individual and whether forced retirement is legal. Some individuals choose, in fact, may look forward to, the opportunity to lessen their active social roles. Other individuals may choose not to lessen their activities and are capable of maintaining active social roles beyond the accepted retirement age. A third option may be a shift to new roles requiring neither disengagement nor the fast-paced roles previously engaged in. Atchley (1980, 219) states that fifteen years of research clearly shows that disengagement is neither universal nor an inevitable response to aging.

Medical advancements have provided additional active years of life. Technology, in turn, has lessened the physical requirements of work. Past income levels established a level of living. Society did not keep pace sociologically with these happenings by advancing (only five years in some cases) or abolishing the retirement age. Job opportunities for elderly people or plans by which they could maintain their past standard of living were not in place. Disengagement was never intended to be defined as despair!

Disengagement can also be seen as a gradual adjustment to one's approaching death. In her studies, Kübler-Ross found that individuals who had gradually withdrawn from some of their many roles and activities accepted the pain of separation that terminal illness produced much more easily (Kübler-Ross 1969, 262).

ELDERLY RESPONSE TO RETIREMENT: ACTIVITY THEORY

The activity theory emphasizes the opposite of the disengagement theory. The disengagement theory encourages withdrawal from past roles; the activity theory encourages the continuation of those roles or of an appropriate substitute. Retirement and widowhood often bring an abrupt end to roles to which the individual was accustomed. The activity theory points out the importance of remaining involved in social activities in spite of these role changes.

The disengagement theory appears to be a neat little package in which the individual withdraws from society and society withdraws from the individual. The activity theory is not quite so neatly wrapped. Society is withdrawing from the individual, but the individual is not withdrawing. Most elderly people do not choose to keep the same high, perhaps even stressful, level of activity associated with the work world, but they wish to be busy just the same. George Burns states the case well for this type of person: "You must have a reason to get up in the morning" (Burns 1983, 133).

For some individuals, the activity theory is associated with happiness and fulfillment. They wish to remain involved to some degree after retirement. To others, the disengagement theory is what they have been waiting for and working toward for sixty-five years. Their idea of happiness and fulfillment is to welcome each new day with, "Well, what am I going to do today?" It is reasonable to conclude that the choice of disengagement or activity will depend on the unique lifelong habits, experiences, and goals every individual brings to old age. Both theories have good and bad points and neither provides all the answers to individual or societal concerns about the aging process.

However, adapting to the changes that psychological, social, economic, and physical changes bring is important to adjustment and happiness. As age brings with it some signs of slowing up, some degree of graceful withdrawal from some past roles must be made. Expectations must be adjusted and more appropriate schedules need to be selected. This can be true of any age in which there is a mental or physical cause for such adjustment. To disengage or change activities in such cases is a valuable move toward a suitable match between one's capacity and one's expectations. Both the disengagement and activity theories also provide an opportunity for people who did not like all their roles. It is an opportunity to withdraw gracefully from the less popular roles and engage in new, more suitable ones.

ELDERLY RESPONSE TO RETIREMENT: ENVIRONMENTAL ADJUSTMENT THEORY

The disengagement theory can be deceiving. It is not meant to imply that adjusting to old age is the same as planning for one's death. Quite the contrary. Demographers remind us that once we have reached sixty-five years of age, we can expect to live an average of seventeen more years. Even a cynic could not expect that so many years are needed in planning a funeral.

The activity theory may not be the perfect substitute, either. To put the theory into practice depends on several factors. First, substitute activities must be available. Second, the individual must have the physical, mental, and economic means to take on those new activities. Third, the person must find these substitute activities personally satisfying and therefore want them as substitutes.

Perhaps the environmental adjustment theory proposes a more attractive option than the disengagement or activity theory. Successful aging is largely dependent on the person's ability to change or adjust the external environment to accommodate the physical, social, psychological, and economic changes aging brings. When these adjustments are appropriately made, the individual can continue to function in a self-satisfying manner. The major focus of the environmental adjustment theory is for the individual to retain self-esteem (Schwartz 1974, 14).

Aging is a part of a total life span. Every individual makes adjustments from childhood on. We make a grave error if aging is not seen as part of that total life span (Figure 4.4). Therefore, adjustment must continuously be made. The adjustments may be less or greater depending on the number or severity of losses that must be compensated for. Throughout life, adjustments were usually made without the loss of self-esteem. The same can be true in the later years. Society can greatly help in these changes by providing social services to assist in both the change and the adjustment.

The environmental adjustment theory presents the life cycle as one continuous process of growth and change. This century has seen dramatic changes in how an individual distributes personal time among such major life activities as education, work, retirement, and leisure. Increased longevity and changing social and work patterns mean children are spending more time in school, both men and women in the middle years are spending more time in work, and older people are spending more time in retirement.

Retirement is no longer a luxury; it is now an institution—as much an expected part of life's course as family, school, or work. The portion of life spent in retirement has increased substantially since the beginning of this century. In 1900, the average male had a life span of 46.3 years. An average of 1.2 years, 3 percent of his life span, was spent in retirement. By 1980, the average male had a life span of 69.3 years and was spending 13.8 years, or 20 percent of his life span, in retirement.

In 1980, males averaged more than five more years in the labor force than in 1900. However, a smaller portion of their life cycle was spent in the labor force, 55 percent, than in 1900, when they spent 69 percent of their life span working.

The number of years spent in school also increased for males from an average of 8 years to 12.6 years from 1900 to 1980. However, the proportion of time devoted to education only increased from 17 to 18 percent.

Changes in distribution patterns of major life activities are similar for women. As more women have entered the labor force, a dramatic

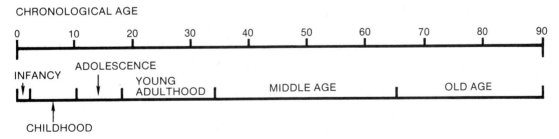

FIGURE 4.4
Total life-span chart (From Atchley, Robert C. **The Social Forces in Later Life. Belmont, Calif.: Wadsworth Publishing Co., 1980, 91.)**

increase has taken place in the portion of time spent in work outside the home. Since 1900, the average number of years spent in the labor force increased from 6.3 to 27.5 years and from 13 percent of the life span to 36 percent (U.S. Senate 1984, 44). These major environmental changes for men and women require social adjustments if they are to maintain high self-esteem throughout these changes. Successful social adjustment is an essential part of the growing and aging processes (Figure 4.5).

The transitions throughout one's life span both for the aging person and society are gradual. Both are flexible enough to allow for successful aging. The goal is realistic and the results can be satisfactory to both.

ELDERLY RESPONSE TO RETIREMENT: SOCIAL BREAKDOWN THEORY

One of the most recently developed social theories of aging is the social breakdown theory (Brown 1985). This theory points out that aging is given bad social reviews. Society emphasizes the poor self-concept of elderly people, the negative response to old age by those who are younger, and the lack of skills older people have to deal with the world.

Prevention of this social breakdown syndrome can happen only when the social system accepts aging in a positive light and demonstrates that attitude change with unbiased treatment. This respectful type of treatment would help elderly people maintain positive self-images. This, in turn, would encourage them to continue to play positive social roles in society.

AGING: A STATUS PASSAGE

Aging, in a social sense, includes multiple status passages. Status refers to the position or rank in relation to other people, and passage refers to the process of moving from one position to another. The aging of the body has social consequences. Three of the many passages include:

1. Physiological aging.
2. Work roles.
3. Family relationships.

According to Glaser and Strauss (1971, 103), passages are described in terms of whether the passage is desirable or reversible. This is determined by:

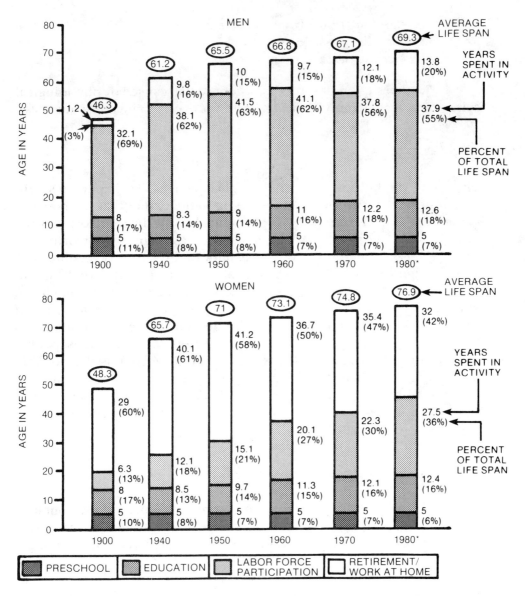

*Data for 1980 is based on 1977 work life estimates.

NOTE: Divisions represent number of years and percent of total life span spent primarily in these activities.

SOURCE: Formal education for 1940 to 1970 compiled from "Median School Years Completed," *Bicentennial Edition-Historical Statistics of the United States*, pp. 380; for 1900 from Best, F., *Work Sharing: Issues, Policy Options and Prospects*, Upjohn Institute for Employment Research, Kalamazoo, Michigan, 1981, pp. 8; for 1980, Bureau of the Census. Worklife estimates from Smith, Shirley; New Work Life Estimates, *Bureau of Labor Statistics Bulletin* 2157, November, 1982. Life expectancy from Bureau of the Census.

FIGURE 4.5
Lifecycle distribution of education, labor force participation, retirement and work in the home: 1900-1980 (U.S. Senate Special Committee on Aging, Aging America: Trends and Projections, 1984.)

1. Who has control over the passage.
2. How long the passage lasts.
3. Whether the passage is anticipated.

The three types of status passages (social, caused by physiological aging; career; and family) have separate yet overlapping consequences.

Social Passages

The aging of the body has social consequences. Each person's self-definition is changed with age according to the extent that the person's sense of self is determined by appearance. In American society, *old* is a negative label. Aging is seen as a gradual decrease of personal worth. This aging process is therefore viewed as undesirable and irreversible. The methods aging persons adopt to control this aging passage are the use of cosmetics, undergoing face-lifts, and dressing in a style that might be viewed as young. This control over the passage may be a measure of reversibility. Chronological age alone does not create clear boundaries for entering or leaving a particular status. This is one reason most people in their seventies still label themselves as middle-aged. It is also possible for the aging person to believe in a middle-aged status because aging is so gradual. Aging is most easily perceived by people who have not seen us over a period of time. Looking in a mirror every morning does not make aging as perceptible to oneself.

Career Passages

Work roles also hold a series of status passages throughout the course of life. Work roles are age-graded and have age implications. Older workers generally have more seniority and command higher wages than younger workers. They are also more susceptible to unemployment. Once older workers lose their jobs, they are less likely to regain their former jobs or find employment with a comparable wage. Retirement, forced or voluntary, is both a luxury and a stigma. Individuals, depending on how far away or how close they are to retirement, view that passage quite differently.

Family Passages

Family life contains many passages, including marriage, (divorce), parenthood, the "empty nest," grandparenthood, and widowhood. Although these passages may occur in somewhat different order for some people, they nonetheless tend to be in a hierarchical order to family careers. Marriage must precede widowhood, and parenthood must come before grandparenthood.

The young family includes such descriptive terms as *father* and *mother;* the elderly person takes on such descriptive terms as *retiree, senior citizen,* or *grandparents.* These status terms signify the passages that the individuals have experienced and are age related.

Status passages, whether associated with work, family, careers, or physical aging, influence relationships with other people. For example, most people see parenthood as marking the entrance into adulthood, with society's assuming the parent will accept adult responsibilities. Retirement is associated with disengagement from the work role. It symbolizes the giving up of the work role and is associated with age.

In America, some neighborhoods also tend to be age graded. Some areas advertise as young neighborhoods, where property is bought by young couples with children. Similarly, in retirement areas, quiet is preserved by sales only to elderly people. Not only do the neighborhoods take on an identity, but the individuals owning the homes also take on an identity.

AGE AND THE DIFFERENT SOCIAL STRUCTURES

As many different social structures exist among the elderly people as among other age groups. These differences include income, gender, race, and ethnicity.

Income level is a major source of variability among elderly people. Their age group includes the poorest and least powerful people in our society and also the wealthiest and most powerful. Three factors to keep in mind when looking at the income level of elderly people include:

1. Being old and being poor are not necessarily synonymous.
2. Although most people experience a drastic drop in income at retirement (50 percent or more), most retirees say that they have sufficient income for living. This income may come from a combination of sources: savings and property, combined with reduced expenses due to the empty nest.
3. Social Security during the past ten years has kept pace with inflation so that the economic status of the aged has actually improved. This does not imply that all elderly needs are taken

FIGURE 4.6

care of by Social Security. Demographers point out that people over sixty-five years of age are still much more likely to have incomes that fall below poverty lines than are people at younger ages.

Gender is a key variable in our society. Economic as well as social differences exist between males and females at all ages. Men and women experience old age differently in the following five ways:

1. The mortality rate is much higher for males. Although both men and women have been living longer, the gender gap in longevity has been increasing.
2. Men are more than twice as likely to be married in old age than women. (In 1980, 80.6 percent of men between the ages sixty-four and seventy-four were married, compared to 49.3 percent for women of the same age.)
3. Older women are much more likely to have economic problems than men. (In 1981, the median income for males sixty-five years and over was $8,173. For females of the same age, the median income was $4,757.) This lower economic condition results

from lower female wages and their inconsistency in the labor market. As a result, few women have pensions and few inherit pensions.

4. Women have a significant advantage over men in terms of social ties and social network systems. Women tend to have closer relationships with both family and friends. Men often establish social relationships with other people through their wives. As a result, widowed males appear to be more socially isolated than are widowed females, especially in the earlier phase of their widowhood, and later may be able to establish companionship with older males.

5. Elderly widowers are eight times more likely than elderly widows to commit suicide. This high suicide rate for widowers is interpreted to mean that the elderly man has faced the loss of two major roles if he is widowed: the loss of his wife, who tended to keep him more socially active, and the fact he is retired and has suffered the loss of his work role. Also due to the wife's domestic role, it would appear more difficult for elderly men to live without their wives than elderly women without their husbands.

Race is another factor that creates differing social experiences in aging. Both economic and cultural differences are related to racial inequality in our society. In 1982, 35.6 percent of the elderly black population was below the poverty level and 30 percent of the elderly Spanish was below the poverty level, compared to 12 percent of the elderly white population (U.S. Senate 1984, 37). Some gerontologists have described being old and black as double jeopardy and being old, black, and female as triple jeopardy. Mortality rates are also higher for blacks, especially males; and, therefore, a higher proportion of black women are widowed. That fact, in addition to black older women being more likely than white women to have a spouse who is absent, may account for the economic deprivation for blacks of all ages.

Cultural or ethnic differences also exist. Black families are more likely to live in three-generation households. Black grandmothers are also more likely to have an influential role in the rearing of the grandchildren when compared to white grandmothers.

Ethnic differences go even deeper. Most elderly white Americans express a preference for intimacy at a distance. They prefer to live near, but not with, their children. In comparison, Polish and Italian Americans prefer a widowed parent to live with the children rather than to live alone. English and Scandinavian elders visit much less with family; they substitute membership in organizations. Social ties appear to vary significantly among ethnic groups.

ROLE CONFUSION

As stated at the beginning of this chapter, the sociology of aging is the scientific study of elderly behavior in society. Confusion occurs when elderly people are unsure of what behavior or role is expected of them. Before people can meet role expectations for themselves or society, they need to:

1. Know what the role involves.
2. Have the ability to fulfill the role.
3. Have the desire to meet the expectations of the role.

The purpose of socialization is to help people gain the knowledge, ability, and motivation to perform a role satisfactorily. Social roles hold great importance. People often define themselves in terms of their roles. Roles also give people a place or status in society.

We know that elderly people have the ability to perform important roles in society. The problem exists in the other two requirements. They are not clear as to what the roles are, and they may not be motivated enough to want to carry them out.

Role confusion occurs when society has not clearly defined what is expected or has not provided any guidelines to meet those expectations. Such boundaries, when given, provide predictability to human behavior. This problem is not unique to elderly people. Historically, role confusion occurred when slaves were freed, when women began to become independent of male domination, and when the legal age for teen-agers kept being changed or differed from state to state.

Reaching sixty-five years of age and retirement is also on the list of role confusion. There are few guidelines regarding this role. Not only are elderly people themselves confused, but society also seems unsure. We have role expectations for chiropractors, nurses, and teachers. But what is our role expectations for retirees? What should they do with the twenty-four-hour day? What should they be contributing to society in general? What actions should be rewarded? From where should come the motivation to take on new roles? Each person addressing these questions may have a different answer.

Retirement became an accepted concept in 1935, when Congress passed the Social Security Act. Then, in 1978, Congress passed the Age Discrimination in Employment Act Amendments, which raised the legal age of retirement from sixty-five to seventy years of age and eliminated mandatory retirement for federal employees. However, during those fifty years, we have made elderly people play a game for which there are no established rules. With nearly 28,000,000 people sixty-five years of age and over, this is not just role confusion, it is mass confusion!

SEX ROLE CHANGES

The term *sex roles* is often used to describe the varied characteristics individuals have because of their sex. It may be more accurate to define sex role as expected behavior of a person because he or she is male or female.

Research on sex roles in the 1970s and 1980s found an apparent shift toward unisex roles—roles common to both males and females—in later life. During postparental years, there is no longer the need for

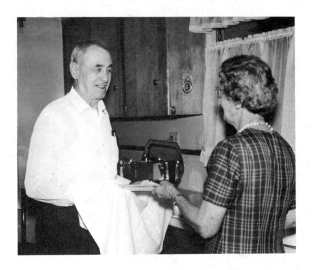

FIGURE 4.7
(From Geriatrics: A Study of Maturity, *4th ed., by Esther Caldwell and Barbara R. Hegner, copyright © 1986 by Delmar Publishers Inc.)*

traditional sex roles. Guttmann's studies (1975) suggest that during the empty nest years:

1. Males no longer have the demanding work role during which they often suppressed the nurturing and tenderness roles.
2. Women's nurturing and caring roles for children are completed and they no longer have to suppress their aggressive feelings.

   With the present emphasis on males sharing the parenting role and females sharing the work-outside-the-home role, fewer traditional sex roles exist. The personality change toward unisex as seen in the past may be but a phenomenon of the present older generation. However, sex role changes or adjustments are not unusual as they are made in each stage of life. More recent studies have shown that both males and females, once having reached middle age, point out that their main goals are the same — accomplishment, independence, and happiness.

FIGURE 4.8

ROLE PREPARATION

How does an elderly person plan for a role when society has no guidelines? In American society, we prepare for almost every role in an organized, systematic manner. When young, we go to school for the prescribed number of credits or hours. We train under supervisors or coaches until we have mastered a prescribed skill. We know what is expected, and we plan our energy, time, and money accordingly. Different roles have different requirements, and past roles may provide limited experience for new ones. In order to change roles, we may need to make plans to meet the new requirements. Through new, formalized training, we are made aware of what to expect in our new role. We approach each new challenge with the eagerness and competitiveness to which we have been accustomed in the past.

Suddenly, the role is retirement, and we have no school to attend for knowledge, no on-the-job training for experience, and no rule book for guidelines. Also, our past eager, competitive spirit is to be exchanged for a passive, more dependent attitude that resembles nothing we have displayed in any past role. Besides being confused, elderly people are unprepared.

WHOM DO THE ELDERLY PEOPLE IMITATE?

Who are the role models who can demonstrate successful aging? Nearly every age and every profession has its role models. Nearly everyone has an idea of whom they want to be like. However, no one wants to be old or like anyone who is old. Even elderly people themselves select younger role models. This youth-oriented standard hampers adjustment to aging. Even the older successful individuals are pictured or portrayed without wrinkles, gray hair, or aging spots. The Louis Harris poll (1974) stated that elderly people themselves chose the age of thirty-four as the ideal age. Added to that is the denial of actual ages by most elderly, famous people. Old is always someone else! This socialization dilemma is a formidable obstacle in adjusting to old age.

SOCIAL TIES AND LONGEVITY

Among the 1,200 centenarians interviewed in the United States by the Social Security Administration, enjoyment of work and a strong will to live emerged as dominant common themes among them. Most had lived quiet, circumscribed, independent lives; were content with their lot; ate a balanced diet; were devoted to family and religion; worked hard and enjoyed it; they had no high ambitions, regrets, self-pity, or combativeness.

The importance of social ties and life satisfaction to longevity was highlighted in a study of nearly 5,000 men and women in California. This study found that the death rate was more than double among the men and nearly triple among the women with the fewest social connections, as compared to people who had the most social contacts. A similar increase in mortality was noted among people who were least satisfied with life (Brody 1984, 8KX).

WHAT DO ELDERLY PEOPLE ACHIEVE BY REACHING OLD AGE?

Do people get rich, become powerful, or gain a position of respect by growing old? Isn't reaching old age an achievement? The positive fact is that old people have survived the alternative. The unattractive truth is that old age often forces the aging persons out of the positions that gave them these social comforts—for example, the work status and paycheck that provided the right and the fee to belong to the country club. Old age, in fact, had decreased or even taken away that economic security, position of authority, and respect. The loss of these socially admired roles forces older people to a much less prestigious, unenviable position. Society has made older Americans ineligible to occupy positions that are valued. The elderly persons lose the status they achieved through career advancement, and upon retirement they are assigned a role they may not want or find acceptable.

Society has entry requirements to positions throughout the entire life span. These criteria center around rights, obligations, and privileges. They are set up for children, teens, young, middle-aged, and elderly adults. Most of the entry requirements are based on age, sex, color, education, experience, and health. Everyone, from the young child to the oldest adult, is expected to abide by these requirements.

RETIREMENT

One of the most common roles forced on elderly people is retirement. Because of the enormity of this role change in the life of an elderly person, this text devotes a separate chapter to it. However, the effects of retirement on socialization require its mention here. The primary cause of retirement is simply age. Health may be a factor for a small percentage of people who have a choice about early retirement. About 80 percent of all men and nearly 90 percent of all women are no longer holding full-time employment at sixty-five years of age or over.

Leaving full-time employment brings with it adjustments. Whether the retirement is forced or freely chosen does not change this fact. Retirement often causes not only a major role change but also peer group and economic changes that affect one's manner of living. The challenge to fill the voids and compensate for the losses is too overwhelming for some people. For a minority of people, the adjustment borders on the impossible. One reason for the adjustment problems is they felt secure in their past role; its rules provided security. Their new role has no direction. It is not a role that offers new security. Thus, for some people this new role of retirement poses a crisis at a period in their lives when an orderly, tranquil setting would be most welcome. What proportion of retirees become disenchanted with their new role? The number is not known; however, cross-sectional surveys indicate that about 10 percent at any one time were highly uncomfortable being retired and another 33 percent encountered significant difficulty in retirement adjustment (Atchley 1980).

Nearly two-thirds of retirees have difficulty with their new role. The remaining one-third have spent greater time in retirement preparation and see themselves retiring *to* some other planned role they foresee as satisfying.

WIDOWHOOD

An often sudden, unplanned, and forced new social role in old age is widowhood. It also requires enormous change and adjustments. In 1980, more than 41 percent of women and 9.3 percent of men were widowed by the time they reached the age of sixty-five. Besides the psychological and emotional impacts, there are great sociological changes. Most social events are attended by couples. Going to a movie by oneself is uncomfortable. Eating out is a social event. Sitting in a restaurant by oneself often evokes a "Will there be someone joining you?" remark from the server. As a result, most of the widowed elderly find themselves more isolated than they are accustomed to living.

Widowhood, like retirement, may not be totally unacceptable to some individuals. Once the adjustment is made to the new role, it may provide an independence and freedom that is enjoyed. It may provide more mobility and an opportunity for new friends and recreation. Nevertheless, these new, positive results depend on the individuals' success in adjusting to their new role.

Successful adjustment can be assisted by society's providing new opportunities and roles for the person. Senior citizen organizations, religious clubs, and neighborhood groups are of vast importance. Often, an urban setting provides more of these opportunities than does a rural setting.

SHIFT FROM INDEPENDENCE TO DEPENDENCE

As seen on the total life span chart, we begin life in a dependent role (Figure 4.9). Our next years are spent, with help from other people, achieving the role of independence. It is a goal in which much effort is spent. Its achievement gives us a new status and feeling of worth. No wonder that the loss of such a status is one of the most dreaded role changes in old age. Dependence often comes in the form of physical and/or financial needs. Whatever the reason, dependency often causes hostile feelings on the part of the elderly person. The changes that role reversal brings touches many lives. After nearly fifty years of independence, the role of dependence is most difficult to adjust to. Add to that dependence on one's own children and we have a highly unusual situation.

Anger and frustration from such a reversal can strain parent-child relationships. The typical abused older person is a white female, aged seventy or over, who lives with the abuser. Most abuse, although by a

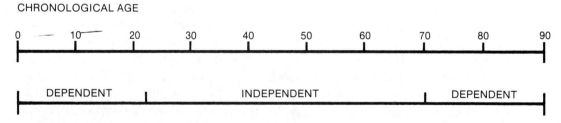

FIGURE 4.9
Dependent-independent cycle (From Atchley,
Robert C. The Social Forces in Later Life. Belmont,
Calif.: Wadsworth Publishing Co., 1980, 91.)

FIGURE 4.10

family member, is not premeditated, but rather crisis-precipitated. Signs indicate that we, as a society, must prepare ourselves to deal with a great increase in elderly abuse.

The battered elderly syndrome is the latest area of domestic violence. It is believed that at least one million aged Americans yearly are physically abused by their families. Some estimates believe the number of physically, psychologically, sexually, and/or financially abused elderly people actually exceeds 2.5 million. It is difficult to achieve documentation of elderly abuse because the victims fear reprisal, removal from the family setting, shame of reporting a family member, and lack of knowledge of how to report the abuse. Most abuse occurs when there are no witnesses, and because of the stereotypic attitude of senility, complaints by the abused may go unchecked. The children of elderly people find themselves in a dilemma. Guilt to provide parental support may put economic and psychological burdens on children. The resentment such role reversals cause in both older adults and their children is a serious sociological problem.

Some elderly adults can balance this dependency role by providing services to the family. Help in housekeeping, child care, or other assisting roles can lessen the feeling of dependence. Dependency roles by older adults are also undefined and unclear. Whose responsibility is the older adult who through health or economic loss becomes dependent, even against his or her will? Society has not adequately answered such questions.

DISABILITY

To be disabled is another new role forced on an individual by illness. Because old age makes a person more susceptible to disability, elderly people are most often the victims. Disabilities restrict the number and kind of roles the individual can play. Nearly 11 percent of the elderly sixty-years of age and over in 1980 experienced a limitation of activities due to chronic conditions. About one-third of the older people suffer from some form of disability that limits their work roles and in some cases their recreational choices.

Moderate to severe effects of chronic illness may prevent individuals from functioning as independently as they may desire. In 1980, 10.8 million people over the age of sixty-five had some degree of limitation in daily activity, from mild to severe, due to chronic illness. Future estimates demonstrate that 16.4 million persons sixty-five years of age or older are expected to have functional limitations at the turn of the century. This figure will reach 23.3 million by the year 2020 and 31.8 million by 2050 (Figure 4.11).

Illness: Role Expectations

The role of the elderly sick or disabled individuals is more clearly defined in our society. We do not expect them to meet the requirements of any position. We expect them to be dependent on others for their needs. If this role of illness lasts over an extended period of time, the elderly sick or disabled may actually be excluded from both present and future social responsibilities. Often, society's only expectation of the ill is that they desire to get well. Society may even soften this expectation for elderly people and accept their illness as a permanent state and hold no expectations for them. If the elderly perceive this giving up by society, they, too,

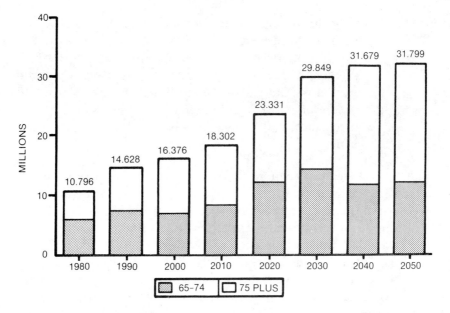

FIGURE 4.11
Limitation in activity due to chronic conditions—persons 65 years and older by age group, actual and projected: 1980-2050 (U.S. Senate Special Committee on Aging, Aging America: Trends and Projections, 1984.)

may adopt the giving-up attitude and prematurely confine themselves to the life of the dependently ill.

Illness: Family Support

A popular myth in our society is that all old, ill people are abandoned by their families and placed into institutions. As a result of this myth, in the mind of many people, being old means spending one's last days in the nursing home. This image is not true for two reasons:

1. Most older people are not so ill or frail that they need institutional care. Only about 5 to 7 percent of people over sixty-five are in nursing homes.

2. Families do care for their elderly. For every elderly person in a nursing home, there are one or two others with equivalent disabilities being cared for at home. Furthermore, that 5 to 7 percent who are institutionalized can be compared to the 10 percent ill being cared for at home. The institutionalized elderly are much more ill and need more highly skilled nursing care. It is also a fact that the care received at home delays institutionalization.

The most dependable family caregivers are spouses. Elderly people who are unmarried are nine times more likely to be institutionalized than are married elderly people (Galle 1985, 38). This is the reason, in part, that long-term care institutions have a higher population of women, for they are more likely to be widowed. Also, adult children, particularly daughters, are caregivers for their elderly parents. The predominance of women (wives and daughters) as caregivers is related to gender expectations. Caregiving can be viewed as part of the female family role because it resembles both mothering and housework. However, this reliance on women as caregivers is becoming increasingly problematic. More and more women have entered the paid labor force. Middle-aged women must face the dilemma of having to juggle their time among their careers, their family responsibilities, and the care of their aged parents. This is why middle-aged couples are often referred to as the sandwich generation. Their time, money, and responsibility must meet the needs of both a younger and older generation.

LOSS OF FAMILIAR ENVIRONMENTS

The role changes brought about by psychological, physical, and/or economic circumstances can also bring about environmental losses. The social roles people play are affected by the familiar environments in which they function. Age can forcefully or voluntarily bring about three major environmental changes:

1. Work environment.
2. Home environment.
3. Community environment.

The effect of such losses is also the study of sociological gerontology. People establish strong attachments to familiar environments. The change of comfortable environments elicits feelings of loss even if the environment is less than desirable. Nonetheless, the environment provided a feeling of security. It is not unrealistic for people to say they miss the familiar dripping faucet or the sound of the old rattling furnace they had lived with and, in fact, had become attached to. Even the prospect of a new apartment across town with new furniture and appliances may not be an acceptable substitute. Few older people change housing in later life. Even fewer older people choose a new community. Such changes cause dramatic adjustments they prefer not to make. New environments do not contain old memories. Even unhappy memories are better than no memories of the people and events that make up the past.

Some older people choose to move south to a warmer climate, often only for the winter months. When their health no longer allows such mobility, they sometimes return to their original homes and communities for good.

Institutionalization is another example of a dramatic environmental change. It may contribute to the reason institutionalized elderly people appear to others as having declined faster than would seem attributable to the illness they suffer.

EFFECTS OF SOCIAL CHANGES ON FUTURE AGING

When we look at the elderly people of American society today, we can get a glimpse of our future.

- The aged are they!
- The aging are we!

As the sociological conditions of our society change, there are likely to be differences in the process of aging. The problems of aging in the future revolve around two issues and their implications:

1. Increasing numbers of elderly.
2. Changes in family structure.

Larger Populations

The increasing proportion of elderly people in our society, particularly the increasing number of old-old (eighty-five years of age and over), will mean rising costs and a diminishing pool of workers to support an increas-

FIGURE 4.12
"So I'm as old as I feel. Would it be such a crime if I were to prefer feeling old?" (© 1986 by Bill Haas. Used with permission.)

ing proportion of dependent, nonworking elderly people. Over the past few years much concern has been voiced about maintaining Social Security, Medicare, and Medicaid programs, which served 26.2 million older Americans in 1985. The costs of these programs are going to be even higher and more problematic as the baby boom generation reaches the retirement years and must be supported by the low birthrate of the baby bust generation.

Social Changes

Changes in family structure include divorce, fewer children, and women in the work force. The rising divorce rate, for example, can bring either greater or diminished family ties. For instance, maternal grandparents may become involved in child care, at least for a short period of time, around the time of divorce. Once the divorce is completed, the grandparents are likely to lose their relationships to their grandchildren. The increasing divorce rates also mean that in the future more elderly people will be unmarried.

Smaller family size is another factor leading to the isolation of increasing numbers of elderly people. The decrease in the birthrate means there will be a greater proportion of elderly people without children. Moreover, the small family size means there will be more families without daughters. Thus, more and more families will lack potential caregivers. Perhaps even more significant, the commitment of increasing numbers of women to careers means that family care will be more costly in the future. As women earn higher incomes, their time becomes more valuable and less easily dispensable.

These same social changes can also create positive opportunities for the experience of aging in the future. The technological advances in medicine potentially can lead to still longer and healthier lives. Furthermore, elderly people of the future are likely to have more education, more economic resources, and better interpersonal skills. These resources reflect current social trends, such as the feminist movement, advances in education, and the increasing acceptance of psychotherapy. The greater participation of women in paid work illustrates the dual-edged meaning of these social trends. On the one hand, women's working creates problems in providing family caregiving and is associated with rising divorce and, thus, potentially with more loneliness in old age. On the other hand, however, women who work for substantial periods in their lives are likely to have considerably more economic resources and financial management skills than women who do not work outside the home.

FIGURE 4.13

SOCIOLOGICAL SOLUTIONS

Society needs to respond in a problem-solving manner and to deal with the present problems, as well as the dilemmas, that the increase in aging numbers will present.

First: Scientific fields of study must not work separately because the successes and failures of one field affect one or several other fields of study. An example is the tremendous energy and money channeled to find a medical fountain of youth. The medical world searched and found methods of prolonging life. Medical breakthroughs like transplants and medications to retard aging have added years to life expectancy. The consequences of longevity have caused a sociological crisis. Unity in the scientific fields could mean simultaneous study of longevity and its consequences. Together, they could consider whether a longer life may even be desirable. As one scientific unit, they could also consider a person's right to die.

Second: The period from birth to death makes up a person's total life span, not the period from birth to retirement. Adding years to the life span necessitates adding education, work, and leisure to the entire life span distributed in such a manner that the entire lifetime is meaningful.

Too much of a good thing ceases to be good. Twenty consecutive years of leisure may be too much of a good thing for many elderly people. Who can support socially, psychologically, and economically twenty years of leisure? Such a poorly balanced life span must necessarily cause problems. The life span must be reprogrammed to be more practical and more livable. When the medical world added ten more years to the life cycle, they forgot to inform sociologists what to tell people to do with those years; nor were the elderly informed about how to pay for them.

Third: Their initial education prepares people for the world of work. For nearly the first twenty years of life, people are taught how to survive the following forty-five years in the work world. Forgotten is the education on how to deal with the following twenty years of leisure. Sixty-five years are spent in learning to live in a harmonious family setting, but people have not learned how to live alone when widowhood is forced on them. People of all ages, and especially the old, must have opportunities to learn to deal with all possible social roles that the extension of life has brought about.

Fourth: All of the sociological solutions need individual, community, and national commitment. These commitments must come in the form of ideas, energy to put these ideas to work, and money to finance that work. State and federal budgets must reflect the sincere intention to meet the sociological problems we face. Demographers have provided the statistics to predict the magnitude of the problems well into the future. Long-range planning, on behalf of all agencies, must demonstrate the commitment to present and future aging generations in solving these problems.

SUMMARY

Demographers have assured sociologists that the graying of America is not just a phenomenon of the present but one that can be expected to continue for many years. The increasing numbers of elderly people have a tremendous impact on the whole social system. Not only society as a whole but also individuals, in particular, must make successful social adaptations.

The disengagement, activity, environmental adjustment, and social breakdown theories may be more supportive of one another to an individual than first believed. As needs differ, so do the approaches to dealing with the role of retirement.

Life is a series of adjustments throughout the life cycle. Among the major changes in the elderly years are retirement, widowhood, and disability. Any of these changes can bring with it not only status changes but environmental changes as well.

Social gerontologists dispel many myths believed about elderly people. Some elderly people anticipate retirement with a positive frame of mind. Others, because of lifelong adjustment habits, meet the new roles this period of life brings with enthusiasm and a sense of challenge. Also, many people are cared for lovingly by family members as they become dependent. The key to harmony between society and its aging members appears to be that individuals and society must make a commitment to meet the challenges that old age brings with it. There are positive and workable solutions.

EXERCISES

1. If not calendar age but obsolete knowledge is an obstacle to older people's employment, what creative methods can you suggest in order for aging people to stay current and up to date?
2. Prepare a three-minute argument about why you believe retirement at sixty-five years of age should or should not be continued. If not at sixty-five, then when?
3. Within a group of four people, assign the following topics:
   a. Disengagement theory
   b. Activity theory
   c. Environmental adjustment theory
   d. Social breakdown theory
   Have each person present the positive and/or negative aspects of his or her theory on how it affects successful adjustment in old age.
4. Life contains many passages. List the passages you have already gone through and rate your success as to poor, fair, good, or excellent.
   Then, list the passages you have yet to experience. For each passage, list at least one thing you think will assist you in successfully meeting these future challenges.
5. List the expectations you have for people sixty-five years of age and over. When you have completed that listing, check all of the items you think should also be applied to you when you are sixty-five years of age and over.
6. List famous people sixty-five years of age and over who you feel are excellent role models for their generation. Share these names with

classmates and see if all are in agreement with your list and you with theirs.

REVIEW

1. Define sociology of aging.
2. How has a longer life expectancy created sociological dilemmas?
3. What major event in American history made us more aware of age than of acquired skill?
4. With the concept of *retirement*, two major adjustments have to be made by individuals and society. List them.
5. Define individual and societal disengagement.
6. List the differences and likeness of the disengagement theory, activity theory, and environmental adjustment theory.
7. Status passages influence what areas of an individual's life?
8. List the four major social structures among elderly people.
9. What are the major reasons role confusion exists during the retirement years?
10. Do elderly people have role models?
11. How do achieved and assigned roles differ?
12. Why does retirement receive such mixed responses from elderly people?
13. In 1980, what was the difference in the percentage of widowed males to females? What are the social implications?
14. Why are dependency roles so threatening?
15. Is the mental picture of most families' taking an elderly parent against their will to a nursing home fact or myth?
16. Who makes up the sandwich generation?
17. How can society best resolve the sociological problems of an ever-increasing elderly population?

RECOMMENDED READINGS
AND REFERENCES

Atchley, Robert C. *The Social Forces in Later Life.* Belmont, Calif.: Wadsworth Publishing Company, 1980.

Brody, James. "Researchers Progress in Delaying Effects of Aging." *Minneapolis Star and Tribune,* December 9, 1984.

Brown, Roger. *Social Psychology.* New York: Free Press, 1985.

Burns, George. *How to Live to Be 100*. New York: New American Library, 1983.

Galle, Bart W., Jr. *Multidisciplinary Perspectives on Aging: Independent Study Guide*. Minneapolis: University of Minnesota, Continuing Education and Extension Department, 1985.

Glaser, Barney and Anselm Strauss. *Status Passage: A Formal Theory*. Hawthorne, N.Y.: Aldine Publishing Co., 1971.

Guttmann, David, *et al*. "Improving the Care of the Aged through Interdisciplinary Efforts." *Gerontologist* 15 (1975): 387-392.

Harris, L., *et al. Realities of Aging*. Washington, D.C.: National Council on Aging, 1974.

Kübler-Ross, Elisabeth. *On Death and Dying*. New York: Macmillan Publishing Co., 1969.

Santrock, John W. *Adult Development and Aging*. Dubuque, Ia.: Wm. C. Brown, Publishers, 1985.

Schwartz, A. N. "A Transactional View of the Aging Process." In *Professional Obligations and Approaches to the Aged,* edited by A. Schwartz and I. Mensh. New York: Holt, Rinehart and Winston, 1974.

Shukers, Joyce. "New Look at Old." *Journal of Practical Nursing* 35 (1985): 24-25.

U.S. Senate Special Committee on Aging. *Aging America: Trends and Projections*. Washington, D.C., 1984.

CHAPTER
5
Psychology of Aging

Learning Objectives

After studying this chapter, the reader should be able to:

- Explain how the senses are the means through which the human mind experiences the world both outside and inside the body.
- Understand that because of the extreme complexity of each human being, no one can expect completely to understand the underlying dynamics of another person's behavior or personality.
- Identify personality changes as a gradual, continuous process throughout all of life's stages.
- Present the findings concerning the effects of aging on intelligence, learning, and memory.

Preview

Psychology can simply be defined as the study of human behavior. The field of geropsychology specifically attempts to identify the behavior styles of elderly people. This chapter answers some of the most often asked questions of geropsychologists:

1. What is the connection between old age and earlier life experiences?
2. Does aging bring about dramatic personality changes?
3. Is memory loss an unavoidable consequence of aging?
4. What is the meaning of mental health for elderly populations?
5. Is there only intervention for the needs of our elders or is there a method of prevention that can be used?

WHAT IS GEROPSYCHOLOGY?

Geropsychologists study the behavior of the elderly to answer these questions and also to be able to predict behavior. By predicting behavior, problems can be anticipated and as a result avoided. If this sounds like a simple process, then it is deceptive. To predict the behavior of a three-year-old is much easier than to predict the behavior of a sixty-three-year-old. Those additional sixty years of individualized, unique experiences create a great diversity among the older population that has not yet been acquired by the very young. The heterogeneity of the older population, the fact they are more different than alike, accounts for the limited understanding geropsychologists have concerning the dynamics of behavior in old age.

More and more people survive into their 70s, 80s, 90s, and even reach the 100-year-old mark. As they do so, it is even more obvious that though there exist some common behaviors used in adjusting to aging, these behaviors are outnumbered by the individualistic approaches used in meeting the challenges of old age.

Geropsychology, when explaining what contributes to psychological well being, must study the evolving patterns of personality, intelligence, and motivation of the aging person.

PSYCHOLOGY OF AGING: OUR ELDERS

Historically, elderly people were not a sought-after group for psychological study. Young adults, adolescents, children, infants, monkeys, and mice were much more popular as subjects of research. A lack of study left the field of psychology without verifiable information concerning the old segment of the population. Paucity of information led to severe misunderstandings about the process of aging. False images, such as people who were mentally and physically ill, as well as socially isolated, became accepted facts. Had researchers studied healthy, community-active elderly people, a positive, more correct portrait of old age would have been portrayed to society.

A humorous story that has been shared for decades emphasizes this point:

> Once upon a time, there was an old man who had gone to a party and had a bit too much to drink. On his way home, he walked through a dark alley, where his keys slipped from his hand and fell to the ground. He tried to search for the keys but could not find them in the dark. Then he noticed light at the corner of the block and went there to look for his keys, under the light.
>
> Eventually a police officer came by, noticed him, and asked what he was doing. "I lost my keys," the man said. "Did you lose them here?" asked the officer. "No, sir," he answered, "but this is where the light is!"

Similarly, research has been done where the light is: on attractive populations, such as the young, and on available populations, such as the older sick. Such studies may have made the work of psychologists easier, but they left enormous gaps and misunderstandings in our knowledge of the process of aging.

During the past twenty years, however, three factors have combined to increase interest in the study of aging and the aged.

1. There has been a rapid increase in the number and percentage of elderly people in the general population.
2. Rapid increases have changed the services, programs, and health care required to maintain quality of life as a person grows older.

3. There is an interest by the aging population themselves to prepare for a more positive old age than that portrayed by myths.

As a result of these happenings, a new awareness of the difficulties
many elderly people face has led to interest and research in the area of
aging. There has been a steady increase in the study of the characteristics,
problems, and behavior of people who are no longer adolescents but are
becoming the old members of society.

AGING AND PERSONALITY

Personality can be defined as how individuals see themselves, and how
they relate to other people as well as react to the events of the world.
Simply defined, personality is the core part of all human beings. It is a
combination of traits, roles, and coping styles developed over time; it
includes such concepts as self-esteem, self-confidence, and self-accep-
tance. Personality involves both stability and change throughout the life

FIGURE 5.1
(From Geriatrics: A Study of Maturity, *4th ed., by
Esther Caldwell and Barbara R. Hegner, copyright ©
1986 by Delmar Publishers Inc.)*

cycle. All normal personality patterns, regardless of age, are usually consistent with general laws of behavior. As old age approaches, personalities remain unique yet are consistent with earlier patterns of life. Different personalities age differently. That statement, however, may oversimplify the definition and role of personality and its effects on aging. Personality, like intelligence, is a multifaceted, hypothetical-assumed, imagined concept.

If people's environment, circumstances, and motivation would remain the same across their life span, then we could expect no changes in behavior from early childhood through the adult years. But we know such unchanging life patterns do not exist. There are instead varying degrees of change in environment, while circumstances and motivation remain nearly constant. Elderly people who met this constant change and challenge with flexible coping skills in earlier years maintain a relatively stable personality pattern in later years. People who were more rigid and fixed in their coping strategies when younger are found to exhibit greater personality change when approaching old age. In other words, personality remains rather consistent with earlier behavior patterns. Unpredictable behavior is the exception rather than the rule. Age, therefore, does not create a sudden personality change any more than one ages suddenly. Each is a gradual, continuous process.

PERSONALITY TYPES AMONG THE ELDERLY

Researchers have established that a relationship exists between adjustment to old age, the activity level of the elderly person, and personality (Neugarten *et al.* 1964). Studies established that there appear to be four basic personality groups or patterns among the elderly. Neugarten, Havighurst, and Tobin (1968) identified them as:

1. Mature personalities.
2. Defended personalities.
3. Passive-dependent personalities.
4. Disorganized personalities.

Mature Personalities

The greater number of individuals and those who had made a positive adjustment to aging belonged in the mature personality group. Members of this group enjoyed life, were content with the past as well as the present, and had close and happy social relationships. They were the kind of people who displayed a sense of humor, were kind to others, and had a generally positive attitude toward life. A new experience presented a mental, as well as physical, challenge that they enjoyed meeting. Such people planned ahead, weighing the consequences of their decision making.

Integrated individuals are not free of ever having made mistakes, but rather they put the past in a proper perspective and do not let it threaten the happiness of their future. An integrated person is verbal and is a stand-up-for-your-rights type of person, but within reason, with respect for the differing opinions of others. High self-esteem and an ability to deal with frustrations give the integrated person a strong foundation for a mentally healthy approach to life.

> Nobody grows old by merely living a number of years. People grow old only by deserting their ideals. Years may wrinkle the skin, but to give up interests wrinkles the soul. Worry, doubt, self-distrust, fear and despair . . . these are the long, long years that bow the head and turn the growing spirit back to dust.
>
> (Warner 1972, 220)

The characteristics of integrated personalities show a successful adjustment on their part to the process of aging. The defended, passive-dependent, and disorganized personalities are considerably less successful in adjusting to aging.

Defended Personalities

The defended personality (sometimes referred to as armored) gives a high priority to staying young. These people are status conscious, body conscious, and age conscious. Their energies are channeled toward achievement in these three areas. Therefore, they are very active and competitive. As a result, they experience an abundance of fear. The loss of status or youthfulness would be very devastating to their mental health. Their busy behavior is an attempt to keep them from thinking about and thus planning for the inevitable fact of aging and some of the losses that process may bring.

FIGURE 5.2

Passive-Dependent Personalities

The passive-dependent personality, or rocking chair group, has two subgroups within it: the poor-me type and the what's-the-use type. Unlike the defended personality, passive-dependent people are very content to let others be responsible for them. This type of personality actually uses age as an excuse not to be independent or capable, although there are no mental or physical reasons for this giving up of work or social roles. This failure to stay independent causes, or is caused by, a poor self-image. These people may turn to food, alcohol, or drugs as a form of gratification.

Passive, what's-the-use individuals are also inactive. They are apathetic and look to retirement as an excuse for not being involved. Their form of withdrawal often makes them submissive to more powerful types of personalities. As a result, this group is subject to abuse. These individuals seem to be aware of their situation but appear satisfied to let it remain so. They appear content with this type of life-style and hold no hostility for those who choose to live quite differently. In their own withdrawn, passive manner, they give the appearance of having adjusted to old age.

Disorganized Personalities

The disorganized personality group appears to be the smallest in number. These individuals suffer from psychological problems, display irrational behavior, and find coping with everyday demands very difficult. Emotional control for these individuals is very difficult. Its lack is demonstrated by extreme displays of anger or depression and by inappropriate displays of emotion. Mental deterioration, which is often incorrectly associated with aging, may more accurately apply to this personality group. These individuals can only marginally adjust to community living but are capable of independent living. They are, however, very unhappy and remain isolated from friend or group associations. The disorganized type of individuals make up a very small percentage of the total elderly population. They need professional assistance in order to cope mentally and socially with their aging role.

PERSONALITY AND FAMILY

Many adaptive requirements within a lifetime are the result of an individual's interaction with his or her family. One's family provides a link

FIGURE 5.3

between the past and the future. Throughout life, events directly related to family, such as marriage and parenthood, have required adjustment and role change. These social events demand new responses that lead to personality and behavior changes. Old age continues to have family-related changes: empty nest, grandchildren, and perhaps even the death of family members. These continuing changes account for continuous personality adjustment and change. In youth, as in old age, it is likely that family ties provide affection and companionship at a time of need. The kinship network, the reciprocal support of marital relations, and the intergenerational support system encompass the entire life span for the majority of elderly people. Even though the family, at times, may fall short of the needs of its elderly members, it nevertheless provides a solidarity essential to the changing and stress-filled period of old age.

A study of daughters, mothers, and grandmothers concluded that all three generations preferred family members as confidants and advisors over friends, community providers, or attempting to go it alone (Brody, Davis, and Johnson 1979). Even when the time comes for children to assume responsibility for their aged parents, there appeared to be little reluctance. Such willingness on the part of the family appears to be widespread. The family network appears to be strong.

AGING AND PERSONALITY DEVELOPMENT THEORIES

Personality studies are based on normal personality development. Studies center around mental health and successful adjustment to demanding changes accompanying life experiences. Just as physical health is not defined as the absence of disease, so mental health does not involve the absence of frustration and stress. Rather, mental health is the ability to cope with the problems and events of life in a self-satisfying, self-fulfilling manner.

Theories of personality provide understanding of:

1. How adulthood is organized.
2. Major events, circumstances, and changes in adulthood.
3. Forces that lead to stability and change in personality during adulthood.

Aging personality development can be divided into four categories: (1) psychological theorists, (2) social theories, (3) learning theories, and (4) life-experience models (Birren and Renner 1979, 113). It is important to realize that the many theories that follow are not competing to be the *one* theory of developmental aging. In actuality, it is usually impossible or impractical to test one theory against another because each theory defines its own area of study and emphasis. Therefore, the following theories may sometimes differ from one another according to what the researcher determined to be the most important aspect of aging; at other times the theories may support one another.

Eight Stages of Life—Erikson

Psychoanalytic theories led to the belief that personality is cemented early in childhood and thus virtually does not change even into adulthood. Few theorists accepted this notion but rather proposed stages in adult

	INFANCY	EARLY CHILDHOOD	MIDDLE AND LATE CHILDHOOD	ADOLESCENCE	YOUNG ADULTHOOD	MIDDLE ADULTHOOD	LATE ADULTHOOD
STAGE 1	BASIC TRUST VS. MISTRUST						
STAGE 2		AUTONOMY VS. SHAME, DOUBT					
STAGE 3			INITIATIVE VS. GUILT				
STAGE 4				INDUSTRY VS. INFERIORITY			
STAGE 5				IDENTITY VS. ROLE CONFUSION			
STAGE 6					INTIMACY VS. ISOLATION		
STAGE 7						GENERATIVITY VS. STAGNATION	
STAGE 8							EGO INTEGRITY VS. DESPAIR

FIGURE 5.4
Erikson's eight stages of development

development that showed reaching old age was dependent on adapting, reevaluating, and merging all of life's experiences in a satisfactory manner. Erik Erikson (1959, 1963) proposed eight stages of life (Figure 5.4). Erikson's ideas about the eight stages of development represent one of the most widely discussed views of lifespan development (Santrock 1985, 348).

Erikson, in a sense, extended the tendency for generativity—the ability to produce and originate—into his eighth and final stage, integrity versus despair. Even though old people could no longer procreate, he believed they could still be productive and creative. For example, when elderly people no longer needed to care for their own children, they could care for other children. Erikson believed there was a relationship between old age and childhood that rounded out the life cycle.

He also believed the key task of any individual was to achieve ego integrity. This was achieved by remaining active, relating directly to society, and integrating all of life's experiences, thus bringing integrity— a sense of worth—to themselves. After all, old age is a time of reflection— of looking back on the events of a lifetime. To the extent that an individual has successfully coped with the problems posed at each of the earlier stages of life, he or she had a sense of wholeness and achievement—of a life well lived. If the elderly person looked back on life with regret, seeing it as a series of missed opportunities and failures, the final years would be ones of despair.

Three Biological Stages—Buhler

Buhler (Buhler and Massarik 1968) divided life into the biological stages of growth, culmination, and decline. After studying countless autobiographies and biographies, Buhler concluded that each of these periods in life had specific goals. The first stage was self-determination; the second, stability; and the third, old age. The aging person determined life's success by whether he or she had met personal goals in terms of productivity and righteousness. If the assessment was positive, then a sense of self-fulfillment and happiness resulted.

No one or combination of the dozen or more theories that exist is designed to deal with the issues of individual differences in personality development. They are theories that describe the magnitude of adult development and personality change. However, they still leave us with the questions concerning how individual personality development is affected by differences in sex, social class, and environment.

FIGURE 5.5

Social Theories of Personality Change

Social theories adhere to the belief that there are no general personality controls. They theorize that personality and behavior result from socialization, experiences, and social roles. Such factors as environment, occupation, and family roles constantly call for new responses and adjustments, which lead to personality and behavior change. It is the ever-changing social demands that require an individual to change throughout a lifespan, and many of these demands are age related. Adulthood is no less demanding of changes. Retirement, relocation, changes of roles and friends, and loss of friends all create a continually changing environment. The number of changes can somewhat be controlled by seeking environments and settings that require fewer changes, but the demand to adjust is ever present.

Learning Theories of Personality Change

Learning theories focus on the internal factors of personality development during aging. Three generally accepted ideas come from the researcher Thomae (1975). The first is how we see ourselves changing as people, which leads to the changing of our behavior. Second, people's beliefs and expectations establish how they see themselves and in turn how they change their beliefs and expectations as a result of that view. Third, being able to adjust to aging depends on how well individuals balance this whole process. Of course, this adjustment process is made simple or complicated depending on how many changes and the degree of changes expected of them throughout their life span. This theory, though appearing complicated, simply attempts to prove that personality does, in fact, change, but that changes are based on a great degree of stability because they are made as a result of reflection and deliberate adjustment.

Life-Experience Models

Life-experience models resulted from studies conducted by Levinson of large numbers of college-aged men to determine the developmental periods of life. Levinson (1974), like Erikson, believed there were stages in life determined by the nature of people and the nature of society. For each age category, he determined that there appeared to be a major goal or task to be accomplished in each of the stages. Levinson's research led to the following life stages and corresponding goals:

Adolescent	Separation from family
20s	Get to the adult world
30s (early)	Making bigger commitments
30s (late)	Totally independent
40s (early)	Assessment: achievement versus aspirations
40s (late)	Reassessment
50+	Achieve a sense of fulfillment and acceptance

Life Review

Robert Butler (1975) gave strength to both Erikson's and Levinson's theories by stating that old age inaugurates the process he calls life review. He found that elderly persons consciously return to past experiences, not only taking stock of themselves as they review their lives, but also attempting to think and plan what they will do with the time that remains. Through this process of life review, Butler believes, their sense of integrity, as described by Erikson, may be achieved and strengthened. The life review allows individuals to integrate life experiences, to tie up loose ends, and to find meaning for their life. Two means the elderly use to achieve this are story telling and reminiscing.

CREATIVE AGING

The terms *creativity* and *aging* appear to be antonyms. We view being creative as an active process and aging as a passive one. The dictionary does little to change this view. *Webster's New Collegiate Dictionary* defines creative as "marked by the ability or power to produce or bring about a course of action." The definition for aging is "to become old ... to acquire a desirable quality by standing undisturbed."

Certainly, our present attitudes of aging do not give to the elderly the quality of emotional health believed necessary to be creative. Our

FIGURE 5.6

society describes aging as a state of mental decline, not a time of imaginative skill.

However, the term *creative* can also be applied to the process of adaptation. Aging is a process that constantly requires a changing sense of self and a continuous adaptation to environmental change. As one moves across the life span, the challenges become more complex. This complexity brings an enrichment composed of commitments and freedoms, self-actualization and pressures, successes and failures. To say the least, the ability to act and react to all these formidable challenges is a creative process!

These constant forces of change do not discontinue automatically at age sixty-five. There is no one point in the total life span when a person ceases to be a human being, devoid of change and challenge. Stagnation is found only in the myths and stereotypes about the old.

In reality, nothing that human beings of any age do or think is free of adaptive responses. We can not forget that people got old because of their successful adaptation to a lifetime of change. Life until death is a developmental process of increasing complexity and enrichment in which creativity is the key to success. Creativity, a mental exercise, is not the sole possession of any one age group.

BEHAVIOR CHANGES

What happens when noticeable behavior changes are evident in an elderly person's behavior? A middle-aged son or daughter may notice that an elderly parent has made a sudden and unpredictable change from traditional behavior patterns; for example, an elderly mother suddenly has stopped baking all those delicious recipes handed down from her mother. There are no goodies in the house when family comes to visit, whereas in the past, there was more than anyone could eat. Can such a behavior change mean that senility has finally set in?

A more careful look at the change that has occurred reveals that the motives for doing all that baking are gone. Her husband, who loved sweets, has passed away, and the time between family visits has gotten longer. The baked goods were getting old, and mother herself never really cared for sweets that much. Also, financial concerns caused the grocery purchasing to be cut down; only the more essential items could be purchased. What has occurred is not a sudden personality or unexplainable behavior change resulting from aging, but rather a practical adjustment to the changing circumstances.

FIGURE 5.7

MENTAL HEALTH

Headlines in the *Minneapolis Star and Tribune* in November 1984 stated that one in five Americans are mentally ill! This article did not identify any age categories that contributed more or less to that 20 percent of the population that suffers from some form of mental illness.

When speaking of the elderly, we tend to associate such words as senility or dementia with mental illness. We also tend to believe that the number of elderly people suffering from such illness is very high. The fact is that no statistics are readily available, only estimates. If the definition used for mental illness is impairment of the individual's ability to function socially, then the review of studies would indicate that somewhere around 10 percent (an estimated 23 million) of the elderly population suffers from disabling mental illness, including 3 percent who are in institutions of various kinds (Atchley 1980). However, these percentages are highly speculative and are not based on hard data; even so, they would be within the national percentage.

Our concepts of mental health and aging are difficult at best to understand because we are unclear as to what is appropriate behavior for elderly people. Our stereotypes and myths concerning the old tend to be negative. If we use the standards of behavior of the middle-aged, we soon discover that many of the terms used to describe that age group also contain inaccuracies. Society does not allow the elderly to retain all of their once middle-aged roles, forced retirement being an example.

We have no standards of behavior for people who may not go to work but are physically capable of doing so. What does a mentally and physically healthy person do with twenty-four hours of leisure for the remaining seventeen years of life? How do people feel about themselves during that period of time?

The personal feelings of self-worth or self-esteem in the later years are important aspects of the psychology of aging. In fact, self-esteem in later years affects the elderlies' quality of life more than any other factor. Proof of this psychological fact is found in the type of statements older people make when describing what makes their life worthwhile. The events they describe are memorable events in which feelings of love, respect, being needed and enjoyed by others, as well as being effective were the focal point. However, should feelings of self-worth begin to fade, which can happen when losses, physical and social, take place, the positive feelings of self, the once strengthening belief of being in control, of being master, begin to erode.

There are many ways, mostly inadvertent, in which well-meaning family members and/or health care workers affect the lowering of self-esteem in the elderly. Schwartz and Peterson (1979) state that perhaps the most prevalent way is infantilizing the aged person. This happens when overzealous helpers do more for the older persons than they actually require or request. Assistance to help them dress, eat, and walk may be given so that they can be quicker, neater, and faster, as though any of those qualities could possibly be more important than the self-esteem involved with independence.

INTELLIGENCE

When a learned individual was asked, "Who is smarter, a man or a woman?" the person replied, "Which man and which woman are you asking me about?" The parallel answer would be just as applicable if we were asked who is more intelligent, a young person or an old person? The answer would necessarily have to be, "Which young person and which old person are you comparing?"

> Not by physical force, not by bodily swiftness and agility are great things accomplished, but by deliberation, authority and judgment; qualities with which old age is abundantly provided.
>
> Cicero

One of the only things an IQ test provides is an IQ score. No one has yet figured out what to do with it after we have it. We know that learning, memory, and decision making are related to intelligence. But the concept of intelligence is an intangible. Too many factors can influence the learning performance of all people, including older adults. Research was inconclusive when testing older adults. Such factors as health, anxiety, and education are variables in which people tend to show a considerable degree of difference. These factors also influence test results. This may be why some researchers found a decrease in mental ability whereas others argued there was actually an increase.

It is valuable to note that how knowledge is used differs. The type of thinking used to bake a cake may be quite different from that used to

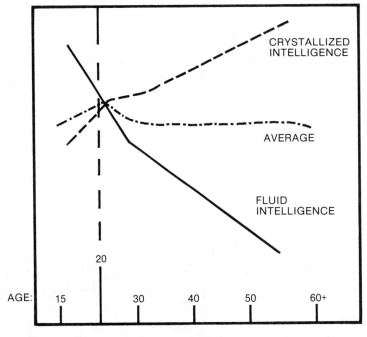

FIGURE 5.8
Fluid versus crystallized intelligence

select insurance. For this reason, when dealing with the effects of aging, researchers divided intelligence into two categories: fluid and crystallized intelligence.

Fluid Intelligence versus Crystallized Intelligence

Fluid intelligence deals with problem solving; crystallized intelligence deals with accumulated general knowledge over a period of time (Figure 5.8). When intelligence was divided into these two categories, then all previous research findings were right—there was both a decline in intelligence and an increase in intelligence. The correctness of both points of view was reflected in the difference between the fluid and crystallized scores. If the two scores were averaged, then the general evidence that little change takes place would also be true. Of course, such factors as physical health and mental health could change these findings for specific individuals.

LEARNING

The old adage that you can't teach an old dog new tricks has been misinterpreted. The key word in this statement is *you*. *You* may not be able to teach it, but the old dog can learn new tricks either from someone else or by itself!

Studies confirm that under most circumstances, age brings about very little change in the ability to learn. Without a doubt, health and motivation may affect the ability to learn, but the ability itself remains. Perhaps the greatest changes are in what individuals want to learn and the length of time they wish to spend learning.

Societal Expectations

Another circumstance affecting the learning of elderly people is the expectations of society. Society expects old people to be unable to learn, and when challenged they are expected to fail. This makes old people hesitant and anxious, doubting their own ability. Thus, the self-fulfilling prophecy is at work to make the stereotyping, which, in fact, has no basis, appear true. There is no question that a lack of self-confidence undermines the ability to learn at every age.

Learning Favors Youth

> "The man who is too old to learn was probably always too old to learn."
>
> (Harry S. Haskings as quoted in Comfort 1976, 96)

The statement that learning favors youth does not imply that there is not a difference between the performance of younger and older learners. In most research comparisons, learning performance favors young adults. But in the past, acknowledging the conditions that may affect the outcome of the test was not identified. Three important questions to determine the validity of the test results are:

1. Was the information tested ever known by the elderly person in the first place, or was it automatically assumed he or she had known it but forgotten?
2. Were there environmental factors that affected the test results of the elderly person—temperature conditions, stress conditions due to timing, poor lighting affecting visual clarity, background noise affecting clear understanding of the directions?

FIGURE 5.9

3. Was there motivation to do well? Why would a person seventy years old care what his or her IQ was compared to a young person's?

Testing bias or limitation can easily reduce a score that is not reflective of the actual learning or memory skill of the elderly person.

The Graying Student

Both formal and informal education on the adult level is on the increase. The older adults make up nearly 50 percent of higher level educational enrollment. Not only the traditional classroom has made room for the older student, but work places, night programs, religious and other organizations, libraries, television, and correspondence courses enroll a large number of these nontraditional students.

The variety of reasons for this new educational trend include:

1. The desire for career retraining before or after retirement.
2. Alleviation of boredom and use of excessive free time.
3. Learning new social skills, hobbies, etc.
4. For mental stimulation and love of learning.
5. For the social contacts such enrollment provides.

Whatever the reasons these older individuals pursued continued education, it was found that the people involved were already well educated and highly motivated. These individuals had made successful role adjustments and were eager to remain informed. Those who chose not to engage in any form of education or reeducation appeared to fall further and further behind in the educational field. Studies show it is not economic factors that keep them from returning to the community classrooms but rather a lack of motivation. This is not different from individuals of other age groups who choose not to complete or continue to participate in some form of education.

Creativity

Creativity is difficult to define and measure. Edison's teachers told him he was too dumb to learn anything. Walt Disney lacked sufficient good ideas and therefore was fired from his newspaper job. Both Einstein and Churchill had problems in school and were sent home. The list of examples of creative genius not recognized could go on and on.

One of the few things agreed on is that intelligence and creativity are not the same thing. Creativity is best defined when applied to people. We label people creative if they make unique and original contributions to society.

Many studies have been done to determine the period of highest productivity in a person's life. Some studies insist that about 80 percent of the most creative contributions occur before the age of fifty. Some argue that productivity is highest in the thirties. Other studies, which consider the fields of art, science, and humanities, claim creative productivity comes later in life. They say it remains high well into the seventies, eighties, and nineties. Researchers who claim that the greatest productivity occurs between one's sixtieth and seventieth years examined more than 400 careers that were the most notable of their time and were considered outstanding in a variety of activities. They found that the decade of years between age sixty and seventy contained 35 percent of the world's greatest achievements; between seventy and eighty years, 23 percent; after eighty years, 8 percent. In other words, 66 percent of the great achievements have been accomplished by people after they passed their sixtieth year (*Meeker REA Pioneer,* April, 1985). (See Figure 5.10.)

MEMORY

Memory differs from learning in that learning is an acquiring of general information. Memory is the retaining of specific information with the ability to recall it at will. Memory can be divided into two kinds: short-term and long-term.

Short-Term Memory

The length of short-term memory varies under different conditions. It has a limited capacity. It does not hold information very long and it cannot hold very much information at a time. Elderly people tend to show deficiencies in short-term memory studies. Whether the short-term memory is negatively affected by social, psychological, or physical factors is not known. It could be attributed to the fact that the elderly may not be highly motivated to remember what they consider unimportant information or be willing to take the time to commit it to memory. Therefore, it is not their inability to remember but their lack of motivation to remember. Also, short-term memory retention is higher when information is pre-

---

SOME EXAMPLES OF CREATIVITY IN OLD AGE

Picasso painted until his death at 91.

Pablo Casals continued to play the cello, conduct, and teach until his death at 96.

Grandma Moses painted until she died at 101.

Willie Shoemaker won his fourth Kentucky Derby at 54.

Vladimir Horowitz, pianist, made the cover of *Time* magazine for his Moscow performance at 81.

Tip O'Neill, Speaker of the House at 73.

President Ronald Reagan at 75.

FIGURE 5.10

sented auditorily rather than visually for all age groups (Kermis 1984). Elderly people may not be able to benefit as much as younger age groups due to possible hearing loss, which could require greater concentration. Kermis also notes that there is an age-related decrease in the ability to recall incidental aspects of a learning situation, which may indicate a degree of attentional rigidity—concentrating on one thing and letting others pass by.

Long-Term Memory

Long-term memory does not have the time or capacity limitations of the short-term memory. Long-term memories can last for months and decades. Most findings show that for the elderly, long-term memory stays intact. This may account for grandparents' not remembering what they bought at the store yesterday (which is really not important to them) but recalling, in detail, many facts about the good old days eighty or ninety years ago (which were important to them at the time).

One myth of old age is the assumption that memory is inevitably lost with age. Some elderly people perpetuate the myth by complaining of poor memory. Of course, there are countless jokes about the loss of memory.

The truth is that their complaints of poor memory do not coincide with their actual memory capability. It is also true that they become much more alarmed and experience an increased sensitivity when they are unable to remember something now compared to when they had forgotten names, dates, and so on at an earlier age. This stress created by worrying about forgetting can actually be the cause of some of the failure to remember.

Minding His T's and 2's

Dr. Irving Wright, President of the American Federation for Aging Research, tells the story of a psychological test that was developed to measure the mental agility of elderly people. A young psychologist was chosen to try out the test on a ninety-one-year-old man.

The psychologist explained that it was a verbal test and that some of the questions were easy, while others were difficult. The first question, for example, was "What two days in the week begin with T?"

"That's easy," the man replied. "Today and Tomorrow."

The psychologist paused, studied his papers, and moved to the next question. "This one is much more difficult. How many seconds are there in a year?"

Without blinking an eye, the man said, "Twelve."

"What did you say?" asked the psychologist.

"Twelve," said the elderly man, smiling. "The second of January, the second of February. . . ."

—Contributed by F.O.
(*Reader's Digest,* December, 1985, 180)

What appears to affect memory the most is that the organization of items to be remembered may not be as efficient or fast as that same process in the young. The change is not in the memory itself but in the moving of information in and out of the memory.

DECISION MAKING

Many characteristics dealing with intelligence are common to more ages than just old age. This is also true of decision making. Fear of being wrong and decision making are common bedfellows at many ages. We attribute to old age the need for more time to make a decision and a reluctance to take a chance on giving a response about something of which the outcome is uncertain. At first, we may attribute it to age. At second glance, it may be labeled as wisdom!

Omission or Commission

A difference commonly observed between the young and old is that older individuals will tend more often to commit the error of omission rather than commission. That is, they are more likely not to respond at all than to risk answering wrongly. This cautiousness may be a means of self-protection. If society expects them to be wrong, to prove them false is not to answer at all rather than to take a chance and maybe prove them right. However, should the occasion call for risk taking, the elderly appear to be no more reluctant than any other age.

Risk Taking

In studies done by Botwinick (1978), this increase in cautiousness was demonstrated. Older adults tended to avoid risk taking by taking no action even if taking action involved very little risk. If an older person was asked to make a decision in a situation in which there was a 90 percent chance of being right and a 10 percent chance of being wrong, or a third choice was to take no chance at all, the person would choose the no action option. However, it was also proven that when the "no action" choice was removed, an older person was just as willing as a younger person to take a risk. Other researchers studying the same concept found that when including middle-aged people in the study, they also were more likely to select the "no action" option. Though the "no action" response was selected more often by the old, it was established that the desire not to be wrong began before old age.

Another variable affecting risk taking was education. The higher the educational achievement, the more willingness there was to take a risk. Since each cohort in the United States is more educated than the previous one, results of future studies will be of interest. However, as long as avoiding failure is linked to maintaining self-esteem, cautiousness may always be a method the elderly use to preserve a positive self-image.

MOTIVATION

IQ scores, learning, memory, and even decision making are all directly affected by motivation. That is true of every age and every person who has even been the subject of research study. Of all these areas, the greatest task of the geropsychologist is to study the effects of motivation on the life-style of an elderly person.

Why does one elderly person continue to lead an active, productive, self-satisfying life and another literally quit living? Motivation appears to be the controlling factor for both instrinsic and extrinsic motivation.

Self-Motivation

Intrinsic motivation affects self-motivation. If it is a positive driving force, it keeps alive the desire for independence, positive expectations, and the determination to retain a positive self-image. When negative internal forces are at work, elderly people see no reason for autonomous—self-governing—behavior and allow themselves to be overcome by depression, a feeling of boredom, and even a deterioration of mental and physical health.

External Motivation

The same positive and negative effects can work involving extrinsic motivation. Positive motivation keeps elderly people physically and socially active. They retain some past roles and substitute others that may be more satisfying. Negative motivation causes a withdrawal and isolation from the public sector. Replacing bridge parties with television, depending on others rather than personally doing the weekly grocery shopping, or failing to keep beauty shop appointments limits both the physical and mental uplifting such occasions would provide.

SENILITY: ARE THE CAUSES MENTAL OR PHYSICAL?

Senility was a term coined to describe a myth. Strictly speaking, senility is not a medical diagnosis. Sometimes it is meant to refer to senile dementia or Alzheimer's disease, which are medical terms for diseases causing brain disorder.

Most often, the term *senility* is loosely used for such conditions as forgetfulness, mental confusion, or a decline of past levels of mental functioning that we attribute to old age. It comes from the Latin word *senex,* meaning old. It is unfortunate that such a term covers such a great variety of symptoms. There could be more than one hundred different reasons for such conditions occurring—reaction to medication or poor diet are just two.

By using the term senile, the condition often goes untreated and the myth that mental decline is an automatic consequence of aging is perpetuated. The word *pseudodementia* is now being used to convey that the symptoms may be resulting from a treatable and reversible condition. The myth that such a condition is to be expected during old age leaves too many elderly people without the medical care to correct a correctable condition. Such misdiagnosis is a grave disservice to elderly people.

SEXUALITY AND OLD AGE

The myths and jokes about sexual activity in later life are alive and well. They are also causing great psychological damage for people considered old. These falsehoods would lead us to believe that sex is either not necessary or not possible. But if it does occur, it is not normal, and if you can consider it normal, it is still not nice! The facts are quite different.

Even though sexual behavior may decline with age, it does not disappear. There is no biological reason older men and women who are capable of sex cannot or should not have an active and rewarding sex life. Sex is a need of elderly people, and it therefore is an important area of study for geropsychologists. Sexuality is linked to an elderly person's sense of self-esteem. Physical companionship and affection are valuable ingredients for psychological health.

Masters and Johnson (1966) pioneered the study of human sexual response, including that of elderly people. Their findings confirmed that the human sexual response may be slowed, but it certainly is not terminated. They also found that there may be as many or more psychological reasons for the slowing down process as physical ones. Perhaps there is a psychological game behind the reason we deny the sexuality of the aged. It may result from a fear among younger adults that their own sexual abilities may be lost as they grow older. One way of handling that fear is to play the game called "Sex isn't important when you're old!" After all, if it's not important then, it won't matter if you cannot enjoy it. This way of thinking creates stereotypes and myths that the elderly have to overcome, or else they become victims by way of the self-fulfilling prophecy.

FIGURE 5.11
"Beats me why these kids are willing to pay 10 bucks to get a set of wrinkles." (© 1986 by Bill Haas. Used with permission.)

SUMMARY

The goal of geropsychology is to study the behavior of elderly so that future problems can be anticipated and solved before they have to be experienced. Aging personalities are difficult to study because the term *personality* is a hypothetical concept. Though behaviors differ due to individuality, some traits are common to nearly all people, young and old.

Personalities are often categorized into types and then rated according to their adaptive abilities. The greater the adaptability to old age, the more likely aging would be rated as a happy and fulfilling experience.

Theories of personality and its continued development in old age shed light on the adapting and evaluating process that goes on in order for each person to establish a sense of self-worth. The feeling of positive self-esteem or lack of it determines whether the final years will be spent with a feeling of wholeness or despair.

Mental illness affects the elderly as well as other age groups. Although the figures are only estimates, it appears that this group is well within the percentage of mental illness reported nationwide.

Studies are inconclusive as to whether personality changes with age. It may be more likely that a person's personality, flexible or inflexible, determines if behavior changes are made in order to adjust to changing environments.

Intelligence and IQ are separate but related concepts. External environments, once ignored in the testing of elderly people, are now respected for their impact on testing scores. When all environments are in favor of the test taker, then scores favor youth. However, when it comes to decision making and risk taking, age is not a negative factor.

The ability to learn, the desire to learn, and the creative contributions made by the elderly are there for all of society to see. People who do not succumb to the fear of being wrong or who make society's expectation of failure their own have the energy and ability to pursue new levels of achievement. The elderly make up nearly 50 percent of the higher level educational enrollment.

The myths and jokes involving sexuality in old age cause psychological damage. Aging does not make one less human nor does it make one any less a sexual human being. Facts disprove the myths but do indicate that the need for sex may lessen with age; the need for loving relationships do not lessen with age. Physical companionship and affection are valuable ingredients for psychological health.

EXERCISES

1. To become familiar with the four personality patterns, and because personality does not change dramatically with age, list at least two people you know who fit each personality pattern. Write a short explanation why you feel these individuals fit the specific group in which you placed them. (If you prefer not to use people, see the next exercise.)
2. Using magazine pictures and carefully reading the body language in the pictures, assign pictures to each of the four personality patterns.
3. Interview several people seventy years of age or older. List any and all skills, hobbies, and/or travel they experienced since their sixtieth birthday. Do your findings prove true or false the old adage, "You can't teach an old dog new tricks"?
4. Discover and write a report on someone not listed in this chapter who was known for the contributions made to the world after sixty years of age. Share these with other findings by classmates and compile a class list of creative seniors.
5. Keep a tabulation (for a specified period of time) of how many times you hear such remarks as, "I must be getting senile" from people sixty-five years of age and over. Keep a similar record of how many times things are forgotten or mislaid by young people that are not attributed to an aging memory. Study the findings and write a concluding statement.
6. If you had to select the loss of one of your five senses, which one would you select and why?

REVIEW

1. Define geropsychology.
2. Historically, the least sought out group of people for research were the _____ .
3. List the two factors that have created interest in the study of aging and the aged.
4. Define personality.
5. Identify the three changes that occur to bring about a change in behavior.
6. Identify and explain the four basic personality patterns found among the elderly.
7. How do family relationships in old age affect personality change?

8. Define mental health.
9. List the four categories of personality development in old age.
10. Which stage of Erikson's eight stages of life directly pertains to the elderly?
11. What did Buhler indicate were the three periods of life? What was each period's specific goal?
12. What do social theorists believe causes personality and behavior changes?
13. Why is creativity a vital part of aging?
14. Are dramatic behavior changes always a sign of mental deterioration?
15. What is the relationship of IQ to learning performance?
16. Compare fluid and crystallized intelligence.
17. Why have some past studies concerning learning been invalid as they applied to elderly people?
18. How does memory differ from learning?
19. What are the major differences between long-term and short-term memory?
20. Why is the error of omission more common among the elderly than that of commission?
21. What potential danger exists in a diagnosis of senility?
22. The link of sexuality and old age affect self-esteem. How do myths about sex and old age strain that connection?

RECOMMENDED READINGS AND REFERENCES

Aging. 3rd ed. Guilford, Ct.: Dushkin Publishing Co., Group Inc., 1983.

Atchley, Robert C. *The Social Forces in Later Life.* Belmont, Calif.: Wadsworth Publishing Company, 1980.

Birren, J. E. and V. J. Renner. *A Brief History of Mental Health and Aging.* Washington, D.C.: National Institute of Mental Health, 1979.

Botwinick, J. "Cautiousness in Advanced Age." *Journal of Gerontology* 21 (1966): 347-358.

———. "Disinclination to Venture Response versus Cautiousness in Responding; Age Differences." *Journal of Genetic Psychology* 115 (1969): 55-83.

———. *Aging and Behavior.* New York: Springer, 1978.

Brody, E., L. Davis, and P. Johnson. *Formal and Informal Service Providers: Preferences of Three Generations of Women.* Washington, D.C.: Gerontological Society, 1979.

Buhler, C. and F. Massarik, eds. *The Course of Human Life.* New York: Springer, 1968.

Butler, Robert N. *Why Survive?* New York: Harper & Row Publishers, Inc., 1975.

Comfort, Alexander. *A Good Age.* New York: Crown Publishers, Inc., 1976.

Erikson, Erik. *Childhood and Society.* New York: W. W. Norton, 1963.

———. *Identity and the Life Cycle.* Psychological Issues. New York: International Universities Press, 1959.

Gergen, K. J. and K. W. Back. "Communications in the Interview and the Disengaged Respondent." *Public Opinion Quarterly* 33 (1969): 17-33.

Kermis, Marguerite D. *The Psychology of Human Aging.* Boston: Allyn and Bacon, Inc., 1984.

Levinson, D. J., *et al.* "The Psychosocial Development of Men in Early Adulthood and the Mid-life Transition." In *Life History Research in Psychopathology,* edited by D. F. Ricks, A. Thomas, and M. Roff, vol. 3. Minneapolis: University of Minnesota Press, 1974.

Masters, William H. and Virginia Johnson. *Human Sexual Response.* Boston: Little, Brown, 1966.

McKenzie, Sheila C. *Aging and Old Age.* Glenview, Ill.: Scott, Foresman & Co., 1980.

The Meeker REA Pioneer. "Ready for Retirement or Ripe for Achievement?," April, 1985.

Minneapolis Star and Tribune. "1 in 5 Americans Mentally Ill," November 21, 1984.

Neugarten *et al. Personality in Middle and Late Life.* New York: Atherton Press, 1964.

Neugarten, B., R. Havighurst, and S. Tobin. *Middle Age and Aging.* Chicago: University of Chicago Press, 1968.

Reader's Digest. "Minding His T's and 2's," December, 1985, 180.

Santrock, John W. *Adult Development and Aging.* Dubuque, Ia.: Wm. C. Brown, Publishers, 1985.

Schwartz, Arthur N. and James A. Peterson. *Introduction to Gerontology.* New York: Holt, Rinehart and Winston, 1979.

Thomae, Hans. *Patterns of Aging: Findings from the Bonn Longitudinal Study of Aging.* New York: S. Karger, 1975.

Warner, Wayne E. *1000 Stories and Quotations of Famous People.* Grand Rapids, Mich.: Baker Book House, 1972.

Woodruff, Diana S., and James E. Birren, *Aging.* Monterey, Calif.: Brooks/Cole Publishing Company, 1983.

CHAPTER
6

Stress
and Aging

Learning Objectives

After studying this chapter, the reader should be able to:

- Conclude that certain major sources of stress seem to characterize older adults more than their younger counterparts. It does not follow, however, that these stressful events will be coped with in a different manner.
- Summarize the evidence that indicates elderly people's ability to cope and adapt is a personality characteristic they have possessed throughout their life.
- Discriminate between the elderly people who are classified as having a chronic, irreversible form of dementia from those who in reality have a potentially treatable disorder.
- Explain that coping resources and strategies are important ingredients in influencing adaptation to stress and the ability to live a psychologically healthy life.

Preview

"Old age is generally a time of serenity." Is this statement fact or fiction? With the increased public awareness of the many problems confronting elderly people within our society, the serenity-in-old-age idea is fast losing ground. Just as the myth that everybody over sixty-five is basking carefree in the tropical sun is not reality, neither is the concept of stress-free golden years. Instead, demographics and social realities confirm that old age brings with it physical decline, loss of income, change in life-style, loss of social status, loss of work-related friends and activities, and fear of physical and mental disease—all of which are stress related. It may be true that no other age group faces and experiences higher stress levels than do the elderly. Added proof may lie in the statistic that the aged account for 11 percent of the population statistics but for 25 percent of the suicide statistics.

WHAT IS STRESS?

Few people regard any stress as positive. However, stress in and of itself is neither positive nor negative. Stress is the expenditure of energy to adapt to the changing situation.

There are two types of stress. The first type, *distress,* is harmful to the body. It cannot be totally avoided, but it can be controlled. The second type, *eustress,* is a healthy type of stress that is beneficial and helps the body.

When the level of stress allows significant time for adaptation and replenishment of energy, an individual can perform at optimum levels. This is eustress. When stress is continuous and loss of energy prevents adaptation, exhaustion occurs. This is distress; it is a much more familiar concept and term to most people than is eustress.

A complete freedom from stress is death (Selye 1974, 20). Too little stress leads to no action—a state of lethargy and lack of performance. Motivators are stressors that cause people to react and change. They can be concrete, such as income, status, or career advancement; or abstract, such as personal or moral ideals. The motivators get people going and keep them moving until they are doing their best. Once that stage is reached, the trick is to stay there (Figure 6.1).

In his research on stress in the 1930s, Dr. Hans Selye uncovered many factors classified as *distress,* or what we more commonly call *stress.*

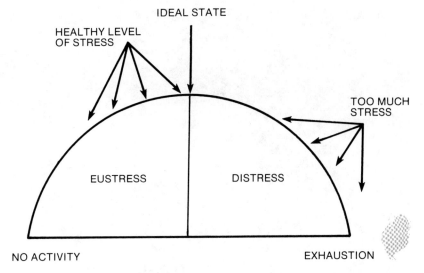

IDEAL STATE

HEALTHY LEVEL
OF STRESS

TOO MUCH
STRESS

EUSTRESS

DISTRESS

NO ACTIVITY

EXHAUSTION

FIGURE 6.1
Diagram of eustress and distress ("Eustress and
Distress," and illustration from **Parent Burn-out** *by*
Dr. Joseph Procaccini and Mark W. Kiefaber. Copy-
right © 1983 by Dr. Joseph Procaccini and Mark W.
Kiefaber. Reprinted by permission of Doubleday
and Company, Inc.)

He divided distress into four basic groups: mental, physical, chemical, and
thermal (Figure 6.2).

Mental Distress

When the term *stress* is mentioned, most people think of mental distress.
This is one of the primary types but not the only one. Mental distress can
have a wide scope, from the death of a loved one to a teen-ager's being
teased about acne. Emotional stress that is met properly is usually overcome rapidly by the body.

In modern society, we have many types of emotional distress that
are not short-term in nature and that take their toll on health. The distress
may be financial—being unable to pay all the bills at the end of the month.
The distress may be the loss of a job or forced retirement. The most
problematic type of emotional distress is distress that is unrelenting, with
few prospects for change.

FIGURE 6.2
(From Geriatrics: A Study of Maturity, *4th ed., by*
Esther Caldwell and Barbara R. Hegner, copyright ©
1986 by Delmar Publishers Inc.)

Physical Distress

Physical distress can be as simple as not getting adequate sleep, or working too many hours—in other words, driving oneself past the body's
endurance. "Physical distress also includes structural problems within
the body, such as spinal imbalance or other body misalignment. These are
especially significant if there is constant pain, because pain itself is a
distress to the body."*

---

*From *Stress,* Pamphlet # PE-615, Systems DC, Pueblo, Colo. Used with permission.

Common physical distresses among the elderly include arthritis and orthopedic impairments. Physical eustress is the "good" tiredness caused by enjoyable activity that can be effectively relieved by adequate rest and relaxation.

Chemical Distress

This form of distress is on the increase in our modern environment. The three major categories in the chemical phase of distress include environmental pollution, such as automobile emissions, pesticides, or a furnace leaking gas; contamination and refinement of food supply, including the many preservatives, food colorings, and artificial flavorings in modern foods; and medications, both prescription and over-the-counter, that may

FIGURE 6.3
(From Geriatrics: A Study of Maturity, 4th ed., by Esther Caldwell and Barbara R. Hegner, copyright © 1986 by Delmar Publishers Inc.)

be stressful to the body and thereby create significant demands on the stress mechanisms.

Thermal Distress

When the body becomes overheated or chilled, a stress reaction is set up to meet the demand. For example, when getting into an automobile with the windows rolled up on a hot, sunny day, the body immediately becomes too warm. Air conditioning then blows directly on the individual as soon as the car is in motion.

"Prolonged thermal stress always affects the adrenal gland. Because the adrenal gland is responsible for many body functions, symptomatic involvement from distress is great."* The problem may surface as ulcers of the digestive system, allergies, migraine headaches, high blood pressure, heart disease, severe fatigue, nervousness, moodiness, or the inability to think clearly. Since the autonomic nervous system—which controls the organs and glands of the body—becomes imbalanced from prolonged distress, any part of the body controlled by that system can develop symptomatic problems, eventually resulting in disease.

REACTING TO STRESS

In addition to the four types of distress, Selye (1976) studied the relationship between prolonged stress and psychological or physical problems. He proposed that when the body experiences prolonged stress, it responds in three sequential steps, which he referred to as general adaptation syndrome.

Alarm Reaction

The first bodily response to prolonged stress is the alarm reaction. Such a stressful situation exists when a condition calls forth all the body's resources in order to increase the energy supply. The direct effect of stress occurs through the fight-or-flight mechanism within the body. This mechanism is a natural body activity that enables one to handle problem situations. It does exactly what its name implies—it enables one to fight a situation or to run from it.

---

*From *Stress,* Pamphlet # PE-615, Systems DC, Pueblo, Colo. Used with permission.

The adrenal gland is important in the fight-or-flight mechanism. It is responsible for increased blood sugar, which provides muscle energy and thinking power; for an increased heart rate and higher blood pressure to circulate energy-giving sugar and oxygen through the body; and for an increased respiration rate, to give more power and thinking ability.

However, for some individuals, including the elderly, the fight-or-flight mechanism does not represent practical options. Losing one's work setting and friends through forced retirement is not a fight-or-flight situation. Tremendous energy is needed to cope with the situation. The energy can be spent in dealing with it in a constructive, problem-solving manner and assuring the person of physical and mental well-being. Or, if the energy is spent in bottling up the hostile feelings, this prolonged stress can cause harm to the body.

Stage of Resistance

The second phase of the general adaptation syndrome is the stage of resistance. As in the first phase, there is a continued sense of pressure and strain. All of the body's physical and emotional resources are combined to ward off the stressful situation. As a result of the prolonged stress, the individual begins to exhibit signs of depression, mood change, sleeplessness and appetite loss.

FIGURE 6.4

The constant erosion of the individual's psychological and biological well-being may, during the resistance stage, tempt the person to resort to sedatives, tranquilizers, or alcohol to induce sleep, create appetite, or settle the nerves. Should any of these drugs prove to lessen the stress problem, dependence may result. Overuse or misuse of them could lead to greater stress problems resulting from the reaction of the mind or body to the level of drug intake. Such habits used to cope with stress at any age, including habits established during later maturity, can influence the quality of life during the remaining years.

Exhaustion

The third phase of the general adaptation syndrome is exhaustion. Stress over a prolonged period of time can exhaust both the mind and body. The individual is simply worn out and wants to give up. The body can no longer maintain a satisfactory amount of energy, and the mind no longer wants to think about the situation. Flight was abandoned in the second stage of resistance, and fight is abandoned in this third stage of exhaustion. All the person's resources are depleted. In fact, the state of exhaustion may be extreme enough to be followed by depression.

DEPRESSION AND LATER LIFE

The topic of elderly depression can be discussed in the chapter on the psychology or biology of aging as well as here, under stress. The causes and/or effects of depression affect the total person.

> "Depression is frequently a confusing concept for older adults and those who work with them. On the one hand, depression is seen as synonymous with the aging process itself: 'It is depressing to grow old.' Though most gerontologists would not accept this view."
> (Blazer 1986, 21)

Myers (1984) believes severe depression is less prevalent in the later years than in earlier stages of the life cycle. These findings are controversial and, it is feared, may suggest a rosier view of mental health in later life than is accurate (Blazer 1986, 21). This statement, however, is not intended to detract from the fact that severe depression among the elderly continues to be a major public health concern. Suicide remains one of the ten leading causes of death among the elderly.

Blazer's community surveys concluded that approximately 15 percent of older adults have significant depressive symptoms. He states that if the figures include individuals in late life who express a decrease in life satisfaction, the percentage would be higher. But of the 15 percent:

a. Approximately 7-8 percent are suffering from either bereavement or adjustment disorder.
b. 3-4 percent suffer a form of "transient" depression, a depression that is severe but lasts for a relatively short period of time—about two weeks.
c. 2-3 percent suffering a "dysthymic" disorder which is less severe but lasts for a longer period of time.
d. 1-2 percent who at any given time suffer severe depression. These severe depressions require professional attention and are often life threatening. (Blazer 1986, 22)

FIGURE 6.5

All four categories of depression are treatable and are often characterized by unhappiness, loss of sleep, loss of weight, indifference, lack of concentration, and, not uncommonly, thoughts of suicide.

It is apparent that one step toward preventing such depression would be professional intervention within the second stage of reacting to stress—resistance. However, since most elderly are so reluctant to use counseling and mental health services, too many continue into the third phase—exhaustion. Education of the elderly is important to teach them how to cope with stress and how to find ways to lessen the consequences of stress so they can avoid the exhaustion phase and regain and maintain a healthy mental and physical level for satisfactory living.

STRESS DIFFERS WITH AGE

All human beings, at every stage in life, experience stress. As people enter later maturity, the kinds and amount of stress to which they are subjected change. Also, the ways and opportunities to deal with stress change. When younger, most stress deals with goal achievement, with wanting to gain a certain social and/or financial status. This stress, although having a physical and emotional price, also has rewards. These active roles are expected and accepted by society, and they serve as a constructive outlet of energy.

As one reaches old age, role expectations change. There are no longer those achievement goals; retirement has ended them. Aggressive behavior is frowned on as society expects the elderly to assume a more passive role. The energy outlets to which the individual had become accustomed are no longer available or acceptable.

The role characterized by activity in the past now becomes one of passivity. The stressful situations have not lessened with age; in fact, they may, in some cases, have increased, but the outlets have been eliminated. Even the adjustments required in old age cannot be met by the past patterns of aggression. Such behavior is of no value when one loses a mate or a family member. It is also valueless against reduced physical ability or the loss of a youthful appearance. Age-related stresses are related to the loss of family, friends, work, status, health, independence, and valued experiences. Past habits of dealing with these types of stress may not be appropriate.

COPING POSITIVELY WITH STRESS

Unfortunately, there is no way that all stress can be eliminated. Some stressful situations, such as loss of a loved one, are permanent and unchangeable. The stress may be extreme, but the individual must make an adjustment for the sake of physical and mental well-being. The coping is even made more difficult in old age because:

1. This may be the first experience with losses, and often the losses are greater in number and occur within shorter time periods.
2. Society provides little or no preparation to teach people how to cope.
3. Unlike in the past, the individual may have no work to get caught up in in an effort to forget or lessen the impact of the loss.

Most of the younger years are spent in learning how to get what we want, how to achieve goals, and how to step over obstacles on the way up the achievement ladder. Little or no time is spent on how to face stressful situations that cannot be changed and that no amount of energy can reverse. Suddenly, the elimination of stress is totally dependent on our own ability to get control of ourselves. For some people, stress becomes a life-shattering experience. The additional stressors of old age, the diminished outlet to cope with that stress and not having learned positive coping skills, influence the psychological and physical well-being of many people in later maturity. Besides the biological illnesses related to stress, there are the psychological ones. Anxiety due to stress manifests itself in terms of real or imagined illnesses, depression, fear, and even suicide.

It must be emphasized that most aged individuals cope exceptionally well with stress. Successful coping may often be aided by friends, relatives, social institutions, and a variety of environmental factors. For the person who has suffered a dramatic loss or has been placed in a highly stressful situation, professional help by an individual or an institution may provide the temporary support the person needs to deal with the adjustments.

Some positive ways to help elderly people cope with stress include releasing emotions, setting new goals, avoiding major changes, remaining responsible, and seeking professional guidance.

Releasing Emotions

People who experience a dramatic change or permanent loss need to be permitted and encouraged to release their emotions in an atmosphere of sympathy, understanding, and acceptance. Society must allow people to cry and to discuss their feelings openly—whatever they are. To be able to talk freely about what has been lost or changed can do much to release pent-up energy.

The expression of strong emotions, such as anger and hate, is often considered taboo. Many people believe these emotions are best not expressed. If a stressed individual feels that friends and family prefer that she or he not express such strong feelings, then the individual's only other choice is to bottle them up and endure the stress-related pressure. Some people see keeping the proverbial stiff upper lip as more acceptable behavior than expressing anger or hate as the result of a personal loss. Only a sympathetic, accepting attitude of all emotions from a distressed person will allow the distressed person to be rid of the stress related to experiencing a crisis.

Setting New Goals

The setting of new or different types of goals or objectives can be helpful in dealing with the expenditure of energy resulting from stress. Substitute goals should not be expected, however, to be the cure for stress or frustration. Whenever a person has an opportunity to pursue activities on which energy can be spent in a positive manner, that person is less likely to exhibit patterns of negative behavior than is the individual who does not have such outlets. Substitute goals can include travel, joining new social groups, or finding new recreation or hobbies. These activities may prove helpful in using energy in a constructive manner.

Substitute goals must be personally meaningful to the individual. Being forced to pursue an activity the person dislikes creates another stressful situation substituted for a past one. When personal interest, enthusiasm, and commitment to a new undertaking develop and grow, the undertaking becomes an outlet for stress-related energy. The goal is to change behavior, because if behavior can be effectively changed, changes in attitude frequently follow.

What seems most tragic is that many stressful losses suffered during the course of the life span are accompanied by the loss or reduction of substitute goals or activities. This means that when the person most needs substitute goals or objectives, they are most likely to be withdrawn.

An example is the highly stressful situation of widowhood. With the loss of her husband, a woman also often loses the other activities and interests she had. She is also likely to be excluded from a variety of social activities, to lose the companionship of some friends who are still married, and to feel unwelcome or uncomfortable in homes or restaurants she formerly went to as a married woman. Her change in marital status is likely to produce many painful and unexpected side effects. Thus, the recently widowed not only must cope with the death of a spouse, but also

FIGURE 6.6

must face the additional loss of interests, activities, companionships, social status, and pursuits that were important during married life. At a time when substitute goals or activities are most needed to vent the emotional energy produced by the stress of a loss, such goals and activities are suddenly withdrawn. This loss of substitute goals and activities can be almost as devastating to the woman's welfare as is the actual stress brought on by the loss of her husband.

Avoiding Major Changes

Stress is often the result of a major change. To attempt to alleviate the stress of a major change by another major change is not a solution but rather another problem. An example is the woman who lost her husband being encouraged to buy a new home, to move in with a family member, or to leave the community in which she is comfortable. These major changes are stressful situations in and of themselves. People under great stress should maintain their current situation until they are emotionally capable of making a decision they will not regret. Should they insist on a major change, arrangements should be made so the change is only temporary and can be reversed. The key is that during stressful situations, additional life changes should be avoided.

Remaining Responsible

It is important that individuals remain realistic. Every type of support possible should be given. But individuals should not separate themselves from all responsibilities that were a natural part of life. Sheltering the individuals from remaining responsible for their personal affairs can be counterproductive, canceling positive goals. It could introduce people to a role of overdependence, which brings with it feelings of personal inadequacy.

A more practical solution is for individuals to receive assistance with the duties that may be new to them as a result of a loss. For example, a widow may not have been responsible for the banking and insurance. Careful and patient help should be given so she learns these responsibilities and can remain independent in handling personal and business affairs.

Performing such duties and responsibilities can be an excellent release for the stress-related energies. Such activities can prove to be as effective an energy release as learning a new hobby. When everything is done for an individual, energy that might have been channeled to constructive activities may be redirected toward self or others in a destructive manner.

Seeking Professional Guidance

When time and the help of friends have been of little value in the healing process, it may be necessary to encourage obtaining professional help.

People cannot always deal with stress successfully without the advice and counsel of trained professionals. However, the suggestion of professional help is not always well received, usually for two major reasons. First, people experiencing extreme stress may be in no emotional condition to realize that their behavior is no longer healthy. Their claims that they are coping successfully and that all they need is more time may seem realistic to them. Second, the idea of professional help is totally unacceptable to them. They may see their problems and their inability to cope effectively with them as a personal defeat. They cannot imagine sharing their problems with a stranger.

Professional help has not been an acceptable solution in the past because some people associate such terms as shameful, degrading, and embarrassing with professional mental health clinics or their personnel. Past generations may have used such terms as crazy or insane to describe people who sought such help. These labels can be powerful deterrents when stressed people receive suggestions to seek professional counseling.

A stigma—disgrace or shame—also may be attached to such needs. Some people falsely believe that such disorders are incurable and that they will always be labeled as mentally ill. It is not surprising that an individual who goes to a dentist for a toothache, a chiropractor for a backache, or an optometrist for vision problems would never think of going to a psychologist for stress-related problems.

America's elderly population underuses the health clinics set up for them more than any other service. Only the education of future generations will help erase the stigma of mental health professions. However, society can ill afford to wait for the next generation and ignore mental health problems of the present generation. Education of the clergy and more geriatric training for physicians are two possibilities to be considered.

EVENTS INFLUENCING THE SEVERITY OF STRESS

The effects of stress—the intensity of the anxiety it arouses and the degree to which it disrupts the individual's ability to function—depend on a number of factors. These factors include some characteristics of stress itself: the situation in which stress occurs, the individual's appraisal and evaluation of the stressful situation, and his or her resources for coping with it.

Predictability

Being able to predict the occurrence of a stressful event—even if the individual cannot control it—usually reduces the severity of the stress. Experiments show that both human beings and animals prefer predictable offensive events to unpredictable ones.

People also prefer immediate to delayed shock. One example is the vulnerability of older people to be unknowingly (and involuntarily) moved from their private home to a nursing home. This highly stressful move can precipitate negative physical effects.

Control over Duration

Having control over the duration of a stressful event also reduces the severity of the stress. In one study (Tallmer and Kutner 1969, 70-72), subjects were shown pictures of painful events. One experimental group could terminate the viewing by pressing a button. The other group were shown the same pictures but could not end the viewing. The group that could end the negative experience showed much less anxiety than the group with no control over the required viewing time. The belief that we can control the duration of an aversive event appears to lessen anxiety, even if the control is never actually used.

Cognitive Evaluation

Two people can perceive the same stressful event quite differently, depending on what the situation means to each individual. The objective facts of the situation are less important than the individual's appraisal of them. Doctors treating wounded soldiers in wartime were often amazed at the calmness with which the soldiers reacted to their serious injuries—compared to civilian injuries for which patients would plead for relief from pain. For soldiers, the wounds meant they would no longer be subjected to the additional danger of combat.

An individual's perception of a stressful event also involves appraising the degree of threat. Situations seen as threatening to survival (for example, a diagnosis of cancer) or to the individual's worth (for example, forced retirement) impose a maximum of stress.

Feelings of Competency

People's confidence in their ability to handle a stressful situation is a major factor in determining the severity of the stress. Having to perform before a large audience is a traumatic event for most people, but individuals experienced in performing have confidence in their ability and feel only minimal anxiety.

Emergencies are particularly stressful because our usual methods of coping do not work. Not knowing what to do can be demoralizing. People trained to deal with emergencies can act calmly and effectively because they know what to do, but the person who lacks such training may feel helpless. Since we tend to fall back on well-learned responses under stress, it is important that people have training in coping with many types of emergency situations.

Social Supports

The emotional support and concern of other people can make stress more bearable. Divorce, the death of a loved one, or a serious illness is usually more devastating if an individual must face it alone. Sometimes, however, family and friends can increase the stress. Minimizing the seriousness of the problem or giving blind assurance that "everything will be all right" may produce more anxiety than failing to offer support.

People with many social ties (marriage, close friends and relatives, church memberships, and other group associations) tend to live longer and be less apt to succumb to stress-related illnesses than people who have few social supports. Stress is easier to tolerate when its cause is shared with other people. Community disasters (floods, tornadoes, fires) often seem to bring out the best in people. Individual anxieties and conflicts tend to be forgotten when people are working together against a common enemy or toward a common good.

MISDIAGNOSIS

Stress, when referring to the elderly, is sometimes misdiagnosed. This happens most often when stress causes depression. For example, when a twenty-one-year-old woman suffers postpartum depression after the birth of a baby, or when a forty-four-year-old suffers from menopausal depression, their depression is acknowledged and treated. But when at the age of sixty-five, a woman suffers from depression, these same symptoms most often are erroneously diagnosed as senility. Such a harmful conclusion often finds the person not encouraged to seek any professional assistance and often sees the support group slowly withdrawing. If the complaint of depression was seen not as a symptom of old age but of possible malnutrition, reaction to medication, infection, or as disease-related, the approach to the solution would be more realistic, immediate, and encouraging to the patient.

STRESS AT ITS WORST: SUICIDE

Most depression does not end in suicide. The reverse, however, is also true: most people who make serious suicide attempts are depressed. This fact is perhaps most true in old age. It is estimated that if a general definition of depression is used, almost 100 percent of elderly suicides

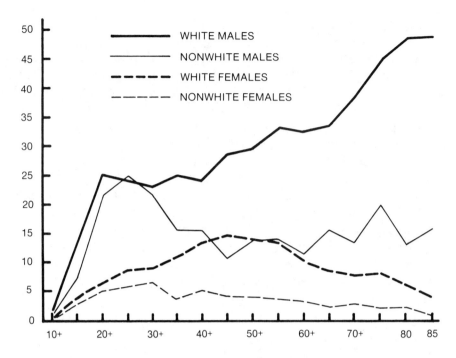

FIGURE 6.7
Suicide rates in the United States for 1980 (U.S. Bu-reau of the Census, Demographic and Socioeconomic Aspects of Aging in the United States, *Series P-23, No. 138, 1984.*)

are preceded by depression symptoms (Stenback 1980). Because older people are more likely to experience depression, they are also more likely to attempt suicide. This accounts for their percentage of suicide attempts resulting in death being higher than that of younger people. Figure 6.7 shows the high percentage of suicides among the elderly and also points out that the category of white, elderly males, at the age of eighty-five, has more than triple the number of suicides compared with other groups in the chart.

Another point to consider about the high suicide statistics among the elderly is that young people are more likely to make a suicidal gesture to manipulate other people or to get attention. However, suicide attempts by older people have a greater chance of being successful because their goal is not attention but to end life. In 1985, the elderly accounted for 11 percent of the population but 25 percent of the suicides.

MEASURING STRESS

"We have found great trouble clustering people into age brackets that are characterized by particular conflicts; the conflicts won't stay put, and neither will the people."
(Lazarus and DeLongis 1981, 16)

Gerontologists are interested in how stress is understood, how it should be measured, and whether elderly people, sixty-five and older, experience more stress than during any other point in their adult life. Any change in an individual's life—whether pleasant or unpleasant—requires some readjustment. Studies of personal histories suggest that physical and emotional disorders tend to cluster around periods of major change in a person's life.

The Life Change Scale was developed to measure stress in terms of life changes. The life events are ranked in order, from the most stressful (death of a spouse) to the least stressful (minor violations of the law). To arrive at this scale, the investigators examined thousands of interviews and medical histories to identify the kinds of events people found stressful.

Because marriage (a positive event, but one that requires a fair amount of readjustment) appeared to be a critical event for most people, it was placed in the middle of the scale and assigned an arbitrary value of 50. The investigators then asked approximately 400 men and women (of varying ages, backgrounds, and marital status) to compare marriage with a number of other life events. They were asked such questions as, "Does the event call for more or less readjustment than marriage?" and "Would the readjustment take shorter or longer to accomplish?" They also were asked to assign a point value to each event on the basis of their evaluation of its severity and the time required for adjustment.

As one reads the list of forty-three events that provoke stress, it becomes readily apparent that most individuals are susceptible to more than one stressful situation at any one time. Furthermore, it is highly unlikely that any one stressful event will occur in total isolation from all other crises or that life will progress for any significant time in the absence of stressful events. According to Holmes and Rahe (1967), if people compute the total life change units to which they are subjected at one particular time and derive a numerical total, they should apply it to the following table:

0-149	No significant problem
150-199	Mild stress;
	35% chance of illness
200-299	Moderate stress;
	50% chance of illness
300+	Major stress;
	80% chance of illness

"The idea that emotional stress shortens life by increasing one's chance of getting physically ill dates back to antiquity but is just being newly appreciated by scientists."

(Belsky 1984, 57)

People whose total is higher than 200 are operating under an extremely high level of stress or pressure, and their ability to cope successfully may be severely taxed. If they have a stress rating of 200 or higher, it may be necessary for them to stop, reevaluate their situation, and perhaps make some significant changes in their life.

Some people may argue that the issues of stress and coping with it are too complex for such a simple rating scale. People's expectations and their past history of adaptation are scale-tipping factors. Rarely do individuals ignore stress; they attempt to change things when possible; and if they are unable to do that, they come up with a satisfactory explanation for themselves as to why this situation should be. These many strategies to cope with stress help elderly people make sense out of what is happening

Life Events	Stress Score	Your Score
1. Death of spouse	100	_____
2. Divorce	73	_____
3. Marital separation	65	_____
4. Jail term	63	_____
5. Death of close family member	63	_____

FIGURE 6.8
The social readjustment rating scale (T. H. Holmes and R. H. Rahe, Journal of Psychosomatic Research, *11 [1967]. Used with permission of Pergamon Press, Inc.)*

Life Events	Stress Score	Your Score
6. Personal injury or illness	53	_____
7. Marriage	50	_____
8. Fired at work	47	_____
9. Marital reconcilation	45	_____
10. Retirement	45	_____
11. Change in health of family member	44	_____
12. Pregnancy	40	_____
13. Sex difficulties	39	_____
14. Gain of new family member	39	_____
15. Business readjustment	39	_____
16. Change in financial state	38	_____
17. Death of close friend	37	_____
18. Change to different line of work	36	_____
19. Change in number of arguments with spouse	35	_____
20. Mortgage over $10,000	31	_____
21. Foreclosure of mortgage or loan	30	_____
22. Change in responsibilities at work	29	_____
23. Son or daughter leaving home	29	_____
24. Trouble with in-laws	29	_____
25. Outstanding personal achievement	28	_____
26. Spouse begin or stop work	26	_____
27. Begin or end school	26	_____
28. Change in living conditions	25	_____
29. Revision of personal habits	24	_____
30. Trouble with boss	23	_____
31. Change in work hours or conditions	20	_____
32. Change in residence	20	_____
33. Change in schools	20	_____
34. Change in recreation	19	_____
35. Change in church activities	19	_____
36. Change in social activities	18	_____
37. Mortgage or loan less than $10,000	17	_____
38. Change in sleeping habits	16	_____
39. Change in number of family get-togethers	15	_____
40. Change in eating habits	15	_____
41. Vacation	13	_____
42. Christmas, Hanukah	12	_____
43. Minor violations of the law	11	_____
TOTAL SCORE		_____

FIGURE 6.8 (CONTINUED)

to them, making the situation more tolerable and, in some cases, acceptable.

The Life Change Scale was not set up based on older subjects. However, it seems to have specific application to later life. Many predictable events in old age are highly stressful. This may mean that some illnesses among the elderly could be environmentally caused. Examples include the high unit value given to retirement and to the death of a spouse. An event, such as moving to a new location, not only has a forceful impact but also has been studied sufficiently to be referred to as the location effect. Relocation stress can include moving from state to state, community to community, or from a private home to a nursing home.

ARE THERE STRESS-RESISTANT INDIVIDUALS?

We noted earlier that a person's evaluation of a situation is important in determining the severity of stress. Some events in the Life Change Scale (such as retirement or change in social activities) might be viewed as threatening by one individual but challenging by another.

Several investigators (Lazarus and DeLongis 1981, 17; Myers 1984, 963) have been studying the personality characteristics that make people resistant to stress. In a study of more than 600 people, each was given a checklist and asked to describe all the stressful life events and illnesses experienced in the past three years. Analysis of the results indicated that the high-stress/low-illness people:

1. Were more oriented toward challenge and change,
2. Were more actively involved in their work and social lives,
3. Felt more in control of events in their lives. (Kobasa 1979, 10)

Other researchers have emphasized stress resistance as being crucial to longevity and immunity to a host of chronic ailments, including heart disease and cancer. The findings suggest that the intensity of stress is less important to survival than is how a person handles it. Excessive reactions to stress have been shown, among other effects, to depress the actions of the immune system, setting the stage for a variety of illnesses.

The most important factor appeared to be attitude toward change. People who view change as a challenge—for example, retirement from a job viewed as an opportunity to pursue new forms of leisure rather than as a serious setback—are apt to experience less stress and to turn the situation to their advantage.

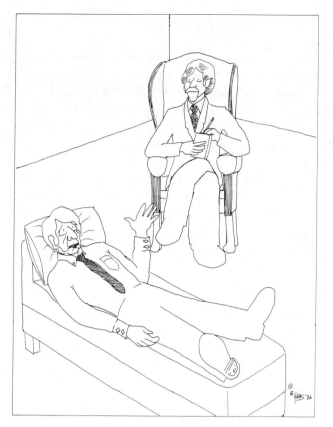

FIGURE 6.9
"I feel like such a failure, Doc. Here I am, eighty-seven years old, but I've still got all my own hair and teeth, keen eyesight, good hearing; senses of smell, taste, and touch, all great; no arthritis, cancer, or heart trouble, I still have my own . . . ." (© 1986 by Bill Haas. Used with permission.)

The personality characteristics of stress-resistant or hardy individuals can be summarized in terms of commitment, control, and challenge. For example, commitment to relationships with other people provides social support in times of stress. The sense of being in control of life events reflects feelings of competency and also influences how stressful events are appraised. People who feel they are able to exert control over stressful situations (instead of feeling helpless) are more likely to take action to remedy the situation. Challenge involves the belief that change is normal in life and should be viewed as an opportunity for growth rather than as a threat to security.

SUMMARY

People at every age are subject to some degree of stress. Individuals cope in different ways and achieve varying degrees of adjustment. Stress, whether real or imaginary, affects one's state of physical and mental health. If stress cannot be dealt with by the fight-or-flight mechanism, the possibility exists that the stress-related energy may be turned against one's self. Some individuals can constructively channel this energy into a form of exciting, new challenge.

As people age, their coping strategies may change. This change most often follows the patterns of readjustment used throughout their mature lifetime. Experience and wisdom may allow a more passive approach to stress, allowing for more constructive use of energy. However, sudden and painful events cannot always be anticipated and prepared for. Therefore, a high degree of stress paired with inadequate coping skills can happen to anyone at any age.

The Holmes and Rahe scale of forty-three events is rated according to the degree of stressfulness each life event is believed to cause. This scale may, more than anything, create an awareness of the situations that are stress producing. The resulting scores emphasize the connection between stress and physical health.

The three phases of the general adaptation syndrome describe how the individual is poised to react. The united forces of the mind and body function under various levels of stress and experience the resulting depletion of energy.

A high degree of relationship exists between people's reaction to stress and their personality makeup. The personality that has always been flexible and not only open to change but also welcoming to challenge is much more successful in coping with incidents that would pose a high degree of stress for less adaptable people.

EXERCISES

1. Take the Life Change Scale and check your own stress level. After adding your own points, add life events you feel are stressful but are not included in the listing. Give each added event a corresponding unit of value. Ask several other people if they agree with your additions and point values.
2. List the present personality characteristics and coping strategies you have that will aid you in the future to cope successfully with stress:

	Personality Traits	Coping Strategies
1.		
2.		
3.		
4.		
5.		

3. Using the diagram of eustress and distress (Figure 6.1), list under *Eustress* the positive types of stress that motivate you to achieve. Under *Distress,* list all of the situations that are negative, energy-robbing situations.
4. Study the Life Change Scale and identify the life events most likely to affect people sixty-five years of age and older. How does the total number of units you have identified affect adjustment in old age?
5. Can the suggestions for coping with stress be applied at any age when faced with stressful situations? Explain how.

REVIEW

1. List the two types of stress and describe how they differ.
2. Explain the four types of distress.
3. What are the three sequential steps when the body experiences prolonged stress? List and define their forms of adaptation.
4. What are some age-related stresses?
5. Why can stress be more difficult to cope with in advanced age?
6. List some positive coping strategies elderly people can use.
7. Identify the factors that determine the intensity of a stressful situation.
8. What is the danger of misdiagnosing stress?
9. How does the Life Change Scale measure stress?
10. List the three personality characteristics that appear to be stress-resistant.

RECOMMENDED READINGS AND REFERENCES

Atkinson, Rita L., Richard C. Atkinson, and Ernest R. Hilgard. *Introduction to Psychology.* 8th ed. New York: Harcourt Brace Jovanovich, Inc., 1983.

Belsky, Janet K. *The Psychology of Aging.* Monterey, Calif.: Brooks/Cole Publishing Co., 1984.

Blazer, Dan. "Depression." *Generations (Quarterly Journal of the American Society of Aging)* 10 (Spring, 1986): 21-23.

Brody, Jane. "Researchers Progress in Delaying Effects of Aging." *Minneapolis Star & Tribune,* December 9, 1984.

Holmes, T. H., and R. H. Rahe. "The Social Readjustment Rating Scale. *Journal of Psychosomatic Research* 12 (Fall, 1967): 213-18.

Kobasa, S. C. "Stressful Life Events, Personality, and Health: An Inquiry Into Hardiness." *Journal of Personality and Social Psychology* 37 (1979): 1-11.

Lazarus, R. S., and A. DeLongis. "Psychological Stress and Coping in Aging." Paper presented at the meeting of the American Psychological Association, Los Angeles, August 1981.

Myers, J. K. "Six Month Prevalence of Psychiatric Disorders in Three Communities." *Archives of General Psychiatry* 41 (1984): 959-67.

Procaccini, Joseph, and Mark W. Kiefaber, *Parent Burn-out.* Bergenfield, N.J.: New American Library, 1983.

Santrock, John W. *Adult Development and Aging.* Dubuque, Ia.: Wm. C. Brown Publishers, 1985.

Selye, H. *Stress without Distress.* New York: New American Library, 1974.

———. *The Stress of Life* Rev. Ed. New York: McGraw Hill, 1976.

Stenback, A. "Depression and Suicidal Behavior in Old Age." In *Handbook of Mental Health and Aging,* edited by J. E. Birren and R. B. Sloane. Englewood Cliffs, N.J.: Prentice-Hall, 1980.

Stress. Pamphlet No. PE-615. Pueblo, Colo.: Systems DC.

Tallmer, Margot, and Bernard Kutner. "Disengagement and the Stresses of Aging." *Journal of Gerontology* 24 (1969): 70-75.

U.S. Bureau of the Census. *Demographic and Socioeconomic Aspects of Aging in the United States.* Series P-23, No. 138. Washington, D.C.: U.S. Government Printing Office, 1984.

CHAPTER 7

Biology of Aging

Learning Objectives

After studying this chapter, the reader should be able to:

- Conclude that principles and habits conducive to overall well-being in old age are the same common-sense behaviors used throughout the earlier years of life.
- Understand that the link between physical activity and mental health is real.
- List the biological processes of aging that are considered universal.
- Define the genetic and nongenetic theories of aging, realizing that we conclude that these are probably the causes of aging.

> Interviewed on his ninetieth birthday, the candid gentleman said, "I'm not as good as I used to be; never was!"

Preview

The body does not feel well when the mind is under stress, and the mind does not function as efficiently when the body is in pain. For too long, we believed that the health of the body was dependent on only its physical parts. In practical living if not in theory, we believed the mind worried, the heart was lonely, and the body caught a cold. Now, we suspect that worry can cause a cold, loneliness can cause migraine headaches, and worrying about money can cause a stress-related heart attack. Our mental, social, and physical activities all contribute to our total well-being or lack of it.

HEALTH AND THE TOTAL PERSON

> Growing old is a fact! How you grow old is a question.

As this chapter discusses the biology of aging, we do not forget the total person (mind and body) (see Figure 7.1); rather, we emphasize the physical aspects of aging. The human being is an incredibly complex biological organism. Aging is one biological condition common to all human beings. New knowledge about how and why it happens is thus our urgent priority. The complicated process of aging is the normal progression of changes related to aging occurring in the cells, organs, and eventually the whole body beginning around the age of thirty. The decline is natural. However, the pace at which this decline occurs separates the person who slides downhill rapidly from the person who ages gracefully. It is tempting to hope that one disease or one defect causes aging. This would simplify the search and eventually end the aging process. However, the existence of only one aging factor is highly unlikely.

Often when people think of the biology of aging, they think of disease. Aging is *not* a disease process. Diseases are random processes

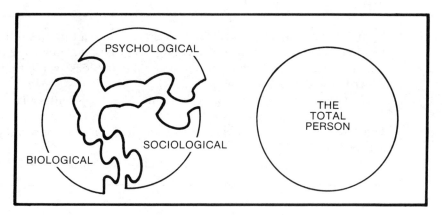

FIGURE 7.1
A person's physical health also depends on his or her psychological and social well-being.

that strike only a small percentage of the population. Aging is also distinguished from a disease process in that it is progressive. That is, it always leads to further deterioration of function. In a disease process, you have a chance to recover. You do not recover from aging.

FIGURE 7.2

Forty-five-year-old golfer Lee Trevino, after winning the PGA tournament last August: "When you're young, you think it's inevitable that you're going to win. When you're old, the inevitable is over with. You never know if you'll win again."

Once on the brink of retirement, Trevino credits his wife, Claudia, with keeping him in the game. "She kept telling me I could win. She'd say, 'Those clubs of yours don't have any idea how old you are, Bubba.' "

(*Reader's Digest,* February 1985, 119)

HUMAN AGING: IS THERE A LIMIT?

What potential the body has for aging is speculation. Sociologists and psychologists may not set limits until 120 or 140 years of living have been experienced. Gerontologists may agree that the age limits are considerably beyond 100 years of age. These sciences do not deal with the number of years in a life span but rather with how those years in the life span are spent. However, biologists have another point of view. They point out that the maximum human life span has not changed, but that more and more people are surviving to the maximum limits (Figure 7.3).

Today, more people live to be 100, but few, now or in the past, survive more than a few years beyond that limit. Biologists believe that the age of 100 appears to be the limit beyond which we cannot go. They have biological theories to support this suggestion and even believe that the maximum life span must be, in some way, predetermined. That is, there may be a genetic basis for death at age 100. They base their argument on the fact that just as there is genetic control over the patterns of growth and development, it follows that there is probably genetic control over longevity. Biologists are uncertain, however, whether this control results from a running out of allotted time or if a body clock triggers the actual time for death.

WHAT IS SENESCENCE?

The study of *biological aging is often referred to as senescence.* Do not confuse senescence with senility. Senility is a nonmedical term generally used to refer to mental forgetting, believed to be the result of aging. We know that the symptoms labeled senility are, in fact, treatable problems.

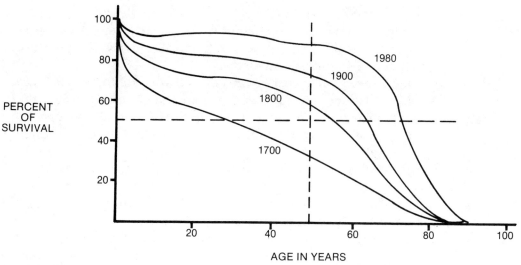

FIGURE 7.3
Human survivorship curves

> *Senescence:* The group of biological processes whereby the organism becomes less viable and more vulnerable as chronological age increases. It manifests itself as an increased probability of disease, injury, and death.

Little is known about actual senescence. We know that chronological age is not the indicator of senescence. Yet, we need to determine what sets senescence apart from other biological processes. The key difference appears to be the word universal. This means that all aging people must experience the same process. Since senescence is not one process but many, finding universal processes to attribute to all aging is difficult.

There appear to be five generally accepted universal processes involved in the process of aging:

1. *The aging process affects every human being.* There can be no exceptions. Every person at the moment of conception begins to age. No one ever becomes younger, and only death stops the aging process.
2. *The body's immune system begins to decline.* The body's first defense against viruses and germs is the immune system. Its job is

to seek and destroy anything inside and outside the body that is foreign to it. This system begins to decline in its effectiveness as chronological age increases, making the elderly person more vulnerable to illness and disease.

3. *The changes that cause senescence must come from inside the body.* It is recognized that environmental conditions affect the aging process. But since these external conditions can be changed and controlled, they do not qualify for the definition of universal.

4. *The processes associated with senescence aid in the decline of bodily functions that eventually cause death.* These processes have a negative effect on the body. This bodily decline is connected to the aging of the human organism.

5. *All the declining processes occur gradually.* Because aging is a slow process, the diminishing of the functions is gradual. Thus, accidents that bring about sudden change do not meet the guidelines of senescence.

THEORIES ABOUT AGING

Since we know little about senescence, it is true that we know little about biological aging. Again, we must study many different theories that can give us information about what probably causes aging. These theories are divided into two categories: genetic and nongenetic.

Genetic Theories

Genetic theories support the idea that the body has a predetermined life span that is inherited through the genes. DNA molecules—DNA stands for deoxyribonucleic acid, the genetic component of the cell—appear to govern the biological process of the human organism. Studies show that each animal species has a unique life span. Life span patterns also appear to occur in genetically related groups. Again, note that environmental factors can influence life spans.

     The DNA theory proposes that aging is a result of the changing DNA functions. As the production of proteins and enzymes does not meet the standards required, the human being ages. As the deterioration process continues, so does aging. However, the question remains about why this diminished production of enzymes and protein begins in the first place.

Nongenetic Theories

The six nongenetic theories are:

1. Wear-and-tear theory.
2. Waste-product theory.
3. Cross-link theory.
4. Stress theory.
5. Single-organ theory.
6. Autoimmune theory.

The wear-and-tear theory is like the car warranty-5 years, 50,000 miles analogy. The car can be expected to run with its original parts for a period of time. After that, the owner can expect to replace or repair parts and eventually to acknowledge the car is worn out. This is not a controversial theory. The analogy can be carried further: not all makes of cars have problems with the same parts wearing out first. Also, the care the car receives could add years to its performance. However, the human body, unlike the car, can repair some of its own parts well into old age.

The waste-product theory is based on the fact that the kidneys eventually lose 50 percent of their capacity to filter out bodily wastes. This lack of cleansing ability plays a key role in senescence.

The cross-link theory states that chronological aging affects the function of the cells. The two major types of cells in the body are:

1. Mitotically active cells: these cells are continuously dividing and making identical copies of themselves. Such cell activity involves the skin, gastrointestinal tract, cells that become red and white blood cells, and fibroblasts that produce structural collagen fibers.
2. Fixed postmitotic cells: these are highly specialized cells that no longer divide. The total number of these cells is determined early in life. Such cells include neurons, skeletal, and heart muscle cells.

Over the years, a body loses both types of cells. Collagen, the gelatin-like substance found in the connective tissue, helps maintain the form and strength of tissue. The cells become attached to each other, for reasons still uncertain. Normally, cells are separate. One effect of this cross-linking is that it immobilizes the molecules. This nonmovement clogs the tissues and cells. The result is that the molecules, tissues, and cells cannot function properly. Cross-linkage is known to be most active and rapid between thirty and fifty years of age. If it were known how to prevent cross-links from occurring, researchers might be able to add years to life (Ebersole and Hess 1981, 24).

The stress theory claims that aging results from the stress experienced across the life span. The origin of the stress can be physical, psychological, or social. It can also come from internal or external causes. It is believed that every person is born with the ability to cope with a certain amount of stress. However, when that ability is depleted by too much stress, the human organism ages. We already know that when the human organism's reserves are exhausted and the high degree of stress continues, the accumulated effect on one part of the body, for example, the heart, can cause death.

Stress resistance appears crucial to longevity and immunity to a host of chronic ailments, including heart disease and cancer. It appears that the intensity of stress is less important to survival than is how a person handles the stress. Excessive reactions to stress have been shown, among other effects, to depress the actions of the immune system, setting the stage for a variety of ills.

The single-organ theory explains aging in terms of a vital organ of the body failing. This failure is caused by disease. Many gerontologists believe no one ever dies of old age. Rather, people die because a disease or wear and tear has caused a vital part to cease functioning. The rest of the body would still be capable of life. Perhaps transplants, or the replacement of the nonfunctioning human organ with artificial organs, is a means of achieving older ages. This means is successfully being used.

The number of organ transplants by December 1984 included:

Organ	Number of Transplants	Artificial Organs
Heart	172	4[*]
Kidney	6,116	
Liver	163	
Pancreas	218	

[*]as of May 1985

The cost to prolong life by this means may be financially prohibitive, depending on the price we place on human life. French novelist André Malraux said, "A human life is worth nothing, but nothing is worth a human life."

Human Transplants Costs		
Organ	Average Cost of Organ and Hospital	1-Year Success Rate
Heart	$100,000	80%
Kidney	30,000	60-85%
Liver	135,000	65%
Pancreas	35,000	35-40%
Artificial Organ Transplant (Example of cost)		
Heart*	$200,000	0%

*Barney Clark's bill; he lived for 112 days after his operation.

The autoimmune theory states that as a person ages, certain body cells become altered. The immune system is supposed to produce antibodies that destroy infections and diseases. However, the alteration of cells causes the immune system to destroy not only diseased cells but also normal ones. Crucial among the declines of senescence is the loss of the immune system to fight off pneumonia. This is why pneumonia is such a common cause of death among elderly people but not among younger people.

Two age-related diseases also believed to be caused by this autoimmune reaction are rheumatoid arthritis and the late onset of diabetes. The importance of a youthful immune system is apparent in a University of Kentucky study of 17 healthy people ranging from 100 to 103 years old (*Minneapolis Star and Tribune,* January 8, 1984). Researchers found that the centenarians' immune systems functioned on a level comparable with younger though still elderly people. The researchers point out that about 10 or 12 out of every 100,000 Americans will live to be 100; at least one-third of this group will be physically active, mentally alert, and free of any major, active disease.

At this time, no single theory explains why we age. In fact, in the description of many of the theories, age started the processes that caused aging! This confusion continues to exist. What we do know for sure is that:

1. We are not sure what causes aging.
2. Aging brings about an element of change.
3. Very few people, if any, die of old age.
4. Old age is not a disease.

FIGURE 7.4
(From **Geriatrics: A Study of Maturity,** *4th ed., by*
***Esther Caldwell and Barbara R. Hegner,** copyright* ©
1986 by Delmar Publishers Inc.)

5. Aging is a universal process that increases one's chances of contracting a disease that may eventually cause death.
6. Not knowing exactly why the body ages does not free us from the fact that it does.
7. The rate of aging differs from person to person, as well as within each person.

OBSERVABLE SIGNS OF AGING

The easiest way to identify an older person is by appearance. Wrinkled skin, gray hair, and aging spots are observable aging signs. However, people use many creative ways to hide or remove these external signs. Another cosmetic change of aging includes the ears elongating, with a thickening of the earlobes. Hormonal changes bring about some facial hair growth in women and in some cases less facial hair in men. The compressing of the spinal discs often causes a shortening of the body and a slightly bent posture. A lack of muscle tone can reduce the size and strength of the muscles. If there is a weight loss, the skull may appear to be slightly larger than before. However, most signs of age changes are biological, and most biological age changes are not externally observable. They occur within the organism.

INTERNAL AGING

In the study of the biology of aging, we need to understand the purpose of different body systems. Some systems in the body (e.g., the cardiovascular system, the respiratory system, the kidneys) have one main function: to keep the internal environment of the body at a constant level.

Single cells in the sea exist in a relatively uniform, unchanging environment. However, it is less likely that the internal environments surrounding each individual cell of a multicellular organism will exist in a constant condition appropriate for cellular survival.

The cardiovascular system sends material around the body, bathing every cell so it has access to fresh nutrient material and so the base material can be removed. This process of homeostasis—a relatively stable state of equilibrium—must be considered when we study aging. In later years, it is the homeostatic condition that begins to fail. People do not just deteriorate. One single biological change does not cause the body to collapse. Rather, there is a general breakdown in the system.

Negative Feedback System

In the biological system, every system (cardiovascular, etc.) has a function. Each system has to maintain a particular variable at a constant level. This is done by a negative feedback system. A common example in our homes is the thermostat connected to the furnace that controls room temperature. A negative feedback system works in such a way that when the room temperature becomes lower than the number at which it was set, the thermostat detects the difference. The thermostat then trips the switch on the furnace, which heats the furnace and thus raises the room temperature.

The negative feedback system also applies to the human cardiovascular system (Figure 7.5). The same process is at work. The pressure of the blood in the cardiovascular system is regulated within a narrow range, assuring blood flow through various parts of the body at a constant rate. Blood pressure that is too high causes the blood vessels to rupture. Blood

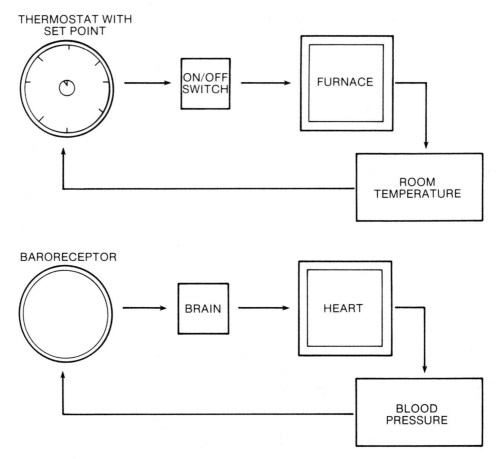

FIGURE 7.5
Negative feedback systems

pressure that is too low causes an inadequate blood flow. Certain receptors (baroreceptors) in the cardiovascular system detect the blood pressure. When blood pressure, for example, is too low, those receptors check it and send this information to the brain, which is in essence the off-on switch; the brain turns on the heart by way of the nerves. This speeds up the heart or increases its strength of contraction, causing the blood pressure to go up.

When the blood pressure goes up too high, the receptors detect that and flip a switch in the brain to slow the heart. These processes work for all systems in the human body. The aging process begins a deterioration in these negative feedback systems—a slow, inevitable deterioration.

Perhaps the receptors are no longer as efficient at detecting changes in the blood pressure. Perhaps the brain is no longer as efficient at responding to the off-on signals. Even the heart may not be able to respond to the same extent as in a younger person. As a result, the regulation of blood pressure may not be adequate.

Another analogy is of one athlete in extremely good shape and another in not such good shape. After running a mile, the athlete in good shape recovers very quickly. The heart rate might drop back to normal in a short period of time. The other athlete takes a longer time to recover. As we get older, we can perhaps do the same things, but not as fast or with as much efficiency. Our reserves are limited.

Because of the extreme importance of the cardiovascular system, we need to study further the age changes that affect it.

Cardiovascular System

The cardiovascular system transports nutrient material around in the body. Some primary elements it transports are gases. The cardiovascular system is connected directly to the lungs. All of the blood comes out of the right side of the heart and passes through the lungs. In the lungs, the gas exchange takes place. Oxygen enters the blood, and carbon dioxide leaves the blood. The blood comes back to the heart from the lungs into the left side, where it is pumped out under high pressure (arterial pressure) to the rest of the body. In the rest of the body, the main arteries service the different organs. The vascular system separates into small capillaries. Because every cell is in intimate association with the capillaries, the real work of the cardiovascular system takes place at this point. The blood converges again into veins that return to the heart to begin another circuit.

The age-related changes that occur in the cardiovascular system are also slow but inevitable. There is an age-related decrease in the amount of blood the heart can put out in a minute. This decreased blood supply limits the reserve energy capability of the body. When a muscle starts to exercise, it needs more blood, and the heart has to work harder. But as we get older, that limit becomes lower and lower. The vessels themselves become more rigid because of changes in the connective tissue in the vessels. Arteriosclerosis occurs—thickening and hardening of the walls of the arteries—and with this increasing rigidity, the pressure goes up and makes the heart work harder. Changes in the tissues themselves in individual organs increase the diffusion distances between the cells, and so the actual cardiovascular contact is not as efficient.

Observable

Hair: Thins and whitens

Vision: Declines; three out of five persons 75+ are affected to some degree, and more often in females than males.

Kidneys: Eventually lose up to 50 percent of their capacity to filter body wastes. This major system shows the greatest decline with age.

Heart: 1st—Between ages 20–90 the amount of blood pumped by the heart decreases 50 percent. 2nd—Muscle fibers contract more slowly. 3rd—Heart and blood vessels are more vulnerable to disease.

Bones: At 40+, the body no longer absorbs calcium efficiently, which contributes to fractures in more than 25 percent of all elderly women.

Joints: 1st—Begin to stiffen, particularly the hips and knees. 2nd—Compressed spinal discs shorten the body and cause a bent posture. Height loss of 1–3 inches is common.

Nervous System: 1st—Hardening of blood vessels create circulatory problems in the brain. 2nd—Aging reduces the speed with which the nervous system can process information or send signals for action.

Circulatory System: Failure in this system is the most common cause of death. Death from cardiovascular disease at age 75 is 150 times higher than at 35.

Nonobservable

Hearing: 1st—Ability to hear high pitches is more difficult. 2nd—Normal sound levels are more difficult to understand.

Skin: 1st—Fine lines around eyes and mouth. 2nd—Lines deepen into wrinkles. 3rd—Skin loses elasticity and smoothness. 4th—Spots of dark pigment.

Lungs: 1st—Between ages 30–75, the amount of air inhaled and exhaled drop by 45 percent. 2nd—Between ages 30–75, the amount of oxygen passing into the blood decreases about 50 percent.

Hormones: 1st—Decline in hormonal flow from the adrenal gland, located atop the kidney, lowers the ability of the elderly to respond to stress. 2nd—For women, menstruation ceases.

Immune System: This system becomes less efficient and therefore lowers the body's resistance to disease.

Muscles: 1st—There is a loss of muscle strength, which reduces coordination. 2nd—Lack of muscle tone causes a sagging of muscles.

FIGURE 7.6
Changes in your body over time

Age-related changes also occur in the valves and the veins. Varicosities—bursting of small blood veins—occur because for blood to get back to the heart requires competent valves—valves that can hold that column of blood against gravity. Aging weakens those valves and forces the heart to work harder. (See Figure 7.6.)

CAUSES OF AGING: DEPENDENT CHANGES

Many theories attempt to unlock the biological secrets of aging. Two main theories emerge as containing the best of the other theories. They try to respond to the question, What causes aging? This apparently simple question has a simple answer: We don't know! However, if researchers take that simple answer as a final one, aging will never be slowed down nor will the negative effects of aging be stopped. A more involved answer is summed up in the following two theories:

1. Error-accumulation theory: aging is a result of many errors made over the years by defectively reproduced cells. The cells were not perfect copies of themselves. These errors or mutations produced faulty, weakened cells, which magnified the error by producing an abnormal protein. This abnormality either could have no effect or could actually destroy the cell.
2. Programmed aging theory: an organism is capable of a certain number of cell divisions that have been genetically determined. Hayflick's experiments (1968) demonstrated that cells double a limited number of times and then stop. He called this occurrence programmed cell death. He counted an average of 50 doublings for human fibroblasts and then found that they abruptly died. Also, when studying fibroblasts from human beings who suffered from the disease that produces premature aging (progeria), he found these cells doubled only an average of 10 to 20 times. If Hayflick's theory of a genetic limitation is true, it would appear that 100 may be the maximum human life span. The theory has no explanation of how or why some individuals live to be older than 100.

HEALTH: A SELF-ASSESSMENT

The most important assessment of a person's health is the one made by the person. Eight out of ten older Americans view themselves as having good

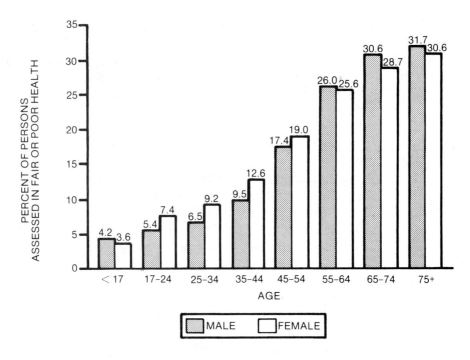

FIGURE 7.7
Self-assessment of health by sex and age: 1981 (U.S. Senate Special Committee on Aging, Aging America: Trends and Projections, 1984.)

to excellent health compared to other people of similar age. Only 8 percent reported their health as poor.

Most Americans generally agree that today's senior citizens are in better health than the elderly were in the 1960s or 1970s. However, note that as the age of the older people increased, so did the percentage of people who reported their health to be fair or poor (Figure 7.7). These figures coincide with the large number of elderly needing hospitalization or nursing care after the age of seventy-five.

However, age is not the only factor involved in how elderly people perceived their health. Sex, race, marital status, education, employment, and income are all factors. For example, elderly people with higher incomes reported excellent health more often than did those with lower incomes (Figure 7.8).

DISEASES: CAUSES OF DEATH

Three out of four people in the United States die from:

1. Heart disease.
2. Cancer.
3. Stroke.

Heart disease is the number one cause of death for people of all ages, including those age sixty-five and over (Figure 7.9). It so outnumbers other causes of death that if it were eliminated, 11.8 years would be added to the life expectancy from birth and 11.4 years at age sixty-five.

The decline in the number of deaths from heart disease and stroke has been primarily responsible for the fact that today people over age

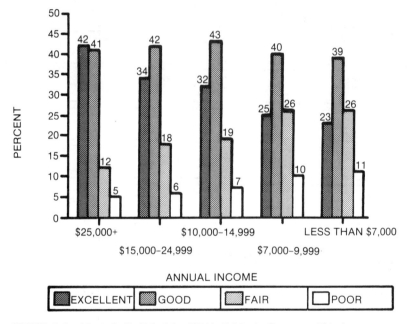

SOURCE: National Center for Health Statistics, 1981 Health Interview Survey, unpublished.

FIGURE 7.8
Self-assessment of health by income range—persons 65 years and older: 1981 (U.S. Senate Special Committee on Aging, Aging America: Trends and Projections, 1984.)

65–74	75–84	85+
1. HEART DISEASE (40.6%)	HEART DISEASE (44.7%)	HEART DISEASE (48.6%)
2. CANCER (MALIGNANT NEOPLASMS) (27.3%)	CANCER (MALIGNANT NEOPLASMS) (18.4%)	CEREBROVASCULAR DISEASE (14.3%)
3. CEREBROVASCULAR DISEASE (7.3%)	CEREBROVASCULAR DISEASE (11.8%)	CANCER (MALIGNANT NEOPLASMS) (10%)
4. CHRONIC OBSTRUCTIVE PULMONARY DISEASE AND RELATED CONDITIONS (4.3%)	CHRONIC OBSTRUCTIVE PULMONARY DISEASE AND RELATED CONDITIONS (3.4%)	PNEUMONIA AND INFLUENZA (5.5%)
5. DIABETES (2.2%)	PNEUMONIA AND INFLUENZA (3.3%)	ATHEROSCLEROSIS (4.1%)
6. ACCIDENTS (1.9%)	DIABETES (2%)	ACCIDENTS (1.8%)
7. PNEUMONIA AND INFLUENZA (1.9%)	ATHEROSCLEROSIS (1.9%)	CHRONIC OBSTRUCTIVE PULMONARY DISEASE AND RELATED CONDITIONS (1.7%)
8. CHRONIC LIVER DISEASE AND CIRRHOSIS (1.4%)	ACCIDENTS (1.8%)	DIABETES (1.4%)
9. NEPHRITIS, NEPHROTIC SYNDROME AND NEPHROSIS (.8%)	NEPHRITIS, NEPHROTIC SYNDROME AND NEPHROSIS (1%)	NEPHRITIS, NEPHROTIC SYNDROME AND NEPHROSIS (1%)
10. ATHEROSCLEROSIS (.8%)	FLU (SEPTICEMIA) (.5%)	HYPERTENSION (.6%)
11. SUICIDE (.6%)	HYPERTENSION (.5%)	FLU (SEPTICEMIA) (.5%)
12. FLU (SEPTICEMIA) (.5%)	CHRONIC LIVER DISEASE AND CIRRHOSIS (.5%)	HERNIAS AND INTESTINAL OBSTRUCTIONS (.4%)
13. HYPERTENSION (.4%)	ULCERS (STOMACH AND DUODENUM) (.4%)	ULCERS (.3%)
14. BENIGN NEOPLASMS (.3%)	HERNIAS AND INTESTINAL OBSTRUCTIONS (.3%)	NUTRITIONAL DEFICIENCIES (.3%)
15. ULCERS (STOMACH AND DUODENUM) (.3%)	BENIGN NEOPLASMS (.3%)	GALLBLADDER DISORDERS (.3%)
ALL OTHER CAUSES (9.3%)	ALL OTHER CAUSES (9.4%)	ALL OTHER CAUSES (8.9%)

SOURCE: National Center for Health Statistics: Advance report, final mortality statistics, 1980. *Monthly Vital Statistics Report,* Vol. 32, No. 4, Supplement DHHS Pub. No. (PHS) 83–1120. Public Health Service, Hyattsville, Md., August 1983.

FIGURE 7.9
Fifteen leading causes of death by age group: 1980
(U.S. Senate Special Committee on Aging, Aging
America: Trends and Projections, *1984.)*

sixty-five represent the fastest growing segment of the population. Among the factors believed responsible for this decline in cardiovascular deaths are the decline in cigarette smoking, the detection and treatment of high blood pressure, and to an unknown extent, changes in diet and exercise patterns.

A study done between 1979 to 1981 found that the more money one earned, the lower the risk of dying of heart disease (Stewart 1985). Apparently, wealthier people have modified the habits that lead to heart disease. "Wealthier people exercise more; they eat more fish and chicken which are lower in salt and cholesterol. Also, wealthier people can afford medical care that might prevent fatalities" (Stewart 1985, 1).

Family Income	Men	Women
to $13,600	460.1*	268.4
to 18,750	401.6	239.1
to 22,600	393.0	219.2
to 28,500	377.6	216.0
28,500+	329.5	211.3
*Figures are deaths per 100,000 population		

Although within the last ten years, the occurrences of death from cardiovascular disease and stroke have decreased, the deaths due to cancer have increased. Death among the 500,000 stroke victims each year has declined 45 percent in 15 years and continues to decline at a rate of 5 percent a year (Stewart 1985). The elimination of cancer would add 2.5 years to the life expectancy from birth or 1.4 years at age sixty-five. An interesting fact about cancer is that it does not become increasingly common in very old people. The peak increase in cancer incidence and mortality occurs between the ages of forty-five and sixty-five, after which cancer risk levels off. Cancer accounts for 30 percent of the deaths among people from ages sixty-five to sixty-nine, but it is the cause of death in only 12 percent of people over eighty.

Chronic Versus Acute Illnesses

Chronic illness—marked by a long duration or frequent recurrence— among the elderly accounts for more than 50 percent of the days lost to disability; chronic illness is rare in younger age groups. Chronic condi-

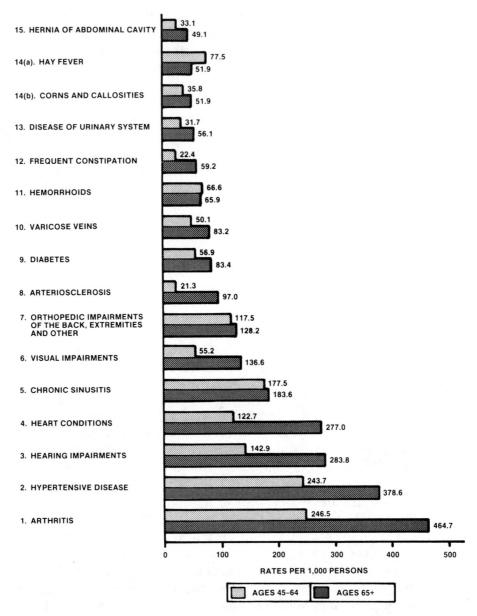

SOURCE: National Center for Health Statistics, Division of Health Interview Statistics.

FIGURE 7.10
Prevalence of top chronic conditions—persons 65 years and older: 1981 (U.S. Senate Special Committee on Aging, Aging America: Trends and Projections, 1984.)

tions account for the majority of disabilities by middle age and are definitely a problem of the aged.

In the early 1900s, acute illness—having a sudden onset and short duration—predominated. This soon changed. Not only did chronic illness become responsible for more than half of the disability days for the elderly population, but it was also responsible for a large percentage of the nation's health expenses. (See Table 7.1, Figure 7.10.)

Leading chronic conditions in 1981 for people over sixty-five were arthritis and hypertensive diseases (high blood pressure, stroke). Many elderly people may be hospitalized for these conditions; their severity can differ tremendously from person to person. However, the people suffering from these conditions are still capable of independent living. Only about 18 percent stated they were not able to perform normal activities due to chronic conditions. After age seventy-five, however, more than 50 percent of the elderly find the chronic conditions to be limiting. Only 22

TABLE 7.1
Prevalence of top chronic conditions—persons 65 years and older: 1981

| Condition | Total Conditions For all Persons | Total for Persons 65 Years and Older | Rate per 1,000 Persons | | |
			17–44	*Age 45–64*	*65 Plus*
Arthritis	27,238,293	11,547,889	47.7	246.5	464.7
Hypertensive disease	25,523,526	9,406,958	54.2	243.7	378.6
Hearing impairments	18,665,650	7,051,238	43.8	142.9	283.8
Heart conditions	17,186,106	6,883,416	37.9	122.7	277.0
Chronic sinusitis	31,036,480	4,562,037	158.4	177.5	183.6
Visual impairments	9,083,717	3,395,397	27.4	55.2	136.6
Orthopedic impairments*	18,416,051	3,185,565	90.5	117.5	128.2
Arteriosclerosis	3,398,230	2,410,125	.5	21.3	97.0
Diabetes	5,499,737	2,073,037	8.6	56.9	83.4
Varicose veins	6,129,874	2,067,311	19.0	50.1	83.2
Hemorrhoids	8,848,365	1,637,487	43.7	66.6	65.9
Frequent constipation	3,599,159	1,471,915	9.2	22.4	59.2
Disease of urinary system	5,689,273	1,395,187	25.8	31.7	56.1
Hay fever	17,873,906	1,290,449	100.2	77.5	51.9
Corns and callosities	4,289,880	1,289,933	14.0	35.8	51.9
Hernia of abdominal cavity	3,697,855	1,220,156	8.9	33.1	49.1

*National Center for Health Statistics, Division of Health Interview Statistics, unpublished.
Source: U.S. Senate Special Committee on Aging, *Aging America: Trends and Projections,* 1984, p. 58.

percent stated that the condition severely hampers normal activities (U.S. Senate 1984, 58). As the elderly population gets even older, the severe effects of chronic illness will begin to curtail independent living for a greater number of individuals. This will have a great impact on the need for future health and long-term care services.

Long-term care services in 1980 had to provide services for 10.8 million elderly people aged sixty-five and over who felt limitations due to chronic illness. It is believed this figure will reach 31.8 million by 2050. Present estimates by caregivers state that one nursing home, with a 100-bed capacity, must be built every day until the year 2000 to meet the growing needs of elderly people. These anticipated needs due to chronic illness mean at least a doubling of all long-term care services if the needs of elderly people are to be met (U.S. Senate 1984, 58).

The type of care in 1981 is reflected in Figure 7.11. Older people, aged sixty-five and over, use more health care services more often than do the young. This means that 11 percent of the population accounts for 33 percent of the country's total personal health care expenditure.

Ninety percent of nursing home residents are aged sixty-five and over. In 1980, the nursing home population was 1.2 million. That number is expected to increase to 5.4 million by 2050. Lest these estimates leave the false impression that practically every old person is in a nursing home, we hasten to add that this number is only 4.7 percent of the population sixty-five years of age and over. To emphasize this fact further—it means 95.3 percent of the population aged sixty-five and over are living independently or with some minimal forms of home care. However, the percentage of nursing home residents increases with age:

Age	Number of Nursing Home Residents
65-74	1 out of 100
75-84	7 out of 100
85+	1 out of 5

Alzheimer's: The Disease of the Century

Because Alzheimer's has been given such a title it deserves a special look. *Newsweek* magazine (December 3, 1984, 56) described Alzheimer's disease as the cruelest of all the incurable diseases because it kills the victim twice. In Alzheimer's, the mind dies first. Then the body dies.

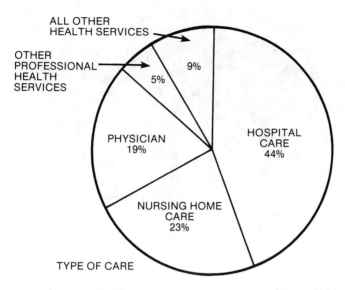

FIGURE 7.11
Health care expenditures for the elderly by type of care: 1981 (U.S. Senate Special Committee on Aging, Aging America: Trends and Projections, 1984.)

Alzheimer's affected up to 3 million Americans in 1984. It kills about 120,000 people a year, making it the fourth leading cause of death. In the next 50 years, the toll is expected to triple. About 27 percent of people aged sixty-five and over in the United States are severely disabled by the disease, and the disease can strike as early as age 40. Alzheimer's disease is responsible for 50 percent of all nursing home admissions. The disease is not a respecter of income or talent. The actress Rita Hayworth suffers from the disease, and artist Norman Rockwell died from it.

The cause of Alzheimer's is still unknown, and the affects irreversible. Scientists are beginning to make progress in analyzing the chemical processes of the brain (Figure 7.12). In the meantime, however, the disease costs this nation $25 billion per year. More important, it cost 3 million minds that were full of acquired information, experience, and wisdom.

This disease gradually, but surely, wipes from the memory names, dates, and places. Soon the simplest tasks, such as combing hair and eating, become impossible. The bodily functions, such as walking, are lost. The body curls up into a fetal position, the mind sinks into a coma,

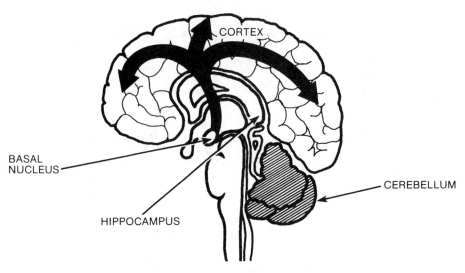

FIGURE 7.12
Researchers are investigating brain cell abnormalities in Alzheimer's victims. Of major focus are the cortex, basal nucleus, and the region next to the hippocampus.

and death eventually occurs. This all happens in an average of six to eight years, although it can linger for as long as twenty years.

Physiologically, Alzheimer's causes brain lesions known as neurofibrillary tangles—nerves in the brain actually twisted around each other like braids. These tangles prevent the passage of impulses within the brain and destroy the patient's intellectual capacity. Other nerve endings also degenerate into clumps called plaques—deformities incapable of sending and receiving information. The greater the number of tangles and plaques, the worse the disease.

All brains change over time, and tangles and plaques often appear in later years. Most people, however, never develop enough of these lesions to lose memory or brain function. The brains of people with Alzheimer's disease, however, are choked by masses of them (Freedman, 1985).

As if that suffering were not sufficient, there is the devastating effect on the family of the victims. Seeing the mental and physical deterioration of a loved one over a period of years is devastating. Along with this, life savings may be exhausted in an attempt to care for the patient.

Is there a cure for Alzheimer's? Scientists compare the current status of Alzheimer's to the challenge thirty years ago with heart disease. Heart disease was once believed, like Alzheimer's, to be an inevitable part of aging. Eventually, proper drugs and diet accounted for the decline in coronary deaths. Perhaps, Alzheimer's itself, in time, will be just a bad memory (David and David 1984, 71). In the meantime, Alzheimer's needs to be recognized as a disease for which great efforts must be made to find a cure. (See Figure 7.13.)

IT MIGHT NOT BE ALZHEIMER'S

Almost half of the old people who are absentminded, indecisive, or incapable of caring for themselves properly do not have Alzheimer's disease. They may have walking pneumonia that has not been diagnosed

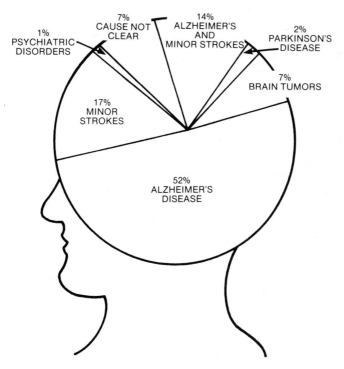

FIGURE 7.13
Alzheimer's and other causes of organic brain disorders

or treated. They may have had a slight stroke, a minor head injury, an adverse reaction to a drug or combination of drugs they take regularly on doctor's orders. They may have a chronic fever. Then, too, they may be lonely or depressed or simply bored. More than 100 disorders mimic Alzheimer's—but unlike Alzheimer's, most of them can be treated or cured. Proper diagnosis and treatment are needed. In any case, many people attribute any deterioration of the mental faculties to old age. Age is not a disease.

DRUGS: USE, MISUSE, ABUSE

The percentage of health improvement and health deterioration due to drugs in the group aged sixty-five and over is unknown. The American Association of Retired Persons believes there is reason for alarm when considering drug abuse and misuse, including prescription drugs, over-the-counter drugs, and alcohol. Drug misuse includes taking the wrong dose, using someone else's prescription, and taking drugs that work against one another. These abuses and misuses take 50,000 lives and cost more than $21 billion a year.

For example, the effects of taking sleeping pills, antipsychotic drugs, tranquilizers, and blood pressure medications may be major causes of crippling falls in people over sixty-five. Tripping and falling in younger people is usually not life-threatening, but older people, particularly women, can suffer broken hips due to brittle bones and/or calcium deficiencies and thus can require lengthy hospitalization. Falls are the leading cause of fatal injury among people over sixty-five (American Association of Retired Persons 1984).

Prescription Drugs

Estimates suggest that on the average, a person over sixty-five years of age uses at least thirteen prescription drugs a year. Eleven percent of the American population is believed to have consumed more than 25 percent of all the prescription drugs sold. Drug misuse often causes symptoms that are misdiagnosed as illnesses directly related to aging. Often, they go untreated or mistreated by prescribing yet another drug that adds to the problem. Some substances, including vitamins, laxatives, cold remedies, antacids, and alcohol, can also lead to serious problems if used too often or in combination with certain other drugs.

> Mrs. W., a ninety-one-year-old woman near death, was rushed to the hospital. She suffered not from a disease, but from the interaction of the eighteen different prescribed drugs she was taking for various illnesses. She didn't need all of them. She went home taking only two prescriptions and in much better health.

Drugs act differently on older people than they do on younger age groups. As the body ages, the percent of water and lean muscle tissue decreases and the percent of fat tissue increases. These changes affect the length of time a drug stays in the body and the amount absorbed by body tissues.

The kidneys and liver are two of the major organs responsible for breaking down and removing most drugs from the body. These organs begin to function less efficiently with age. As a result, drugs leave the body more slowly. This accounts for the fact that older people tend to have more undesirable reactions to drugs than do younger people.

Alcohol Abuse

Estimates concerning the problems of alcoholism among elderly people vary from 15 percent generally to 40 percent in some urban locations. There are two groups of elderly alcoholics:

1. The group who were lifelong alcoholics and have now reached old age.
2. Those who were unable to deal with the stresses of aging (such as loneliness and depression) and turned to alcohol as a solution.

Retirees often develop a feeling of inadequacy and a sense of never again being needed by society. Boredom and loneliness spawned by failures in retirement can easily lead to the beginning of the morning drink. Retirees no longer need to control their intake of alcohol for social or business reasons. They no longer have to work at pleasing people and building a personal image. Without a job to go to, the elderly alcoholic is often left to personal resources (Carle 1984).

Many older people drink in response to the stresses of life—the loss of a spouse, fear of being alone, loss of self-esteem, isolation from family, poor health, and other reasons. Drug use is not an acceptable outlet

FIGURE 7.14

among the older generation, but alcohol is. A drink in the afternoon is believed to stimulate the appetite. A drink at night helps one sleep. Older people may find themselves showing signs of alcohol abuse even though their drinking has not increased. Having grown older, the body metabolism has changed and is more quickly affected by alcohol.

NUTRITION

Physicians of long ago were more concerned with the profound effects of food than they are today. Greek physicians in 500 B.C. insisted that diet was the foundation of healing. How often have you heard, "We are what we eat." Not only is the food we eat influential over our physical health, but it is also a powerful influence over our mental health. Nutrition is a great unexplored area in science, medicine, health, and gerontology.

Convenience Foods

Americans are a nation of processed, packaged, and preserved people. We spend more than $70 billion for convenience food. People aged sixty-five and over are among the consumers. The typical American's diet is low in fiber and whole grains, high in fats and refined carbohydrates, and deficient in fresh fruits, vegetables, and proteins. This kind of diet with inadequate vitamins, minerals, roughage, and energy can cause confused states of mind and depression, conditions we often blame on old age.

Nutrition: A Lifelong Habit

Health is a state of physical, mental, and social well-being, not merely the absence of disease or infirmity. It is a positive quality of life. It means taking care of the physical self, using the mind constructively, expressing emotions effectively, and being concerned about the environment. The total-person approach referred to in the beginning of this chapter is related to nutrition. From the beginning of life and as an infant, normal healthy growth and development require a proper nutritional base. Increasing age may require an even more careful assessment of nutrition if wellness is to be maintained.

Social and financial factors, as well as lifelong purchasing and eating habits, affect the dietary patterns of elderly people. Other factors that at first may be overlooked also affect the eating patterns of elderly people. A contributor to poor nutrition may be a lack of, or poor-fitting, dentures. Periodontal disease affects 90 percent of people sixty-five to seventy-five years of age. Pain, discomfort, or the inability to chew more substantial foods may cause the elderly person to eat unbalanced or high calorie, low nutritional foods.

Also, gastrointestinal changes may occur with age. Eating some foods may cause discomfort. There may be a lack of appetite altogether. However, most nutritional deficiencies appear to be caused more by income level and the person's evaluation of personal health status than actual factors brought on because of old age itself. Recent reports (Stewart, February 21, 1985) suggest that the American population may be undergoing a positive change in nutritional habits. There are decreases in the use of tobacco, animal fats, and highly sugared and salted foods. Corresponding decreases in the number of cerebrovascular and coronary reports seem to support the fact that the consuming public is becoming more health conscious.

FIGURE 7.15
Logo of Zins & Associates (Used with permission of
Dr. Bryan F. Zins)

Health food is not the new fountain of youth nor is it the single answer to longevity and health. However, adequate and appropriate nutrition remains the primary means to improve health and quality of life. The well-known Zins Chiropractic Clinic in Minnesota uses its logo to remind patients, "If you don't take care of your body, where are you going to live?" (Figure 7.15).

EXERCISE

"If I had known I was going to live this long I would have taken better care of myself."

Unknown (from Byrne, 1982)

Contrary to popular belief, exercise has never been shown conclusively to prolong life. However, according to experts, exercise can retard some of the functional declines that accompany aging, such as the loss of muscle mass, capacity for physical effort, flexibility, endurance, bone strength, and efficiency of the heart and lungs. Exercise also may help to normalize blood pressure, blood sugar, and blood cholesterol levels.

Continued studies show some evidence that people who are active and fit have longer life spans than those who are not and that for most people, it is never too late to exercise (Briley 1985, 91). An added reward of exercising is that it may ward off depression and dependency. Recent findings in a study at Purdue University found physically fit subjects between the ages of twenty-seven and sixty-four to be consistently less depressed than their poorly conditioned counterparts. The Purdue study concluded that "there is increasingly strong support for the hypothesis that exercise is a natural medicine which brings about favorable emotional changes" (Briley 1985, 91).

One bonus of exercise is that if done appropriately, it brings about a tranquilizing effect. This is a plus without any of the undesirable effects that medication tends to have. For example, a twenty-minute walk may provide this relaxing effect for an hour or so afterward.

The key to exercise for elderly people is for it to be appropriate (Sheekan 1981). When carefully regulated, the benefits are maximized

FIGURE 7.16

FIGURE 7.17
(From Geriatrics: A Study of Maturity, *4th ed., by*
Esther Caldwell and Barbara R. Hegner, copyright ©
1986 by Delmar Publishers Inc.)

and the risks minimized. The natural, everyday kind of activities like walking, dancing, bike riding, and swimming are some appropriate exercises for the average person aged sixty-five and over. One cardiologist stated, "The weakest among us [the elderly] can become some kind of athlete but only the strongest can survive as spectators. Only the hardiest can withstand the perils of inertia, inactivity, and immobility" (Briley 1985, 36).

SUMMARY

Well-being at any age, including old age, is a combination of social, psychological, and physical factors. The *wellderly,* (well elderly), the great majority of America's old, maintain good physical health, function well socially, have made healthy adjustments to old age, and relate well psychologically with their environment and themselves.

There are no guarantees that old age will include good overall health, but neither is there reason to believe that old age automatically brings ill health. Aging is a group of processes that affect the human organism. These processes reduce the body's effectiveness and increase its vulnerability to disease. Explanations as to how and why this happens are many and varied. The complexity of the aging process has prevented modern science from slowing the process of aging dramatically or even eliminating it.

Aging does produce noticeable changes in the appearance and functioning of the body. However, many of these changes are only cosmetic and do not have to interfere with the physical, social, or psychological facets of an elderly person's life. The gradual decrease in organ functions does not necessarily cause difficulties until after the age of seventy-five. Even then, adjustments can be made to accommodate age changes. The key to well-being in both cosmetic and internal changes is the attitude of the individual.

Environmental factors—such as working conditions, nutritional habits, and exercise—all have an effect on the degree of the aging process and at what age these effects begin to affect everyday living routines. This is why aging is so individual both in rate and degree. Such biological aging depends less on chronological aging than on daily living habits.

EXERCISES

1. List some physiological changes that occur with age. Divide your list into changes you believe can be avoidable, slowed down, or inevitable.

	Physiological Changes	
Avoidable	*Slowed Down*	*Inevitable*

2. Describe the basic principles of several theories of aging. Begin with the one you believe to be the most likely to cause aging and end with the one you believe least likely to cause aging.
3. Identify some factors that may have potential value in delaying the aging process.
4. Keep a log of your eating and exercise habits for one week. Ask another student of gerontology to assess your living habits and to determine those habits that will speed up your aging and those that will delay it.

REVIEW

1. Explain what is meant by the totality of the person affecting aging.
2. Provide a sound argument for the fact that aging is not a disease.
3. What potential does the body have for chronological aging?
4. How does senescence differ from senility?
5. What are the five generally accepted universals concerning the process of aging?
6. List the genetic and nongenetic theories on aging and explain their effects.
7. Explain the negative feedback system.
8. What effects do aging have on the cardiovascular system and how can those effects be compensated for?
9. Explain the two most common and accepted theories concerning the slowing down of the negative effects of aging.
10. Is self-assessment concerning one's health a dangerous thing? Why?
11. List the three causes of death for elderly people in the United States in the order of highest to lowest percentages.
12. Can money possibly affect the risk of dying from heart disease?
13. Equate chronic and acute illness and their effects on elderly people.
14. Why is Alzheimer's disease referred to as the disease of the century?
15. What is the danger of assuming that all memory loss in elderly people may be Alzheimer's disease?
16. To what degree are drug abuse and misuse part of the health problems related to aging?
17. What should be the total person approach to nutrition?
18. Is exercise an effective method to prolong life? What are its major benefits to the elderly?

RECOMMENDED READINGS
AND REFERENCES

Active Senior. "Elderly Alcoholics," February 1985, 9-10.

American Association of Retired Persons. *Prescription Drugs: A Survey of Consumer Use, Attitudes, and Behavior.* Washington, D.C., 1984.

Blue Cross and Blue Shield Association. *Feel Better.* Chicago, 1980.

———. *Put Pep in Your Step.* Chicago, nd.

Briley, Michael. "The Physically Fit Do Live Longer." *Modern Maturity,* February/March 1985, 34-36.

Byrne, Robert. *The 637 Best Things Anybody Ever Said.* New York: Atheneum, 1982.

Carle, Cecil F. *Letters to Elderly Alcoholics.* Center City, Minn.: Hazeldon Educational Services, 1984.

David, Lester, and Irene David. "The Mist Lifts." *Health,* February 1984, 67-71.

Ebersole, Priscilla, and Patricia Hess. *Toward Healthy Aging.* St. Louis: C. V. Mosby, 1981.

Finch, C. E., and L. Hayflick, eds. *Handbook of the Biology of Aging.* New York: Van Nostrand Reinhold Co., 1977.

Findlay, Steve. "More of Us Now Recover from Stroke." *USA Today,* February 21, 1985.

Freedman, Gail A. "Age and Memory Loss." *Family Circle,* February 26, 1985, 78.

Hayflick, Leonard. "Human Cells and Aging." *Scientific American,* March 1968, 32-37.

Minneapolis Star and Tribune. "The Human Immune System, the Fountain of Youth?" January 8, 1984.

Newsweek. "The Slow Death of the Mind," December 3, 1984, 56-62.

Reader's Digest. "Personal Glimpses," February 1985, 119.

Sheekan, George. Editorial in *Senior Spotlight,* November/December 1981, 2.

Stewart, Sally Ann. "Heart Disease Decreases as Income Goes Up." *USA Today,* February 21, 1985.

U.S. Senate Special Committee on Aging. *Aging America: Trends and Projections.* Washington, D.C., 1983.

CHAPTER 8

Death and Dying

Learning Objectives

After studying this chapter, the reader should be able to:

- Distinguish between death as an event and dying as a process.
- Discuss the relationship between age and death.
- Identify the stages of dying and the normal reaction to these stages.
- Understand the psychological impact the thought of death has on elderly people since they, more than any other age group, are closest to experiencing it.

> "Ladies and gentlemen, in certain instances death is preceded by old age!"
>
> Ralph Robin (as quoted in Butler 1975, 402)

Preview

The word *d-e-a-d* appears to be the new four-lettered, pornographic word. It seems to be the topic human beings are least willing to talk about. Historically, people were more comfortable with death, not because they found the idea more appealing, but because it was more familiar.

The acceptability of death depends on the psychological context in which it occurs. Death was always regarded as a natural act until recently, when real death hidden away in institutions has begun to take on the appearance of an unnatural act. The miracles of science and the shelves loaded with wonder drugs give young and old alike the false impression that the incompetencies of modern medicine cause death. Lost is the realization that life is limited. It will end. It will end with death.

Interestingly enough, due to the tremendous increase in the world's elderly population, death is occurring in far greater numbers today. This chapter looks at how death affects the lives of older people more often than it does other age groups. It is a fact that 75 percent of the people who die each year are over 65 years of age—that is about 6 percent of the total older population every year. How are elderly people and society viewing their reaction to death as an event and to dying as a process?

DEATH: A DEFINITION

Death, as a physical process, is the permanent stopping of all vital functions. The process starts with dying and ends with being dead. This dying process does not occur in a single instant. When we hear that someone died last night, we really mean that the dying process ended last night.

In truth, from the moment of conception, life begins an uninterrupted progression toward death. Some body cells are dying while others are being replaced by new ones. This dying and renewing is a process that continues throughout life. However, as a person gets older, the dying of

FIGURE 8.1

cells and structures exceeds the renewing rate. When vital bodily functions are affected and a condition exists from which no recovery can be expected, we say the person is dying.

The moment at which a person can be pronounced *dead* has become a topic of considerable discussion. It was once a simple issue. The development and use of machines that can artificially produce breathing and heartbeat have made the traditional definition of death obsolete. This fact, however, does not preclude that there is a new, precise definition of death. It is just such a lack of definition today that troubles both the courts and the physicians. In the past, death was defined as the "cessation of heartbeat and brain activity." Whether the artificial function of those vital systems constitutes life is a debatable issue.

Social Death

A person can also be socially dead. When people are treated as nonhuman, social death has taken place. If a person is treated as a nonfeeling, non-thinking, non-decision-making object, the person is only physically alive. This concept is best illustrated when people capable of hearing and responding are talked "about" but not "to" in their presence. Social death can happen long before physical death takes place.

Dying Trajectory

Dying trajectory is the term used to refer to the length of time between dying and death. This time period is determined from the time at which no recovery can take place; the organism begins to fail until the brain and heart have ceased all functioning. For some people, the dying trajectory is fast; for others, lingering. During the dying trajectory, the person has also been assigned the social role of a dying person. A longer dying trajectory allows the dying persons time to deal with their dying. It also permits time for survivors to deal with the grief the loss will bring. This fact may be the reason that survivors sometimes manifest relief rather than grief when death finally occurs.

Terminal Illness

The term *terminal* is an age-related term. Older people diagnosed as terminal are expected to deal with their condition in an accepting manner. Passivity is an expected role of the old, whereas the will to live is expected to be demonstrated by the young. The young may continue to express anger and frustration at their impending death, but the old are expected to manifest acceptance. In old age, an awareness of limited time and impending death may bring about some behavior changes. There is no way to predict just what changes will take place. Six of the more common changes are listed here.

1. Elderly people may be hesitant to make any new commitments or undertake any new projects if they foresee they may not be able to complete them.
2. They may value the remaining time and become concerned about spending it in ways they see as the most valuable.
3. Things or people they perceive as wasting their time will be eliminated because they wish to maximize their use of time.

4. Some elderly people will begin to withdraw from external distractions and turn inward toward thought and meditation—a more pronounced form of disengagement.
5. Realization of too little time to change the past may cause depression, anxiety, and regret.
6. Some elderly people will use the remaining time to take care of business and finalize any legal, financial, and/or personal affairs they feel are unsettled.

The Study of Death

Thanatology—the study of death—was not always a subject of study and inquiry. Historically, death was a reward or weapon of the gods. The mystical surroundings of death made it taboo as a concept to be understood.

Today, dying is studied from many perspectives: biological, psychological, sociological, philosophical, legal, and moral. The conclusions of these sciences and other areas must be applied to a society in which values and traditions are constantly changing, and this makes their application questionable. No wonder that people about to enter another of life's stages become stressful. Consider a person entering into marriage when divorce statistics are so high, or choosing a career when the concept of work is for the less fortunate? Can growing old be less than traumatic when it means being isolated from family in an institution set apart from the activity of modern society? What does death mean when science has challenged the biblical belief that there is "a time to be born, and a time to die" (Ecclesiastes 3:1), and when society attempts to replace the warmth of medieval spirituality with the coldness of modern technology?

DEATH: A STATISTIC

Nearly 70 percent of all the deaths in the United States occur in a hospital or care facility. In 1900 and 1985, the four major causes of death were the same: heart disease, cancer, stroke, and pneumonia. This differs from younger age groups, for which the major causes of death now include accidents and suicide. The big difference between 1900 and 1985 was not the causes of death but the number of individuals who lived to reach the age for which these were the leading causes of death.

Although everyone dies sometime, there is a noticeable difference in the death rates for different people:

1. Males die at a higher rate than females at *all* ages (including the fetal period).
2. After age seventy-five, there is a decline in the death rate difference between males and females.
3. The black population has a higher death rate than the white population.
4. Black males and females do not have as great a death rate difference than the corresponding white population.
5. Married people have lower death rates than single people.
6. Older people with low incomes have higher death rates than elderly people with high incomes.

(Death rate = people per thousand dying at a given age.)

Statements about death rates and retirement are stereotypes, not facts. Stories about people dying shortly after retirement often point an accusing finger at retirement as the cause. The fact is many people retire because of poor health.

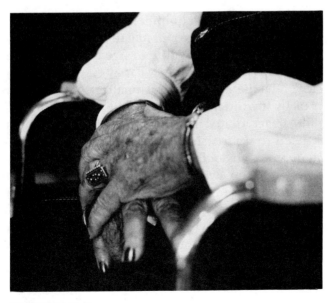

FIGURE 8.2

DEATH: PAST AND PRESENT

In the past, when childhood diseases were not yet controlled by immunization, death was very common among the young. In America in 1900, life expectancy from birth was 46.6 years of age. Adults who died were not old by today's standards. People usually died at home surrounded by the warmth of family and friends. This home atmosphere of both life and death reinforced the idea that death was an accepted part of life. Also, in the past, agrarian communities saw death as a daily event. As death brought to an end the life of animals and human beings, it was seen and acknowledged by all.

Villages and early cities were built around burial sites. Ancestors were at home both in life and death. The dead were honored many times throughout the lifetime of relatives by pilgrimages and rituals. Since the dead could no longer travel, the living remained close to cemeteries; therefore, cities of the dead became cities of the living as well (Lifton and Olson 1974, 20).

Death in Modern Surroundings

In modern times, cities are for the living only. The city and its residents have no place for the old, sick, or dead within their limits nor any time for them in their minds.

The use of modern medical equipment in hospitals and care facilities has brought about both positive and negative changes. It has lengthened the life span, enabling more people to live to an older age. The life expectancy from birth in 1984 was 74.7 years.

The negative change is the institutionalization of death. Dying is largely done for us by the old, tucked away, out of sight; or by the young who die by suicide, in accidents, in war, or from drugs. People do not die at home as they used to. Increasingly, they die in hospitals and institutions. Removing death from social view has a dehumanizing effect. The dying person feels forsaken, which introduces a fear voiced by many people today—the fear of dying alone. The institutionalization of death also provides the living with an "out of sight, out of mind" philosophy. Death is no longer a part of living but rather apart from living. The negative thoughts of death and the negative reaction to older people who reminded us of death are now out of sight. This makes it easier for people to deny the inevitability of death.

"To most of us the dread of death is such that we go to any lengths to avoid it ourselves or postpone it indefinitely in others. In our long and obsessive passion for youth, we have—more than any other modern society—avoided direct approach to age and to dying by denying them in word, in fact, and above all, in worth."

(Simpson 1979, 96)

A Changing Vocabulary

People do not really die; they "expire," "pass away," "depart," "pass on," "go to their rest," or even just "go to sleep." The dead body or corpse becomes "the deceased," "the departed," "the remains of the loved one," or "a beautiful memory picture." We do not simply bury them, we arrange for "funeralization," and the ceremony is called a "life appreciation service." We do not do anything so crude as to buy and sell a grave, although we may admit that the "purchase of memorial property before need" is a "wise family investment" (Simpson 1979, 4). Modern technology, in a subtle but eroding manner, has begun to take death out of the life cycle. It has brought about the population's denial of the fact that there is death at the end of every life. Perhaps historian Arnold Toynbee had a vision of twentieth-century America when he said that death is un-American. Our culture, with all its emphasis and energies placed on youth, vitality, and beauty, can seem to find no time or place for death in life's cycle. Dying thus is punished by abandonment, institutionalization, and loneliness. The pornography of death is so hidden and exploited that it is clouded in false ideas and fearful misunderstandings.

If death is seen as a defeat by medical science then it cannot be accepted as a natural human event. Perhaps that is the goal of a prominent engineer who said, "We will lick the problem of aging completely so that accidents will be the only cause of death (Lifton and Olson 1974, 18).

HOSPICE CARE

The first well-known hospice, and the one that made the concept popular, was St. Christopher's Hospice in London, started in 1967. This was a revival of the hospices located in medieval towns that had provided care for the sick and poor. Dr. Cicely Saunders, medical director and creator of the contemporary hospice concept, had as goals to:

1. Consider the possibility of the patient's dying at home.
2. Relieve patients from the distressing symptoms of their disease.
3. Provide security in a caring environment.
4. Provide sustained, expert care.
5. Assure patients and their families that they would not be abandoned.
6. Take no heroic measures to extend the life of the patient.

Training for hospice care goes beyond training the immediate staff members. Family members are trained to have a new attitude toward death so that the dying person will be surrounded by a positive support group. The patients themselves also receive help in dealing with their terminal illness. Patients often go back and forth between the hospice and home. The median length of stay at St. Christopher's Hospice is about two to three weeks; about 50 percent of the patients return home to die.

The patients at St. Christopher's also help researchers better understand the needs of the terminally ill. Dr. Saunders's visit to the United States encouraged people in this country to establish more than 300 hospices between 1977 and 1985. The issue to be resolved in the United States is whether to establish more hospice facilities or to educate present hospital medical and nursing staff to carry out the hospice philosophy.

DEATH: A PHILOSOPHY

> "In the old days there was no plug. No life-supporting premortem umbilical cord silently proclaimed the presence of a fellow human being surviving only by grace of the physician's technological defiance of nature. Doctors knew their place: their allegiance to life was nearly absolute, but they understood when death had won."
>
> (Doxsey 1959, 4)

Dying, like living, is simple, but not easy. The difficult part lies in the *fear* of death and dying. Each person defines death in a personal way. That interpretation of both death and dying affects each person's own death and response to another's death. The age of the individual also affects that philosophy. Research reveals that people over forty-five years of age begin to put death into a more realistic perspective. They see the future as time remaining. Perhaps their age or their health makes them more cognizant of time as a factor. The fact that they are more often faced with the death of family members or friends may also be a factor.

Sex differences also influence one's philosophy of life. Males see death as an aggressive pursuer. Females view death as a more benevolent event. This philosophical approach by females creates a more accepting atmosphere for death than does that of males.

Regardless of age or sex differences, two common reactions to death are denial and fear. The degree of fear is unique to each person. However, age seems to draw some distinctive lines:

1. Older people do not experience the same intensity of fear as younger people do.
2. As a person gets older and seemingly closer to death, death fears do not necessarily increase.
3. Terminal illnesses do not bring about increased fears in the old but they appear to do so in the young.

FIGURE 8.3

DEATH: FIVE PSYCHOLOGICAL STAGES

When dealing with terminal illness, Dr. Elisabeth Kübler-Ross (1969) identified five common psychological stages:

First.	Denial
Second.	Anger
Third.	Bargaining
Fourth.	Depression
Fifth.	Acceptance

She emphasized that these stages are typical but that not all people go through every stage or go through them in the same order or for the same length of time.

Denial ("Who me? It can't be true!") is one of the most common responses to impending death. This stage is often recognized by the statement "They can't mean me!" This psychological response may not be denial; it may be a means of gaining more time to adjust to the predicted death. It is important to a person in this stage to have time. This time provides an opportunity to talk about personal feelings as well as to get a second medical opinion to confirm the truth of the condition.

Anger ("Why me!"), the second stage changes from "Who me?" to "Why me?" Denial is no longer of value to the person, who now lashes out in anger at anyone who can be blamed for the condition. Often, these people are family members and friends because they are convenient targets for the dying person's angry emotions. This angry release of temper, the accusations, and the general indisposition need to be met with understanding. People who are the targets must realize that the anger is not related to them personally.

Bargaining ("If you'll just give me . . . I promise . . .") usually follows denial and anger. The dying person is trying to make a trade, promising anything for a retraction of the death prediction or an extension of time. This is a technique learned early in life—if we want something badly enough we must be willing to sacrifice something else. Bargaining takes many forms, including promises to family, doctors, or God. The dying person, bargaining for more time in order to dispose of some guilt feelings, needs to share this guilt with someone in order to be rid of it and better prepare for oncoming death.

Depression ("What's the use?"), the fourth stage, may be brought about by exhaustion. Denial is no longer practical because the dying person has lost a job or can no longer be in a responsible position for family roles. Other role losses also may occur. Anger may have depleted the energy, and the body has taken on the appearance of serious illness.

Even bargaining has failed to produce the desired results. Depression may not be only the acknowledgment of these losses; it also creates an atmosphere of preparing for an even greater personal loss—life itself.

Acceptance ("I've had a good life"), the final stage, if time allows, is the peaceful acknowledgment of the inevitable. The dying no longer desire to fight death, but rather wish the closeness of a few family members or friends to help face death. However, this acceptance of death should not be interpreted as the desire to die.

These five stages may be common to many people, but they are not inevitable. Each dying person must be allowed to deal with dying in an individual manner. Dying is something we do, and as in our past life, we must each be allowed to do it in our own unique fashion.

> "Death used to be a door, albeit one-way, leading to a fairly definitely agreed-upon further existence. As traditional beliefs have waned, it is for many people today more like running head-on into a solid wall."
>
> (Simpson 1979, 7)

FIGURE 8.4

DEATH: AS INEVITABLE

Physical death is inescapable. Older people seem better able to cope with that fact. Kalish (1976) found that older people accepted the inevitability of death and thus displayed less fear because:

1. Older people have fewer expectations of the future.
2. Older people, because of their diminished expectations of the future, placed less value on the future.
3. Older people who reached an age beyond their expectations talked about living on borrowed time.
4. Older people are more often faced with the death of family and friends, thus assisting them in the acceptance of their own death.
5. Older people, due to disengagement, have already begun a social withdrawal process.
6. Older people tend to view death as fair, having already enjoyed years that friends or family members may not have had.

DEATH: A RELIGIOUS CONCEPT

It is a myth to assume that age differences in religious behaviors are a product of increased age or growing older. The older generation did not become more religious as they aged; they may have been more religious in their youth. This fact needs to be established before determining the role religion plays in the dying thoughts of an elderly person.

Mathieu (1972) conducted research into what provided comfort when thinking about death. In studies of three geographical areas, these averages were reflected:

Memories of a full life	39.70%
My religion	33.96%
Love from those around me	26.33%

As noted in the percentages, one-third of the people studied turned to their religion for support when thinking about their own death. Nearly 40 percent found comfort in reflecting on the type of life they had led. Religion may have been included in their interpretation of a "full" life.

Riley and Foner (1968) found attitudes toward death were less negative among the well-educated and among people with strong religious beliefs. However, less negative should not be interpreted as non-fearing. They found there was still sufficient negativism to make people feel anxious and inadequate when dealing with the topic of death.

DEATH: THE SURVIVOR'S RESPONSE

The funeral rite has served many functions historically as well as in the present. Funerals are held to honor the deceased and also to serve as a therapeutic function for the living. The word *death*—a Sanskrit word for *smoke*—may have come from India, where the dead were burned and widows threw themselves on the funeral pyre of their deceased husband. This practice was eventually forbidden by the British in the nineteenth century. In some cultures, the body of the deceased was accompanied by the items it was believed would be needed in the other world. Other

FIGURE 8.5

funeral rites handed down were the wearing of arm bands or black, walking in procession, holding a wake, and giving eulogies.

Funerals continue to serve as public acknowledgment of the death of a person and as the practical method of disposing of the body. The therapeutic function of the funeral service provides the survivors with an opportunity to adjust and orient themselves to the role of survivors.

Purpose of Grief

Mourning for the deceased and grief because of their death are part of the process of getting over another's departure from this life. The death of a loved one or a spouse is a very stressful time. The grieving process can be concluded in a short period of time or it can never be finished. Lopata (1973) did a study that showed nearly one-half the widows said they had gotten over their husband's death within a year. Another one-fifth of those studied said they had never gotten over it and did not expect ever to do so.

Types of Grief

Bereavement is dealt with on three levels:

1. Physical.
2. Emotional.
3. Intellectual.

A host of physical reactions accompany grief. Many of them are more pronounced immediately following the death of a loved one and appear to subside over a period of time. Such ailments as stomach upset, bodily fatigue, headaches, shortness of breath, sleeplessness, crying, and a loss of appetite are common. More serious reactions can include those that may bring about the death of the widow or widower.

The most common emotional reaction appears to be depression. Other common emotions include anger, indifference, and guilt. Often, widows or widowers complain of poor health and may need a doctor's care for a period of time.

The intellectual facet of grieving is often assisted with eulogies and memorial services. It is taboo to speak ill of the deceased, so the mind must be cleansed of any negative memories one may have. By retaining only positive thoughts, we can more easily believe that the dead person's life had meaning. This memory is a great comfort to survivors.

Researchers Bowlby (1960) and Gorer (1965) support three forms of bereavement. They list the three stages as initial shock (creating physical reactions), intense grief (bringing about emotional reactions), and gradual reawakening of interest (dealing with the loss intellectually).

DEATH: WIDOWS

Age Relationship to Widows
Young widows are widows for only a short period of time and then they are considered single. Women aged sixty-five and over when widowed are considered widowed throughout the remainder of their lives.

Since life expectancy beyond 65 years of age in 1983 favored females by 4.4 years (83.9 years for females, 79.5 years for males), many more women than men experienced the death of a spouse. The percentage of widows, 36 percent, along with the low rate of remarriage creates for elderly women a social position. As in all social roles for the elderly, however, the role for widows is not clearly defined. Atchley (1980) noted five generalizations concerning widows:

1. Ties with the husband's family are usually drastically reduced by widowhood.
2. Older widows are supposed to try to keep the memory of their husbands alive.
3. Widowhood changes the basis of self-identity for many women because their dominant role had been that of a wife.
4. Loneliness is generally thought to be a widespread problem among widows.
5. Widowhood means a lower economic status for most working-class women.

DEATH: WIDOWERS

Fewer studies have been done concerning widowers; therefore, the social role of a widower is even less defined than that of a widow. What widows and widowers have in common is the problem of dealing with the loss of the significant other. There is no evidence that widowhood is any less difficult to adjust to for males than for females.

The role with which an individual most clearly identifies has an impact on the individual's adjustment to the death of a spouse. Males do not consider their most significant role as that of husband. They identify most strongly with their work role. Thus, the loss of a spouse does not have a similar identity crisis as it does for a widow. Although widowers, too, are expected to preserve the memory of their wife, they remarry at a higher rate. The remarriage rate per 1,000 widowed and divorced persons was 15.6 for widowers sixty-five years old and over, and 1.8 for widows sixty-five years old and over (U.S. Bureau of the Census 1984, 86). Due to the life expectancy differences between males and females, fewer males are widowed.

Widowhood of Persons 55+ by Sex	
Age 65-74	6.9 males
	37.4 females
Age 75+	20.6 males
	67.6 females
	(U.S. Senate 1984, 82)

Race also has an impact on widowhood. Black females are most likely to be widowed, and black males are more likely to be widowed than white males.

Widowhood of Persons 55+ by Race		
	Females	Males
Age 65-74	37.4 (white)	6.9 (white)
	47.3 (black)	15.7 (black)
Age 75+	67.6 (white)	20.6 (white)
	77.9 (black)	34.0 (black)
		(U.S. Senate 1984, 82)

Note: as of March, 1982

Never Married
4% of elderly men
6% of elderly women

Few facts about widowhood are agreed on. More often, conflicting findings are the rule.

FIGURE 8.6
(From Geriatrics: A Study of Maturity, *4th ed., by Esther Caldwell and Barbara R. Hegner, copyright © 1986 by Delmar Publishers Inc.)*

Fact agreed on: Widowhood comes earlier for females than for males.

Conflicting facts from:

Berado 1968	Bell 1971
Older men find widowhood more difficult than older women...	Widowhood is harder on older women than on older men...
. . . because . . .	. . . because . . .
1. Men are ill-prepared to fend for themselves—cooking, cleaning, etc., so they tend to give up independent living.	1. Widows face uncertain financial futures since they have fewer financial skills.
2. Men have more difficulty finding substitute sources of intimacy—friends and	2. a. Women are given less encouragement to remarry.

family see them as too old
"to need that sort of thing."

b. Widows are more iso-
lated because they are
not expected to be so-
cially aggressive.

c. The higher death rate for
males makes remarriage
difficult for all but a few
older widows.
In addition, nearly 50
percent of widowers re-
marry women under 65.

3. Men find it difficult to move
in with their children and
to find a role to play.

3. Being a wife is more important to women than being a
husband is to men, so
women suffer a severe identity crisis.

4. Widowhood, along with retirement, creates a severe
identity problem.

DEATH: THE FINANCIAL SIDE

The bereaved have many business and financial decisions to make before
and after the funeral. Handling medical bills, burial expenses, and insurance policies can be overwhelming for someone in a nonstressful situation. The decision-making requirements and the added responsibilities at
a time of a highly emotional loss can prove nearly impossible. No pre-
funeral planning leaves virtually every detail to be decided by highly
stressed family members.

Survivors often are eligible for some death payments. In January
1985, the lump sum payment of Social Security was $255. That amount has
not changed in many years. Other benefits may include veteran's benefits
and life insurance policies. Remember that a standard funeral costs an
average of $6,500 without cemetery plot, monument, and other inciden-
tal expenses.

The funeral industry is a competitive one; however, few people
choose to shop around ahead of time. Rather, once a death has occurred,
they follow the recommendations of friends. Bereaved persons in highly
emotional states may also incur expenditures that later create financial
hardships. They often choose the best at this emotional time, less con-

scious of cost than they would be for any other major purchase and in a hurry to make a decision. People tend to think that if they can get the funeral over quickly, their grief will go away quickly. This is a time when family and friends can be of valuable assistance.

> "To me, funerals are like bad movies. They last too long, they're overacted, and the ending is predictable. Another thing I don't understand about funerals: all the mourners show up in their somber clothes—black veils, black ties, black handkerchiefs. The deceased is the only one wearing a beige suit with a powder-blue shirt and a polka dot tie. He looks great and we all look pathetic."
>
> (Burns, 159)

DEATH: A RIGHT

In 1914, the Supreme Court ruled that an individual has the right to ultimate control over his or her body.

FIGURE 8.7

> "Every human being of adult years and sound mind has a right to determine what shall be done with his body; and a surgeon who performs an operation without his patient's consent commits an assault for which he is liable in damages."
>
> (Society for the Right to Die 1984, 2)

Unwritten but implied in that ruling is the right to refuse treatment, even if the consequence should be death. This ruling appears not to have had the impact that was intended. Three reasons may be:

1. Patients are not aware of their rights.
2. Patients feel they cannot reject the advice of the doctors.
3. Doctors conclude that the patient is not competent to make this decision.

In June 1984, 1,593 Americans were surveyed at random by the New York Times/CBS News Poll. They were told that "Medical technology now enables doctors to prolong the lives of many people who are terminally ill. Do you believe doctors should stop using these techniques if the patient asks, even if that means the patient will die?"

Response	Percent
Yes	77
No	15
No opinion	8

(Society for the Right to Die 1984, 2)

Living Wills: What Are They?

In the case of incompetency, family members may be called in for the decision-making process. To avoid the burden for family members and the legal burden for physicians, many people feel the Living Will may be an answer (Figure 8.8).

A Living Will is a document that, when witnessed by two other individuals, allows a person when still of "sound mind" to make known personal wishes concerning his or her death. The main goals of such a document are to make known wishes as to treatment during terminal illness should the person become incompetent or unconscious, and to

LIVING WILL DECLARATION

To My Family, Doctors, and All Those Concerned with My Care

I, _____ , being of sound mind, make this statement as a directive to be followed if for any reason I become unable to participate in decisions regarding my medical care.

I direct that life-sustaining procedures should be withheld or withdrawn if I have an illness, disease or injury, or experience extreme mental deterioration, such that there is no reasonable expectation of recovering or regaining a meaningful quality of life.

These life-sustaining procedures that may be withheld or withdrawn include, but are not limited to:

SURGERY   ANTIBIOTICS   CARDIAC RESUSCITATION
RESPIRATORY SUPPORT   ARTIFICIALLY ADMINISTERED FEEDING AND FLUIDS

I further direct that treatment be limited to comfort measures only, even if they shorten my life.

You may delete any provision above by drawing a line through it and adding your initials.

Other personal instructions:

These directions express my legal right to refuse treatment. Therefore, I expect my family, doctors, and all those concerned with my care to regard themselves as legally and morally bound to act in accord with my wishes, and in so doing to be free from any liability for having followed my directions.

Signed _____ Date _____

Witness _____   Witness _____

PROXY DESIGNATION CLAUSE

If you wish, you may use this section to designate someone to make treatment decisions if you are unable to do so. Your Living Will Declaration will be in effect even if you have not designated a proxy.

I authorize the following person to implement my Living Will Declaration by accepting, refusing and/or making decisions about treatment and hospitalization:

Name _____

Address _____

If the person I have named above is unable to act on my behalf, I authorize the following person to do so:

Name _____

Address _____

I have discussed my wishes with these persons and trust their judgment on my behalf.

Signed _____ Date _____

Witness _____   Witness _____

FIGURE 8.8
Living Will declaration (Used with permission of Society for the Right to Die, 250 West 57th Street, New York, NY 10107)

give written consent for the withholding or withdrawal of life-support equipment that will protect health care providers and assist family members in the decision-making process.

Several different kinds of standardized forms of Living Wills are available. The differences between such documents can be major. Some call for steps not generally legal or likely to be carried out. Some reject all artificial means of life support; these would, if strictly interpreted, include all medications, pacemakers, and even oxygen. Most Living Wills focus on the point at which there is "no reasonable expectation of recovery"; this time often requires a calculated guess on the part of other people. It is a fact that recovery from terminal illnesses is rare. Some Living Wills state that life should be ended in the event of any "permanent physical disability," which could include the loss of an eye or amputation of a foot!

Another difficulty with such documents is the courts' inability to determine if the person's earlier preference is still the individual's choice months or even years later. What may seem intolerable to a healthy, active person may not be intolerable once it has really occurred. The human body and mind are very adaptive, and some people may find they value life, even at a reduced state, more than they admitted or realized at the time of writing and signing the Living Will.

Living Wills: Are They Legal?

Living Wills are not valid or legally binding in all states. By the fall of 1984, twenty-two states plus the District of Columbia had enacted Living Will legislation. Living Wills have not been definitively tested in the courts. Is legislation and court intervention necessary? Nearly three-fourths of the population responding to a 1984 Society for the Right to Die poll said, "No!" Popular opinion says the patient should be able to choose death over an extended life when there is no cure.

DEATH: NATURAL, MURDER, OR SUICIDE?

What do we call refusing medication, not accepting artificial assistance, pulling the plug, or choosing when and how to die? When are these decisions right, legal, neither, or both? The debate started when the medical world could intervene in the natural process of dying. When a patient has an incurable, painful illness, most people now agree that heroic technological intervention should not be used. The National Opinion Research Center of the University of Chicago has noted a marked change in the response to a related question it has been asking since 1947: "When a person has a disease that cannot be cured, do you think doctors should be allowed by law to end the patient's life by some painless means if the patient and his family request it?"

Year	Response	Percent
1947	Yes	37
1973	Yes	50
1983	Yes	63

(Society for the Right to Die, 2)

The majority opinion considers that allowing a person to die is neither suicide nor murder. In the United States, suicide is not a crime. Most religious groups, however, feel that under no circumstance is suicide an acceptable means of death. Other people argue that personal autonomy includes the right to choose when and how to die.

All views of the right to die with dignity are a struggle to deal with this delicate question. Not only does death have physical, psychological, social, medical, and legal implications but it also has moral ones. With that many disciplines involved, it is not likely that the controversy will be ended any time soon.

SUMMARY

Death is an inevitable fact of life, the inevitable end of biological life. Despite that statement, death is often a topic that is taboo in polite conversation. More than at any other time in history, however, it is important to discuss death as a fact and as a personal event.

Modern medicine has made more complex the legal time and definition of death. It thus is nearly impossible to find a definition that is accepted by medical, sociological, and religious groups. Such confusion complicates the acceptance of death itself.

Elisabeth Kübler-Ross has suggested five psychological stages of dying. Continued research has been unable to verify that dying people go through the stages in sequence, or need to, in order to deal with their impending death. However, her contribution has helped society understand the dying process.

The environment in which people die is very important. Hospitals and institutions have medical expertise and advanced equipment but perhaps lack the most essential needs of the dying—family intimacy and personal choice as to where to die and when to be permitted to die. Such alternatives as hospices and Living Wills are a step toward humanizing death.

Funerals, an institution to assist people who mourn, take many forms. This is a time that requires rational thought and decision making. Because most individuals over sixty years of age have not prearranged their own funeral, such decision making is often left to people who are in the grieving process.

EXERCISES

1. Scan the obituary column of a small-town newspaper. After having read several death notices that contain information about the person's life, ask yourself, "Is that what I would want written if that were my obituary?" If not, write your obituary exactly as you would wish it to appear in the newspaper on your death.
2. Research the definition of death to see how it has changed throughout history (go as far back as your sources will allow). What is the most accepted definition of death at the present time?
3. In 1972, Mathieu asked elderly people what three areas of their lives gave them the most comfort when thinking about death. List in order his findings in one column and in another column list the three you would choose and compare them with Mathieu's and other class choices.

Three Greatest Comforts When Thinking about Death

	Mathieu	You	Class
1.	_____	_____	_____
2.	_____	_____	_____
3.	_____	_____	_____

4. Visit a funeral home. Take pencil and paper along and list all services and costs as though you were in charge of planning a funeral. Compare your findings with other class members who have visited different funeral homes. How do prices compare? Is it advantageous to shop around for a funeral? Why is this type of shopping usually not done?

REVIEW

1. What is the difference between death and dying?
2. Define social death.
3. What impact does the term *terminal* have on a person's behavior?
4. How do sex, race, and marital status affect death rates?
5. The institutionalization of death has had an impact on modern society. How does it affect society, and why is that effect permitted?
6. List and explain the five common psychological stages of death.
7. Kalish states that older people accept death more easily than do younger people. What reasoning does he give for that conclusion?
8. To what three comforts did Mathieu find that people turn when thinking about death? In what order of importance were these three comforts ranked?
9. What are the main functions of a funeral?
10. What is the effect of widowhood on males and females and how does it differ?
11. What does the 1914 Supreme Court ruling state concerning the right to die? Has the ruling essentially changed today?
12. The public has made known their wishes concerning natural death. What are those findings?
13. Do Living Wills solve the problem of an individual's choice when being allowed to die is in question? If not, why not?
14. Explain the hospice movement.

RECOMMENDED READINGS AND REFERENCES

Adler, Charles S., *et al. We Are But a Moment's Sunlight.* New York: Gulf & Western Company, 1976.

Atchley, Robert C. *The Social Forces in Later Life.* Belmont, Calif.: Wadsworth Publishing Company, 1980.

Bell, Robert. *Marriage and Family Interaction.* 3rd ed. Homewood, Ill.: Dorsey Press, 1971.

Berado, Felix M. "Widowhood Status in the U.S.: Perspectives on a Neglected Aspect of the Family Life Cycle." *The Family Coordinator* 17 (1968): 191-203.

Bowlby, J. *Attachment and Loss,* vol. 1. New York: Basic Books, 1960.

Burns, George. *How to Live to Be 100.* New York: New American Library, 1983.

Butler, Robert N. *Why Survive?* New York: Harper & Row Publishers, Inc., 1975.

Doxsey, John. "Some Psychological Aspects of Aging." Paper presented at Department of Psychiatry, Wayne University, April, 1959.

Fair, Charles M. *The Dying Self.* Garden City, N.Y.: Doubleday & Company, 1970.

Gorer, G. *Death, Grief, and Mourning.* Garden City, N.Y.: Anchor Books, 1965.

Harris, Louis, and associates. "Widowhood, Morale, and Affiliation." *Journal of Marriage and Family* 36 (1974): 97-106.

Heifetz, Milton D. *The Right to Die.* New York: G. P. Putnam's Sons, 1975.

Kalish, R. "Death and Dying in a Social Context." In *Handbook of Aging and The Social Sciences,* edited by R. Binstock and E. Shanas. New York: Van Nostrand Reinhold, 1976.

Kübler-Ross, Elisabeth. *Death: The Final Stage of Growth.* Englewood Cliffs, N.J.: Prentice-Hall, Inc., 1975.

———. *On Death and Dying.* New York: Macmillan Publishing Co., 1969.

Lifton, Robert Jay and Eric Olson. *Living and Dying.* New York: Bantam Books, Inc., 1974.

Lopata, H. Z. *Widowhood in an American City.* Cambridge, Mass.: Schenkman, 1973.

Mannes, Marya. *Last Rights.* Bergenfield, N.J.: The New American Library, Inc., 1973.

Mathieu, J. T. "Dying and Death Role-Expectation: A Comparative Analysis." Doctoral dissertation, Department of Sociology, University of Southern California, 1972.

Riley, Matilda W., and Anne Foner. *Aging and Society, Vol. 1: An Inventory of Research Findings.* New York: Russell Sage Foundation, 1968.

Russell, O. Ruth. *Freedom to Die.* New York: Dell Publishing Co., 1975.

Santrock, John W. *Adult Development and Aging.* Dubuque, Ia: Wm. C. Brown Publishers, 1985.

Simpson, Michael A. *The Facts of Death.* Englewood Cliffs, N.J.: Prentice-Hall, 1979.

Society for the Right to Die. New York: Fall, 1984.

U.S. Bureau of the Census. *Demographic and Socioeconomic Aspects of Aging in the United States.* Series P-23. No. 138. Washington, D.C.: U.S. Government Printing Office, 1984.

U.S. Senate Special Committee on Aging. *Aging America: Trends and Projections.* Washington, D.C., 1984.

CHAPTER
9
Preretirement-Retirement

Learning Objectives

After studying this chapter, the reader should be able to:

- Summarize that the process of retirement involves the transition people experience when they move from a job role to a retirement role.
- Discriminate between a job, which is a position of employment from which an individual retires, and work, which is a never-ending activity.
- Debate that retirement requires an economic system to support people without jobs, a political system to safeguard a viable retirement program, and a social system to accept retirement as a legitimate adult role.
- Realize that retirement is more possible, practical, and palatable when preretirement planning is undertaken.

> We built our retirement home on a hilltop in southern Indiana
> and finally settled on a name for the place—Mount Rush-No-More!
> (*Reader's Digest,* May 1974, 140)

Preview

Employment and retirement are among the major issues of gerontology. Today, aging and retirement are viewed as the same. The reasoning goes something like this:

> Retired people are old.
> Old people are retired.
> Therefore, retirement equals old age!

This situation is not always true, however, and it is not likely to be any more true in the future. To be old and retired may be a luxury both the individual and society cannot afford.

Retirement does not equal old age, which is signified by the age sixty-five because:

1. Many people retire before age sixty-five.
2. Some people never did work and therefore cannot retire.
3. Some people's work life contains several announced retirements, which are followed by a return to work.

This chapter defines such concepts as *retirement* and the *work ethic.* It compares the historical meanings of these concepts to their present definitions. This difference in meaning necessarily affects individuals faced with the prospect of being put out to pasture.

Employment and retirement are affected by Social Security, pensions, and other income sources. These economic provisions can prove to be a solution or another problem depending on the many other factors affecting retirement, such as health, attitude toward the job, and attitude toward retirement.

LIFE PLAN

An increasingly common way of life for Americans is the pursuing of a line-like life plan (see Figure 9.1). Following formal education, a period that has lengthened due to the greater technological demands, are about forty years of consecutive work. This period is followed by an every-increasing time period of retirement.

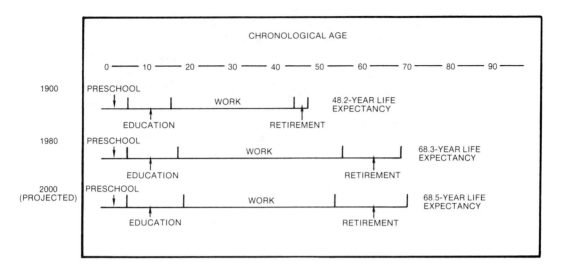

SOURCE: The chart reflects number of preschool, formal education, work, and retirement years in a male lifetime.

FIGURE 9.1
Line-like life plan

FIGURE 9.2

This line-like life plan is the result of major forces in today's living. These similar forces working on each person's life make these line-like life plans not only very similar for most Americans, but natural as well.

First: We acquire the basic skills and knowledge when young;
Second: We move on to major work activities to reach a peak of ability and responsibility;
Third: Finally, we withdraw from work when abilities and responsibilities decline.

Competition for jobs in our society has created a situation in which labor market forces tend to push older people into earlier retirement and hold younger people in prolonged years of schooling.

"WHO I AM" VERSUS "WHAT I DO"

Brent Fredrick has worked for the Willi company for thirty-one years. He had long been accustomed to thinking of himself and introducing himself as "Fredrick of Willi." He was used to thinking of himself as part of the company. He felt comfortable knowing he had a fixed position in the business world.

Then Brent Fredrick turned sixty-five years of age and retired. Some weeks later he walked into a room filled with strangers and he heard himself say, "I'm Brent Fredrick." It jarred his consciousness to realize he was no longer Brent Fredrick of Willi. He was just Brent Fredrick. He was on his own. He felt the loss of his company identification. His Willi anchor was gone and he felt like he was floating in space without identity even though he had a name and was a member of the human race. "I'm Brent Fredrick and I belong to the human race" was not adequate identification!

Mr. Scott was called to the company office every month for a year before he turned sixty-five. He was reminded of the company policy of mandatory retirement at age sixty-five. Co-workers jokingly reminded him to oil the old fishing rod. He only laughed. When the day came that he had been repeatedly told about, he couldn't believe it. He went home and went to bed although he was in perfect health. Within a few months his wife became desperate. Mr. Scott refused to get out of bed, refused to read, or watch TV. He would talk about nothing but the job that was taken away from him.

WORK: A CONCEPT WITH MANY DEFINITIONS

All human societies have found it essential to their survival to develop a system by which goods would be provided. It was also important for society to develop a method by which the goods were efficiently distributed. These processes of production and distribution still make up the ingredients of a work concept. How the concept of work was defined, however, changed from one culture to another and from one time period to another.

To ancient Greeks, the word work meant *sorrow*. Therefore, it was fit only for slaves. Rich Greeks felt work was degrading to the mind and that it corrupted the soul.

The Hebrews looked on work as Adam's punishment. It was punishment for past sins that made it necessary to work for a living.

The Christians at the time of the Protestant Reformation gave work a totally new meaning. Work was a form of religious devotion.

The Calvinists equated work with prayer. They believed that only through hard work could you prove you had been chosen by God for salvation. Work was considered a personal mission.

Today, work is seen as an ethic, a standard of conduct. We often read that Americans are guided by a strong work ethic. An understanding of this all-permeating work ethic is essential to understand the personal struggles before people facing retirement. What force does this work ethic have on the human mind?

Functions of Work

Many sociologists subscribe to the theory that work performs five general functions in the lives of individuals:

1. A job gives people income or some type of monetary return so they can purchase essential goods. This function of work is perhaps the most obvious.
2. A job creates a type of life schedule. It preplans certain days and hours for a major portion of an individual's life. It creates a routine and an order to life.

3. A job gives a person a sense of identity. People describe themselves in terms of their work. Work creates a type of personalized business card. Even though people have many roles throughout life, they often select their work role as the one that counts most in terms of their identity.

4. A job serves as a major source of social contacts. Friendships are often formed as a result of having met in work-related situations.

5. A job provides many and varied life experiences. It is a source of meeting new people, sharing new ideas, and being exposed to different challenges. Work brings the world to the worker. Workers are enriched and gain a self-concept and a world concept through their work contacts.

Definition of Retirement

Preparation for retirement requires dealing effectively with the changes that a nonworking role would present. For clarification purposes, we use Robert Atchley's definition of a retired person (Atchley 1980, 159). He defines that person as:

1. Any person who performs no gainful employment during a given year;
2. Any person who is receiving a retirement pension benefit;
3. Any person not employed full time for a given year.

PRERETIREMENT PREPARATION

> Some sage once said that being retired is being tired twice—first, tired of working, and then later, tired of not working.
>
> Unknown

Certain situations and developments occur when a person retires. Understanding what these are and preparing for them are two important steps in planning for a successful retirement. Often, when planning does take place, it is limited to income planning and legal planning. These aspects are only two of seven areas in which planning is essential. Check your

FIGURE 9.3
*"Actually, I never gave much thought to running
until my Board of Directors said that I was too old
to do useful work and retired me." (© 1986 by Bill
Haas. Used with permission.)*

knowledge concerning your health, housing, income, expenses, legal affairs, social roles, and free time by answering the following questions*:

1. In retirement, health frequently
   a. ＿＿＿ deteriorates
   b. ＿＿＿ stays about the same
   c. ＿＿＿ improves
2. In retirement, housing usually means
   a. ＿＿＿ moving to smaller quarters in the same general area
   b. ＿＿＿ staying in present housing
   c. ＿＿＿ moving to some retirement Shangri-La
3. In retirement, income may be realized from
   a. ＿＿＿ more sources than expected
   b. ＿＿＿ fewer sources than expected
   c. ＿＿＿ the sources one expected
4. In retirement, expenses usually will be
   a. ＿＿＿ about the same as they were just before retirement
   b. ＿＿＿ less than they were just before retirement
   c. ＿＿＿ more than they were just before retirement
5. In retirement, legal affairs often become
   a. ＿＿＿ more complicated than they were before retirement
   b. ＿＿＿ less complicated than they were before retirement
   c. ＿＿＿ about the same as before retirement
6. In retirement, roles will probably undergo
   a. ＿＿＿ little or no change
   b. ＿＿＿ considerable change
   c. ＿＿＿ varied and flexible change
7. In retirement, free time for most people means
   a. ＿＿＿ resting and taking it easy
   b. ＿＿＿ doing anything to keep busy
   c. ＿＿＿ doing something meaningful that they themselves choose to do

(Answers: 1-c, 2-b, 3-a, 4-b, 5-a, 6-c, 7-c)

In every stage of life, from preschool through middle age, people have had to plan ahead and make adjustments due to physical and social requirements. These changes have been made with knowledge, skill, and forethought that may have even included acquiring further education or

---

*Reprinted with permission from *Retirement Planning Handbook*. Copyright 1984 American Association of Retired Persons.

training. Retirement in old age also calls for additional changes based on the additional knowledge and skills acquired over the years. The retirement phase, besides requiring adjustment and preplanning, also provides new and exciting opportunities.

ATTITUDE TOWARD RETIREMENT

Considering Atchley's definition of retirement, and being aware of the five general functions that work plays in our lives, we can see the important role that attitude plays in successful retirement. Employment had set the stage for growing old. It has affected each individual's sense of identity, health, and income. Retirement became the symbol of transition to old age. As a result, retiring individuals must redefine themselves apart from the identity they formed in response to their work role. Changes in income, life schedule, job identity, social contacts, and work experiences force an identity adjustment that is crucial to retirement adjustment. Depending on how successful these adjustments were made, retirement is viewed as a crisis or as a normal part of aging.

FACTORS NECESSARY FOR SUCCESSFUL RETIREMENT

Of all these factors, two factors are more of an indicator than the others when it comes to successful retirement adjustment:

1. The *kind* of work the individual was involved in.
2. The individual's preretirement *attitude*.

Type of Work

The kind of work the individual was involved in does or does not allow for the development of other social ties. Work is one of the most important avenues for integrating the individual into the social system.

> Work provides:
> 1. Identity.
> 2. Style of life.
> 3. Social participation.

Work places the individual and the individual's family in the hierarchy of the social structure. Retirement undercuts the individual's major social support.

> Retirement is not responsible for the individual's lack of security and adjustment in retirement. Rather, the person's work history may not have allowed the development of other social ties.

If in the individual's work history, that person has negotiated numerous other changes in status throughout life, this fact seems to make the retirement transition much less painful.

> "What am I doing on this earth? What good am I here? . . . Not having learned how to play or not having formed any kind of hobby in almost fifty years of hard work, I now find myself at a loss to know what to do with the life I must continue to live. What do I do?"
> (Sixty-six-year-old retiree, in conversation with the author, June 1974)

Willingness or reluctance to retire appears to be a critical factor in retirement adjustment. It appears that individuals who are favorably disposed toward retirement are much more likely to retire. They also are more likely to adjust favorably. They are more apt to expand their activities to other ongoing roles (wife, grandmother, grandfather, friend, volunteer, for example) that assist in retirement adjustment.

Significant Others

The group of individuals who exist in the expanded roles provide a person with another or substitute reference group. This group of significant others, apart from the work setting, can rank high in importance for an individual. Some researchers even state that the healthiest and happiest older people often seem to be involved in close personal friendships. They were people who had established a social life that contained all three spheres of social involvement (Figure 9.5).

FIGURE 9.4

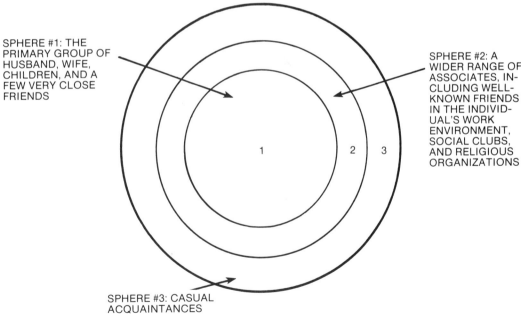

SPHERE #1: THE
PRIMARY GROUP OF
HUSBAND, WIFE,
CHILDREN, AND A
FEW VERY CLOSE
FRIENDS

SPHERE #2: A
WIDER RANGE OF
ASSOCIATES, IN-
CLUDING WELL-
KNOWN FRIENDS
IN THE INDIVID-
UAL'S WORK
ENVIRONMENT,
SOCIAL CLUBS,
AND RELIGIOUS
ORGANIZATIONS

SPHERE #3: CASUAL
ACQUAINTANCES

FIGURE 9.5
Three spheres of social involvement

Since the first two spheres make up a person's major reference groups, it is critical that the worker's social world contains people other than those in their work world. Most people at age sixty-five can look forward to sixteen or more years in reasonably good health. To face these later years with only the immediate family or one or two very close friends would be to place too great a limitation on the social world of older people.

It may be correct to state that significant others are the single most critical determinant of retirement adjustment! Preretirement planning is becoming more crucial every decade for a larger number of people. In 1776, every fiftieth American was a so-called older person (aged sixty-five and over). The total was only 50,000 out of an estimated total population of 2.5 million, or 2 percent. In 1985, the total was 27 million, or more than 11 percent of the total population.

> "Since I retired it seems I am living in a different world. My old business associates don't know that I am still in the world. My social acquaintances seem also to have forgotten that I am still here."
> (Sixty-seven-year-old retiree, in conversation with the author, December 1981)

THE SHRINKING WORK WEEK

Other forces appear to create a "why can't I continue to work" effect on the elderly. Rather than work's being the forceful lever by which the elderly are ready physically to take it easy, it is creating an opposite reaction. The average work week has declined during the last century:

In 1880, the work week consisted of sixty hours.
In 1986, the work week consisted of forty hours.

The increase needed in education and the early age of retirement have actually resulted in less and less time spent working using an ever smaller portion of the total life span and life energy! This compression of work into a shorter work time in the line-like life plan has created a growing set of problems. As life expectancy increases and work years decrease, the older person will experience more years with little or no work or work income. Retirement planning becomes a juggling act. Balancing fewer years of income to meet increasing years of retirement poses a monumental problem. Added to this is the continued improving physical health of our older population. Shorter work hours, plus less physically demanding work, are leaving older workers fully capable of continued employment and income. Retirement planning could be made easier if the opposite were true. If the income generated from work was sufficient throughout retirement, and if individuals' health left them looking forward to leisure time so the concept of the work week was not so inviting, the body might assist the mind in looking forward to retirement.

Without these helpful forces, retirement becomes not only a monetary concern; it also poses a larger challenge—psychologically preparing one's self for an increased number of retirement years, with a decreased income, and a mind and a body that have much to contribute to the work world.

DECLINE OF PEOPLE AGE SIXTY-FIVE AND OLDER IN THE WORK FORCE

Retirement concerns face an increasing aged population not only because of the larger number of people sixty-five years of age and over but also because fewer of that population remain in the work force. The following table shows the percentage of males and females age sixty-five and older in relationship to gainful employment. Female employment figures have been compiled only since 1950.

		Percent
Year	Male	Female
1870	80.6	-
1880	76.7	-
1890	73.8	-
1900	68.4	-
1910	63.7	-
1920	60.2	-
1930	58.3	-
1940	42.2	-
1950	48.8	9.7
1960	33.1	10.8
1970	26.8	9.7
1980	19.1	8.0
1990*	16.8	7.5
2000*	10.9	7.1

*estimates
(U.S. Bureau of the Census 1984, 116)

During World War II, there was a temporary reversal of the long-term trend toward decreasing labor force participation of older men. In 1940, the participation rate for men age sixty-five and over was 42.2 percent. The rate began to climb with the outbreak of the war, reaching 50.8 percent in 1945. When women entered the work world to assist the war effort, the federal government began to compile statistics for female participation in the labor market.

The decline in the percentage of working males does not reflect a declining desire to work. Some research studies have shown that approximately one-half of the people who have retired would like to return to some form of work (Kingston 1979; Morgan 1980).

HISTORICAL CONCEPT OF THE ELDERLY WORKER

In many places, retirement, as we know it, is a rarity. Cessation—stoppage—of work in most preliterate—before the invention of writing—societies occurred only when the individual was too feeble to perform any type of productive activity. The aged were expected to engage in whatever economic functions they were capable of performing, such as shifting from heavy labor to lighter, less strenuous tasks. In this way, these people maintained a sense of usefulness and a place in the group's productive activities.

> In a village in the Andes, many of the centenarians work on the land as farmers. Michaela Quezda, who is 102, spins sheep's wool in front of her house.
>
> In Abkhasia and Ecuador, the people do not retire from working. They exercise a great deal working on the farm and walking errands to the village.
>
> In peasant economies and medieval guilds, the concept of work was a way of life that was generally accepted. Not many people lived to become old in those days; those who did continued to be employed until they grew feeble or died. Since there were no provisions for gaining income in any other way, people worked as long as possible.
>
> Under the feudal system, the lord was obliged to take care of his workers in case of sickness, accident, or old age.
>
> The artisans or laborers in medieval times ordinarily continued to work as long as they could produce something.

In the early stages of the industrial revolution, the economic relations between workers and employers were interdependent and of a permanent character. The labor contracts were usually lifelong, and the employers took a personal interest in the welfare of their workers.

RETIREMENT: A MODERN CONCEPT

Retirement is a relatively recent development in modern, industrialized society. Old age was not universally dreaded before the industrial revolution or the advent of the modern factory system. On the contrary, it was even looked forward to with a certain feeling of satisfaction and accomplishment.

The first use of *retirement* as a mandatory concept was in 1777, when the first American mandatory retirement laws were enacted in New York. However, the law pertained only to judges. By 1820, six more states had passed similar laws, but only for aging judges. Mandatory retirement outside of this isolated profession was little heard of for nearly another 100 years.

Retirement got its foothold in the United States when the government introduced civil service pensions in 1920. By 1935, Congress had passed the Social Security Act, and *retirement* became a household word, an institution. With Social Security developed the idea that a person had a right to share in a nation's prosperity in later years without having to work.

"I can never forgive New York, Connecticut or Maine for turning out venerable men of sixty or seventy . . . when their judgment is often the best."*

(John Adams [1735-1826] as quoted in Fischer 1978, 81)

*John Adams was eighty-nine years old when he made that statement.

Retirement: A Personal Definition

Retirement, like work, did not have the same meaning for all individuals. For some people, retirement was the realization of a lifelong goal and represented the happiest time of their life. For others, it was a time of bitterness and frustration. Others viewed it with shock and disbelief, something they never thought would happen to them.

> Of the two hardest problems facing aging, the first is simply the lack of preparation, the lack of a natural or acquired provision or experience. We observe other people in the condition all our lives but fail to learn from the spectacle, and secondly, we fail to believe that the same can and will happen to us.

In today's technological society, we have become more productive with fewer working hours. Added to that are reduced death rates and prolonged life.

With this highly industrialized society also has come:

1. Urbanization.
2. Residential mobility.

These two factors affect many facets of traditional life. We cannot overlook their direct effect on retirement. They have created a need for different kinds of services. The wage-earning concept (where men and women are dependent on their daily toil for their daily bread) created changes in the traditional roles of family members. It also established a new bond between the individual and the government. These were not small changes; they were permeating changes that would cause waves, not ripples, for future generations.

The traditional family changes were:

1. Family professions were traded for individual employment pursuits (crafts were exchanged for jobs).
2. Outdated skills were a reality as people aged and new technology was introduced.
3. Dependence on the state for retirement care took the place of responsibility by the family unit.

The mental attitude established by the work ethic had to be replaced by an attitude that a person could, with a sense of dignity as an adult, live without holding a job. However, this right was earned by having been employed for a given period of time during one's work years.

The Selling of the Retirement Concept

Perhaps many of the myths connected with the elderly worker got their start when the concept of *retirement* was sold to the public! Retirement was introduced to the public primarily under the guise—pretense—of a means of supporting people who were physically unable to hold jobs. The truth of the matter was that retirement's main function was to keep down the number of people holding or looking for jobs. It was obvious that the humanitarian—welfare of the people—concept would be better received by the public, and of course it was. However, the long-term effect was the linking of physical disability and incapacity with the age of sixty-five, which was an arbitrary age, based on a whim, to begin with. There was not then nor is there now a sound basis for that linkage. Sadly enough, as the retirement age has crept lower, the association between disability and inability has crept right along with it.

ELDERLY WORKERS: THE MYTHS

Once a myth is established, it becomes easier for others to be established as well. The more accepted of the additional myths were:

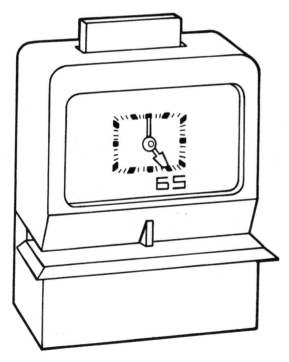

FIGURE 9.6
Retirement at age sixty-five: time to punch out

1. Older workers were too slow—they could not meet the production requirements.
2. Older workers could not meet the physical demands of their job.
3. Older workers were not dependable—they were absent from work too often.
4. Older workers were not adaptable—they were hard to train because they could not accept change.
5. Hiring older workers increased pension and insurance costs.

With the widespread acceptance of these myths, it is little wonder that older workers had a disadvantaged position in the labor force. Add to that some factual information—such as older workers have lower educational attainment, their skills become obsolete, and that management prefers younger workers—and job hunting for an older person becomes a fruitless effort.

THE HIDDEN UNEMPLOYED

> "If there were fifteen months in every year, I'd be forty-eight."
> (James Thurber as quoted in Comfort 1976, 107)

Statistics of elderly unemployment are misleading. Despite the fact that older workers encounter great problems in finding another job once they are unemployed, the unemployment rates for older workers are low. This paradox is explained by the hidden unemployed. The unemployment rates reflect only people actively seeking work. The rates omit older workers who become discouraged and drop out of the labor force after finding their search for employment futile. These people are then no longer classified as unemployed. Workers over sixty-five who declare themselves retired and deny they are seeking work thus avoid the demoralizing experience of referring to themselves as unemployed. Being out of the labor force is more respectable than being unemployed.

What Age Is "Too Old" to Work?

Note that sixty-five is not always, or the only age, at which discrimination takes place.

A forty-eight-year-old woman in Atlanta was dismissed from her job when her company decided to eliminate older employees and retain younger workers.

One man was turned down when he applied for the position of an FBI agent on the grounds that he was too old. He was forty-five.

A report in 1965 revealed at that time one-fourth of the job openings were closed to applicants over forty-five years of age, and one-half were closed to applicants over age fifty-five.

Pressure from Industry

It was not the inabilities of workers over sixty-five, or the government's deep concern for the care of its aged population that provided the major impetus—force—for the concept of retirement. Facts point more to industry. A simple solution to many concerns of industry seemed to be the concept of mandatory retirement. Here are some of industry's arguments.

1. Retirement assured everyone equal treatment. An employer did not have to discriminate among employees by telling some workers they could continue to work and others that they had to leave.

The annual retirement party at the Darrick Company was one of celebration and fun. The company was not saying poor old Dick no longer has the mental or physical power so he's got to go. Everyone knew that sixty-five was the retirement age at the Darrick Company. There was no stigma attached to retiring. It happened to everyone when they turned sixty-five.

2. Many companies believed that a fixed retirement age was needed to open job opportunities for younger workers. It was believed that the job market had a limited number of jobs for an ever-increasing work population.

> In the year 1977, *if* the retirement age had increased from sixty-five to sixty-eight years of age, there would have been an additional 3 million workers in the labor force. That year there were already 7 million unemployed workers.

3. Companies believed that mandatory retirement provided promotional opportunities and strengthened incentives for younger people. With no fixed age for retirement, seniority and tenure policies would result in a slowdown or blockage of the upward mobility of younger employees.
4. The companies' most popular argument was that older workers were not as productive as younger workers.
5. A key argument for companies was that without mandatory retirement, health and pension plans would be more difficult to administer.
6. It was argued that mandatory retirement allowed a company and its employees to plan better for the future by having a fixed date on which retirement must take place.

> "When did I start to feel old? Why, when I stopped working. I was always real proud that I'd come to Minneapolis and got a job and supported my family. Then when they told me I couldn't work anymore, why, I wasn't good for anything!"
> (Anton Fritz, in conversation with the author, October 1984)

Industry Has Second Thoughts

Some companies have turned to older workers to round out their ranks of part-time and full-time workers. They report strong satisfaction with the results. Employers believe that what older workers may lack in agility and physical endurance, they make up for in reliability and a strong work ethic.

> "A company that doesn't consider older workers isn't doing itself a favor."
> (Said of Wier-Burger King Corp. in Brophy, August 16, 1984)

A survey commissioned by the Worker Equity Initiative reported in May 1986 that employers give older workers their highest marks for productivity—critically important to American business today—as well as for attendance, commitment to quality, and satisfactory performance. Lower marks were given for competitiveness, flexibility, and acceptance of new technology. However 90 percent of employers surveyed believed that even the higher salaries and benefit costs of older workers were justified when they considered their value to the company (Brickfield 1986).

RETIREMENT: THE "CONSPIRACY OF SILENCE"

Simone de Beauvoir (1973) called forced retirement the "Conspiracy of Silence." She stated:

> We must stop cheating. The whole meaning of our life is in question in the future that is waiting for us. If we do not know what we are going to be, we cannot know what we are. The economy is founded upon profit; and in actual fact, the entire civilization is ruled by profit. The human working stock is of interest only in so far as it is profitable. When it is no longer profitable, it is tossed aside.
>
> At a congress a few years ago, Dr. Edmund Leach, a Cambridge anthropologist, said, in effect, "In a changing world, where machines have a very short run of life, men must not be used too long. Everyone over 55 should be scrapped."
>
> The word *scrapped* expresses his meaning admirably. We are told that retirement is the thing of freedom and leisure; poets have sung "the delights of reaching port." These are shameless lies. Society inflicts so wretched a standard of living upon the vast majority of old people that it is almost repetitive to say *old is poor.*
>
> At the same time, exceedingly poor people are old. Leisure does not open new possibilities for the retired man; just when he is at last set free from compulsion and restraint, the means of making use of his liberty are taken from him. He is condemned to stagnate in boredom and loneliness, a mere throw-out. The fact that for the last 15 or 20 years of his life a man should be no more than a reject, a piece of scrap, reveals the failure of our civilization. If we were to look upon the old as human beings, with human life behind them, and not as so many working corpses, this obvious truth would move up profoundly.
>
> It is this old age that makes it clear that everything has to be reconsidered, recast from the very beginning. That is why the whole problem is so carefully passed over in SILENCE.

The past may have known silence, but the rumblings of the present forecast an uproar in the future.

> The Townsend Plan of 1935 had 5,000,000 supporters in Cleveland demanding an improved pension plan. They marched to "Onward pension soldiers marching on to war"!
>
> (Jones 1977, 230)

WHY DO PEOPLE RETIRE?

This is one of the most important questions in industrial gerontology. Answers to this question are important so that employers can keep control over the makeup of their labor forces. They can provide either incentives or disincentives for retirement. The federal government needs answers to that question so it can develop retirement policies that eliminate age discrimination in employment, reduce unemployment, and finance Social Security.

The answer to that question can also help individuals plan better for their own retirement.

Reasons for retirement are as varied as the people who retire. However, retirees usually give these five common reasons:

1. Boredom or dissatisfaction with their jobs make them want to leave employment.
2. They do not feel they are physically able to continue working.
3. Mandatory retirement forces some from work while it encourges others to leave because of inviting pension benefits or incentives.
4. A life of leisure has some people voluntarily leaving the work force to enjoy the remaining years.
5. Changes in health, family relationships, or company policies make others retire unexpectedly and/or unwillingly.

RETIREMENT AGES

Just as everyone does not retire for the same reason, neither do they retire at the same age. Retirement ages fall into four main categories (Woodruff and Birren 1983, 337-338):

1. Very early	ages 61 or earlier
2. Early	ages 62-64
3. Average	age 65
4. Later	ages 66+

Very Early Retirees

The very early retirees retire early for a wide variety of reasons. They are either in a very high income bracket, have reasonably good health, or are in poor health with a low income. Some people retire early because they can afford to; some are in so-called hazardous occupations (policemen or airline pilots), and others have poor or chronic health problems. Most very early retirees appear to be in the last category of poor health and low income. A large number of these retirees died within a few years of their retirement (Kingston 1979).

FIGURE 9.7

> The average police officer in Los Angeles was forty-eight at retirement, in New York, forty-nine.

Early Retirees

The early retiree, between the ages of sixty-two and sixty-four, in 1979 accounted for nearly two-thirds of all workers. By accepting reduced retirement benefits at age sixty-three, this group of workers qualified for Social Security. Again, the reasons for retirement were varied.

Researchers (Woodruff and Birren 1983, 339) found the four determiners of an early retirement were:

1. Finances.
2. Health.
3. Retirement attitudes.
4. Job-related attitudes.

Of these four factors, finances appeared to be the most important factor in early retirement decisions. The higher the income the retirees could anticipate on their retirement, the more likely they were to retire early. The opposite was also a factor for not retiring—the more inadequate or uncertain the income, the more likely the individual was to remain in the job market.

Health was also a highly considered factor. Poor health made individuals want to retire early, whereas good health encouraged them to continue working beyond the normal retirement age.

Attitudes about retirement and the job were considerations, but much less so than were finances and health. The most people likely to retire early were those who had positive attitudes about retirement and negative attitudes about their work.

Late Retirees

The average aged and later-than-average aged retiree tend to be the exception rather than the rule. Fewer and fewer workers are remaining in the work force until the average sixty-five years of age. Those who do remain in the work place appear to have some things in common. More often than not, they are self-employed. These people intend to work as long as they choose, which is usually as long as possible. It appears that for these individuals economics and health are retirement factors, in that order. Their high degree of self-satisfaction, plus the freedom from external policies, encourage them to work as long as they choose.

RETIREMENT AND HEALTH

One widespread myth among Americans is that retirement is hazardous to your health. Support was given to this myth by the American Medical Association's Committee on Aging when, in 1968, they published this often quoted passage (p. 2):

> Compulsory retirement on the basis of age will impair the health of many individuals whose job represents a major source of status, creative satisfaction, social relationships, or self-respect. It will be equally disastrous for the individual who works only because he has to and who has a minimum of meaningful goals or interests in life, job-related or otherwise. Job separation may well deprive such a person of his only source of identification and leave him floundering in a motivational vacuum with no frame of reference whatsoever.

No one disputes the fact that the loss of work is stressful to some people. Many stories give strength to that fact. A large amount of research also shows that many older people are happy and well adjusted to their retirement status. These are people who do not miss their jobs, suffer from no identity crisis, feel useful, and are neither depressed nor lonely.

How can such opposite reaction to retirement exist among the elderly? The answer appears to lie in each individual's lifelong adaptation habits. Some people bring to retirement the personality factors that make retirement another positive happening in their lives. The responses are as varied as backgrounds. Backgrounds differ according to occupational status, income level, health status, the nature of one's job, the state of the economy, marital status, sex, ethnicity, and so on. With all of these differing factors, it follows that retirement is good for some people, bad for some, and neutral to others.

Four common threads for people who experience a positive retirement include these facts:

1. Retirement is voluntary rather than forced.
2. Income and health are listed as "good" so that the individual can live comfortably in retirement.
3. Work is not the most important thing in their lives.
4. Retirement has been prepared and planned for.

ECONOMICS: A MAJOR RETIREMENT ISSUE

The economic status of retirees is dependent on a number of circumstances, including individuals' decision-making habits throughout their lifetime, public policies concerning benefits, and luck. Some sources of income are within the control of the individuals; others are not. The four major sources of income for the elderly are:

1. Earnings,
2. Social Security benefits,
3. Other retirement benefits (public and private pensions, annuities, IRA accounts), and/or
4. Income assets (interest, rent, dividends).

Inflation and unemployment are serious threats to retirees. These factors threaten the purchasing power of their sources of income. Also note that not all retirees enjoy income from all of these sources. In 1980, more than one-fourth (28 percent) of all retirees were forced to live on the payments of Social Security only. This statistic has created a crisis in the Social Security financing. For this reason, the Social Security system is undergoing some important changes. Beginning in the year 2009, full retirement benefits will not be paid until age sixty-six; and in 2027, the eligibility age will rise to age sixty-seven. It is believed that these age changes will save the Social Security system $3.6 billion a year and keep another 200,000 people in the work force (Pekkanen 1985, 48).

However, many economists believe the Social Security system is financially sound. They project optimistic figures for the future:

	Social Security Benefits	
If You Reach the Retirement Age in:	Average Earner: $21,410 in 1990	Maximum Earner: $49,800 in 1990
1990	$6,713	$9,089
1995	7,091	9,826
2000	7,611	10,939
2005	8,175	12,174
2010	8,785	13,451
2015	9,436	14,720
2020	10,141	15,875
2025	10,892	17,057
2030	11,701	18,322

The normal age for full retirement benefits will rise in slow steps from 65 to 67 (in 2027) for people born between 1938 and 1960.

(Ramsden and Mullikin 1985, 63)

Added to the Social Security source of income is the possibility of retirement planning, which includes tax deferred income. An individual starting such an account at the age of twenty-eight and investing $2,000 a year at an estimated 12 percent interest per year, as shown on the following chart, at the age of sixty-five would have a savings of $1,235,557. This type of preretirement planning can significantly change the economic status of future retirees.

Tax Deferred Retirement Plan					
Age	Account	Age	Account	Age	Account
28	$2,240	41	$65,832	54	$343,318
29	4,509	42	75,732	55	386,516
30	7,050	43	86,820	56	434,898
31	9,896	44	99,239	57	489,085
32	13,083	45	113,147	58	549,776
33	16,653	46	128,725	59	617,749
34	20,652	47	146,172	60	693,879
35	25,130	48	165,713	61	779,144
36	30,146	49	187,598	62	874,641
37	35,763	50	212,110	63	981,598
38	42,055	51	239,563	64	1,101,390
39	49,101	52	270,311	65	1,235,557
40	56,993	53	304,748		

EARLY RETIREMENT: WHOSE IDEA?

The average retirement age in America is sixty-two. If economics is a problem and if 50 percent of the retirees wish they were working, why does the retirement age get younger instead of older?

A major reason appears to be that the retirement system provides more disincentives to work than incentives. Many pension programs provide no monetary reason to continue on the job. Even Social Security places a limit on the earnings an individual may have without being penalized by a reduction in Social Security payments. Benefits are reduced $1 for every $2 of wages earned above a specified annual limit. Private pensions also encourage early retirement by designating a normal retirement age—usually sixty-five—and are set up so the individual cannot accrue any additional benefits after that. These are powerful incentives for elderly individuals to leave the work force voluntarily!

RETIREMENT AND THE DEPENDENCY RATIO

Of particular concern regarding long-range financing of Social Security is the ratio of the beneficiary population to workers. Around the year 2010, the large post-World-War II baby-boom generation will begin retiring. The labor force at that time will be relatively small, since it will be made up of persons born during the low birth rate period, which began in the late 1960s. Using the current projected statistics, it is believed the number of beneficiaries for every 100 workers is expected to increase from 31 in 1983 to 57 by 2030. That is an 83 percent increase. This substantial increase raises questions about the ability and willingness of the work force to provide certain benefit levels. Because Social Security is a pay-as-you-go system—that is, contributions made by workers are immediately transferred to retirees—the projected change in the dependency ratio creates a national dilemma. Some solutions to preserve the system are to increase the burden on workers through higher taxes, to reduce benefits for retirees, or both. Employment of elderly workers is one solution to the apparent dilemma.

RETIREMENT TRENDS

"Retirement," writes John Pekkanen (1985, 48), "is when you work for years and you deserve some time off, and darned it you're not going to get it."

But retirement is not just a personal decision-making process. Today, retirement is big government, big business, and a big dilemma.

Nearly one-fourth of the federal budget is spent on retirement benefits of some kind, and nearly $100 billion is placed in private pension plans. With a decreased work force and the retirement age getting younger, are we, as a nation, putting our valuable national resources—experience, wisdom, and money—to the best possible use?

SUMMARY

America's elderly population may be getting gray but the work force is not. The trend toward earlier retirement is contributing to a younger work force. Few workers remain employed beyond sixty-two years of age.

The majority of older Americans retire for many different reasons; the major ones are economic and health reasons. If a person's income and health are good, retirement is usually a positive experience. Unfortunately, retirees find that inflation affects their retirement income and savings so that nearly 50 percent of retirees would like to return to some form of work.

Obstacles to continued employment are the confusing and contradictory retirement policies. This entangled mesh of inconsistencies often entraps people. Benefits claim to protect the remaining years of a retired worker, when, in truth, many provide incentives to potential retirees too strong for the elderly individual to ignore.

Not only have Social Security and retirement benefits run into financial problems, but perhaps our nation has run into resource problems. America may not be able any longer to afford the going price of retirement. Is it advantageous to pay extremely qualified people *not* to contribute to our national well-being? Futurists must address this question.

EXERCISES

1. Engage in a conversation with several people thirty years of age and older whom you have not met before. Within a few minutes, see how many of these individuals, without your asking, include their occupation as part of their description of who they are.
2. Research the concept of the *Protestant work ethic.* Is the concept still alive and well today? Explain.
3. What have you done by way of preretirement planning? Next to each category, write the activities that are presently part of your planning or things you would like to have as part of your preretirement planning.

	Do	*Would Like to Do*
Hobbies/Leisure:		
Financial planning:		
Social organizations:		

4. Since dreaming and planning have some things in common, write the story of your retirement. Include your financial status, living arrangements, social activities, state of health, and number of years anticipated in retirement. Also include what you retired from, at what age, and how you used your work years to plan your retirement.

5. Prepare and present a three-minute presentation on what you believe is the most popular myth about older workers. In your preparation, gather information to prove the myth is fact not fiction, or fiction not fact.

REVIEW

1. How has the definition of work changed from culture to culture?
2. What function does work serve in the lives of individuals?
3. What is the definition of a nonworking or retired person?
4. List the two factors that seem to be indicators of successful retirement adjustment.
5. Describe the three spheres that a person's social life comprises.
6. How has the line-like life plan changed over time?
7. Compare 1870 with 1970 and the present in terms of the percentage of workers age sixty-five and older in the work force.
8. What prompted enactment of the Social Security Act of 1935?
9. List some of the myths that force the retirement of or prevent the hiring of persons aged sixty-five and older.
10. Who are included in the hidden unemployed?
11. Why is it to the advantage of big business to have a mandatory retirement law?
12. What is Simone de Beauvior saying in the "Conspiracy of Silence"?
13. What appear to be the major reasons people retire?
14. List the four main categories of retirement ages and the corresponding age for each.
15. Is retirement hazardous to your health?
16. List the major sources of income for retirees.
17. How does the change in the dependency ratio affect the Social Security system?

RECOMMENDED READINGS
AND REFERENCES

Action for Independent Maturity. *Retirement Planning Handbook*. Long Beach, Calif., 1978.

American Medical Association, Committee on Aging. *Retirement: A Medical Philosophy and Approach*. Chicago, 1968.

Atchley, Robert C. *The Social Forces In Later Life.* Belmont, Calif.: Wadsworth Publishing Company, 1980.

Beauvoir, Simone de. *The Coming of Age.* New York: Putnam, 1973.

Brickfield, Cyril F. "Executive Directors Report". *AARP News Bulletin,* May 1986, 2.

Brophy, Beth. "Retirees: USA's New Work Force." *USA Today,* August 16, 1984.

Comfort, Alexander. *A Good Age.* New York: Crown Publishers, Inc., 1976.

Fischer, David H. *Growing Old in America.* New York: Oxford University Press, 1978.

Jones, Rochelle. *The Other Generation.* Englewood Cliffs, N.J.: Prentice-Hall, 1977.

Kingston, E. "Men Who Leave Work before 62: A Study of Advantaged and Disadvantaged Very Early Labor Force Withdrawal." Unpublished dissertation, Brandeis University, Waltham, Mass., 1979.

Morgan, J. "Economic Realities of Aging." Paper presented to the Convocation on Work and Retirement, University of Southern California, Los Angeles, 1980.

Pekkanen, John. "No Idle Matter." *50 Plus,* March 1985, 48, 51.

Ramsden, Kathrine L., and Patrick Timothy Mullikin. "How Can I Think About Retirement When I'm Busy Making a Living?" *Sylvia Porter's Personal Finance,* April 1985, 36-41.

Reader's Digest. "Quotations," May 1974, 140.

U.S. Bureau of the Census. *Demographic and Socioeconomic Aspects of Aging in the United States.* Series P-23, No. 138. Washington, D.C.: U.S. Government Printing Office, 1984.

Woodruff, Diana S., and James E. Birren. *Aging Scientific Perspectives and Social Issues.* Monterey, Calif.: Brooks/Cole Publishing Company, 1983.

CHAPTER
10
Myths

Learning Objectives

After studying this chapter, the reader should be able to:

- Define myths as a collection of beliefs about the nature of a particular category of people—in the case of old age, these myths are overly negative and biased.
- Realize that myths cause incorrect preconceptions and foster misconceptions about old age.
- Conclude that there are a large number of myths that cause unnecessary fears about the elderly and/or growing old.
- Determine that the stigma of old age is an unjust and unearned result of myths.

Preview

In his book *Thirty Dirty Lies about Old,* Hugh Downs (1979, 8) states:

> Some lies [myths] are conscious and vicious, employed to suit convenience, express annoyance, or reinforce prejudice. Others are unconscious, widespread and perhaps well intentioned—but nonetheless devastating—and they fall from the lips of the young and not-so-young alike. Some are silly, and some downright harmful. All should be examined, exposed, and retired. Because regardless of our age, if we hang around long enough, loose lies will victimize all of us.

This chapter presents facts concerning the sixteen more popular myths so that in examining them from every viewpoint and exposing them for what they are, a final blow can be struck to force their retirement.

THE LIES THEY TELL ABOUT US

As a society, we pay dearly for our fictions about aging. At birth, everyone in our country stands a better than 50-50 chance of reaching retirement age. Therefore, our untruths turn out not to involve someone else but

FIGURE 10.1

become self-measurements. They tell us our worth in later life. They tell us the worth of later life. If we use these myths—any fictitious story—as the measuring sticks of our future, we will come up short of what we could have been and what we could have had.

People of all ages in our society keep the myths and stereotypes alive. Recent studies show that children have generally unpleasant images of growing old and of old people. Children from ages three to eleven describe the elderly in negative ways:

1. They are "wrinkled, short, and are gray-haired."
2. They "chew funny."
3. They "don't go out much."
4. They "sit all day and watch TV in their rocking chair."
5. They "have heart attacks and die."

When asked how they felt about growing old themselves, all but a few of the children stated that they simply did not want to do it.

> A twelve-year-old was asked how he would describe "old people." He said, "They are good people. They are wise because they learned through problems and mistakes they have made along the way." He was then asked, "Would you like to get old some day?" "No!" "Wouldn't you like to be wise?" "No, I'd just like to be young!"
> (Brent Williamson, in conversation with the author, November 1985)

Such stereotypes and attitudes, communicated by parents, teachers, and peers, appear in many famous books and on television programs and are even shared by professional people.

Results of other studies with subjects from age eight to college level confirmed the negative images of elderly people in those age groups as well (Blenkner 1967, 104; Neugarten 1964, 269). College students tended to:

1. Downgrade the appearance of old people.
2. Feel that the old resented the young.
3. State that they preferred to avoid direct personal contact with old people.

Adult Americans also harbor many misconceptions about what old age is really like. Surveys show that the general adult population expected:

1. Poor health,
2. Insufficient money to live on, and/or
3. Loneliness.

They believed these were serious problems. However, one-fourth or less of the elderly people sampled actually reported these as problems. It was interesting that many of the old people who were questioned gave different answers when asked about other people than they did when asked about themselves. They tended to see themselves as having fewer problems than other old people, such as the "old fogey" or "old biddy" down the street.

Many elderly people do have problems—inadequate money, poor health, loneliness, poor medical care, fear of crime, and/or difficulties in getting from place to place. These problems, however, are not as serious as the general public believes. Perhaps the greatest problem of the elderly is the attitude of the public toward them.

The truth is that many old people frequently look at themselves in a negative light, thereby continuing and reinforcing the sociological, psychological, and biological myths about old age. Evidence shows that the elderly themselves have some problems dealing with the reality of their age (Blenkner 1967, 105; Neugarten 1964, 270). These studies found that people over seventy were consistently labeling themselves as "middle-aged." A group of sixty-year-olds and older gave the following responses:

1. Sixty-one percent labeled themselves as middle-aged.
2. Sixty-seven percent thought that others viewed them as middle-aged.
3. Sixty-two percent stated that they felt younger than most people their age.

A fifty-two-year-old male said, "If I would think of any age as 'old' I think it would be seventy!"

A seventy-one-year-old woman was asked, "Do you consider yourself old?" Her reply was, "No, people who are eighty are old."

Negative attitudes toward the elderly are very difficult to change. As a result of these myths, there is a continuation of the fear and even denial of one's own aging. Denial of aging and the aged is, however, a two-edged sword. In so doing, we, in the end, deny ourselves.

> "We don't all grow Black or Chinese, but we do grow old!"
>   (Butler 1975, 11)

An observation was made not long ago by nonagenarian George Burns. He thought that people could convince themselves to act according—to think of themselves as unproductive, decrepit, and passive. Burns states, however, "You can't help getting older, but you don't have to get old" (1983, 138).

SOCIOLOGICAL MYTHS ABOUT AGING

Even though myths affect the entire person, some are more harmful to certain facets of everyday living. The following myths are discussed here because of their impact on the social needs of the elderly person.

> MYTH 1:   All the needs of the elderly can be met by the services of a nursing home.

> "We have the right not just to exist, but to live out the rest of our lives to the fullest."
>   (Nursing home resident,
>   in conversation with the author, January 1985)

The right to exist obviously includes the things needed for basic survival—food, clothing and shelter. Certainly, these needs are met by nursing homes. The right to live "to the fullest" can perhaps be summed up best by the word *love*. Is this need met in the nursing home, or should it even be expected of a nursing home?

> Seven to 8 percent of the elderly population are cared for in nursing homes.
>   (U.S. Senate 1984, 64)

The desire for personal care, closeness, and love is not dormant in the elderly. It is overtaken only by the need for the basics of survival.

Until retirement, most people are close to spouses, families, or friends. But in those later years, when many loved ones have died or moved far away, the need to belong increases. Some institutionalized elderly are forced to make the shattering discovery that institutions often have rules that minimize or eliminate opportunities for close relationships.

The quotation by the elderly nursing home resident who believed she had the right not just to exist but to live out the rest of her life to the fullest was made by a woman who had been denied the intimate rights of a married woman with her husband.

The elderly are, perhaps, the most emotionally deprived people in our society. Nancy Littell Fox (1980, 90) sums it up well when she says, "There is really no excuse for American nursing homes to be emotionless mortuaries for the living!"

Patients do not forfeit their civil rights because they have reached a particular chronological age. The dignity and worth of every human being must be upheld. Nursing homes can be said to meet all the needs of the elderly patient when each person because of the care feels that "the sunset is no less beautiful than the sunrise!"

MYTH 2:   All older people are neglected or ignored by family.

The relationships between old age and the family are attacked by a number of stereotypic beliefs. Such stereotypic beliefs or myths are often started on the basis of a single observation and then generalized to the entire population. If an elderly neighbor never sees her children, for example, we might conclude that all older people are neglected or ignored by their sons and daughters. Myths also can be based on unrealistic patterns of the past. It is not unusual for a person to complain about the passing of "the good old days" when the elderly were respected—venerated for their wisdom—and functioned as important and contributing members of the multigeneration family.

However, such reminiscing—recalling the past—ignores the fact that multigeneration families have never been the rule in the United States. Since relatively few people survived to advanced age in the past, there is little evidence to support the notion that older individuals were happier, better adjusted, or better off financially or physically when included within the multigeneration household.

Myths concerning old age and family are sometimes strengthened by media coverage. Elderly people who have unnecessarily been placed in nursing homes, who have been forgotten and neglected by their family,

FIGURE 10.2

and who have lived solitary and isolated lives make for sensational news reports and story scripts. However, older people who interact happily with family members and continue close family ties, although in the majority, are not considered newsworthy.

The majority of elderly in the United States (90 percent) maintain their own home throughout later maturity. This majority believes that living with their children is not desirable. They wish to keep their independence as long as possible.

Although older individuals manage to maintain separate and independent households, they also maintain involvement with their children. Ninety percent reported having seen at least one of their children during the preceding month, and 75 percent had at least one child who lived fewer than thirty minutes away. Within our society, it is normal and common for parent-child interactions to continue throughout old age.

MYTH 3:   Most elderly people feel it is their children's responsibility to care for them in old age.

Time does not stand still, and age takes its toll all around. Even if one remains healthy and feels as well as ever, old friends die or move to other localities and one's circle of contemporaries—other people about the same age—begins to thin out.

With the narrowing of these human contacts, the aging person becomes more and more aware of the need to lean on some person or group of peers. This is not a new event but only a new awareness that this fact exists. Beginning with birth, people must lean and depend on someone if they are to survive. They lean first on their mother; later, on their friends; still later, on their spouse. They do not think about these dependencies for they have more or less always been there in the form of relationships. One is not always conscious of this need to lean as well as to be leaned on. One of the most important elements in life is the ability to depend on and be depended on in return. Without this mutuality, normal adjustment to life could not take place. This fact is so important and plays such a large role in our existence that we are not aware that it is absolutely necessary for a well-balanced way of life.

> Margaret Blenkner describes this dependency in old age "as a state of being, not a state of mind; a state of being in which to be old . . . is to be dependent. Such dependency is not pathological—due to disease; it is not wrong; it is, in fact, a right of the old, recognized by most, if not by all societies."
>
> (Blenkner 1967, 103)

Although most children feel that responsibility for aged parents lies with them, most elderly individuals do not believe such responsibility exists. In the opinion of most older people, responsibility during retirement and later maturity should be shouldered by aged people themselves rather than by their children. They want to live near their family but not with them. In most instances, children's responsibility for aged parents is to provide information. Such aid is in the form of advice in investments, pensions, purchases, Social Security, taxes, insurance, and banking, for example. Children frequently act as advisers, mediators, and facilitators without assuming significant responsibility for the care and well-being of their parents.

MYTH 4:   Grandparenting is universally enjoyed.

No single relationship or behavior pattern exists between all grandparents and all grandchildren. Just as mothers and fathers differ greatly in their handling and interacting with children, so is there a variety of grandparenting styles. Research studies (McKensie 1980, 211) reveal five styles of grandparenting[*]:

1. Formal: Do not interfere with the parenting role but relate in a concerned manner.
2. Fun seeker: Really enjoy grandchildren and tend to spoil them.
3. Surrogate parent: Parental duties and responsibilities are, in part, assumed by the grandmother, who may be helping the working daughter.
4. Reservoir of family wisdom: Maintain authority over grandchildren.
5. Distant figure: Contact with grandchildren is minimal.

"A grandma is a lady who has no children of her own, so she likes other people's boys and girls."

"A grandfather is a man grandmother!"
(3rd grader, in conversation with the author, October 1981)

The age of the grandparents also has some relationship to how they react to their grandchildren. Younger grandparents are more likely to be somewhat fun-seeking in their role, as if they were the children's play-mate. Older grandparents tend to be more distant and formal in their behavior toward their grandchildren, becoming close only on special occasions (distant figure).

"Grandparents are usually fat, but not too fat. They wear glasses and funny underwear. They can take their teeth and gums off."

"They don't have to be smart, only answer questions like why dogs hate cats, and how come God isn't married."

Over the past decades, the family cycle has speeded up. As people married at younger ages, they became parents and also grandparents at earlier ages than in previous generations. Becoming a grandparent had traditionally been seen as a sign of aging. Grandparenthood had the

---

[*]From *Aging and Old Age* by Sheila C. McKensie. Copyright © 1980 by Scott, Foresman and Company. Reprinted by permission.

traditional image of a kind, white-haired, elderly citizen. Grandparent-hood now has become a middle-aged event, and great-grandparenthood is an old-age phenomenon. Perhaps great-grandparenthood will soon assume the meaning of grandparenthood.

Today, with increased longevity, children have more living grandparents than ever before.

Percentage of Ten-Year-Olds Having Living Grandparents			
Year	Number of Living Grandparents		
	1	2	4
1920	80%	40%	11%
1970	95%	75%	71%
		(Neugarten and Weinstein 1964, 272)	

Some individuals may still see grandparenthood as signaling the beginning of the end and may be reluctant to admit their new role to anyone. Others, less fearful of aging, welcome the first grandchild as a ticket of admission to a group known as SOGPIP (silly old grandmother with pictures in purse). They also take pleasure in the evidence of continued immortality through the family.

FIGURE 10.3

MYTH 5:   As people grow older they become more alike.

Note the difference:
homogeneous = having similarities

heterogeneous = differing

The idea that individuals become more alike as they grow older is a
widespread myth imposed on older citizens by our society. Although
people are willing to acknowledge the uniqueness or individuality of each
child, this perceived difference is not often extended to older adults.
When faced with assessing the characteristics and qualities of aged adults,
many people treat this particular segment of society as though it were a
homogeneous group whose members had lost their individuality as a
result of time. Contrary to popular opinion, as we grow older, a narrowing
of characteristics does not develop. Just the opposite is true. With increased age come increased diversity, increased individuality, and increased uniqueness (Maddox and Douglas 1974).

Every day, approximately 5,200 Americans celebrate their sixty-
fifth birthday. These newcomers have experienced a different life history
from those already sixty-five and older and are worlds apart from centenarians who were born about twenty years after the Civil War.

In an attempt to explain and better understand this increased
age-related diversity among people, we must consider two developmental
realities:

1. As people grow older, their varied experiences exert a diversify-
   ing influence.

With the passage of years, each individual learns different things, faces
varied situations, and develops a unique pattern of response. In essence,
as a person grows older, he or she experiences a constant and gradual
emphasis on individuality and uniqueness. Diverse experiences create
heterogeneity rather homogeneity.

2. Chronological age, or the number of years a person has lived,
   affects each individual differently.

Some people are old at sixty-five, and others are young at the same age.
Also, within each individual, various facets of aging are progressing at

different rates. People do not just age; they age biologically, socially, psychologically, as well as chronologically. The potential for diversity within each aging process is enormous.

> "I wouldn't swap one wrinkle of my face for all the elixirs of youth. All of these wrinkles represent a smile, a grimace of pain and disappointment . . . some part of being fully alive."
>
> (Hayes 1965, 238)

PSYCHOLOGICAL MYTHS ABOUT AGING

The myths discussed under this heading undermine the self-confidence and self-esteem of the elderly person. They may be more devastating than social myths because of the silent, unobserved pain.

> MYTH 6:   Elderly people, as individuals or as workers, are less creative, productive, and efficient than younger people.

The drive to discover and create appears natural to human beings. The desire to be creative must be nourished or it will wither. The problem is that society discourages the attitudes and actions that would nourish innovation and creativity in the old. To the elderly, society preaches:

The inappropriateness of:	1. ingenuity
	2. courage
	3. imagination
and instead encourages	1. resignation
	2. humility
	3. self-centeredness.

Society tells the retired that they may find stagnation difficult at first, but that they will get used to it. We reward them for this with promises of benefits, highrise apartments, and senior citizen discounts.

The dangers are not only that the aged are prohibited from freely involving themselves in creative activity, but also that society's tactics will ensure that eventually they will be incapable of performing them. The shame is that society creates the pressures to make the elderly less creative, productive, and efficient and then isolates them on the basis of these conditions.

Perhaps the myth of unproductivity and lack of creativity in old age stems from our society's tendency to equate productivity and creativity with paid employment. Regardless of employment status, many older citizens continue to be productive, contributing, and creative members of society well into later maturity. If society denies, ignores, or suppresses the creative potential of the sixty-five-and-over population, all members of that society will suffer a significant loss.

This myth cannot be allowed on a scientific basis when talking about work unless referring to feats of strength and endurance, which occupy little of the work force in our highly mechanized society. The biological changes that come with normal aging tend to have little, if any, practical application in most jobs. Disease, of course, is another matter. The ability of human beings to compensate for deteriorations or to adapt to new occupational demands often seems bound only by motivations and expectations.

> "Everyone is too old for something, but no one is too old for everything!"

MYTH 7:   Older people tend to be inflexible.

Inflexibility refers to a frame of mind characterized by rigid resistance to change and the inability to adapt to new situations. Some older people are indeed inflexible. Their behavioral patterns are rigid, and they are very resistant to change. However, it is also accurate to say that some children, some young adults, and some middle-aged individuals are also characterized by inflexibility.

In some cases, actual lack of available opportunities to develop, grow, and change may be incorrectly labeled by the outside observer as inflexibility in old age. Note, however, that economic, social, and physical limitations may prove significant barriers to change regardless of the elderly individual's personal desire or ability to behave in an adaptive or flexible fashion. This lack of opportunity to change and develop should not be confused with inflexibility.

Chronological age does not produce an inflexible personality. Not only do older individuals change, but they must, by necessity, adapt to major events that are frequent and expected occurrences of later maturity, including:

1. Retirement.
2. Change in income and status.
3. Loss of loved ones.
4. Illness and disease.
5. Change in life-style.
6. Change in residence.

> An elderly man understood the need for flexibility when he
> said, "The doctor says I'm getting old and should increase my fluid
> intake. I do. I've started taking my Scotch with water instead of
> straight. You've got to adapt!"
>
> (*Reader's Digest,* June 1978, 89)

Although research suggests that older individuals change attitudes
and opinions somewhat more slowly than do younger people, changes
noted among older people tend to mirror existing habits observed in
society in general (Cutler and Kaufman 1975). Most older people remain
open to change throughout the entire course of later maturity. Contrary
to what many people believe, old people do not become inflexible;
inflexible people get old!

Perhaps the word *cautious* is a better description of the elderly
than *inflexible* or *rigid*. A lifetime of experience has taught them not
to expect miracles and to become more practical about what can
be accomplished.

MYTH 8:   The performance of elderly people on intelligence
tests is lower than that of young adults.

It should come as no surprise that no single definition of intelligence is accepted by all individuals. This is because intelligence is a
hypothetical idea created by human beings in an attempt to explain
individual differences in behavior.

Intelligence represents many things. But IQ and intelligence are
not synonymous.

Overall intellectual decline cannot be proven as a natural part of
growing old. Some measured abilities show no pattern of decline in later
maturity; indeed, some abilities seem to improve with increased age.
When intelligence tests are given to the elderly, factors that influence the

testing should be noted and given consideration. Five such factors include:

1. Response time.
2. Level of education.
3. Test-taking sophistication.
4. General health.
5. Social forces.

1.   Many measures of intelligence depend on an individual's ability to respond to a physical or mental activity with accuracy and speed. Most tests of intelligence also have strict time requirements and give no credit for correct answers if such answers are not given within the set time limit.

As a person ages, a physiological change occurs that results in a slowing down of reaction time or an increase in time required to respond to various activities or stimuli. With advanced age, nerve impulses are slower.

> When younger, nerve impulses travel 140 miles per hour. When older, nerve impulses travel 110 miles per hour.

We do react more slowly as we grow older. However, in terms of intellectual functioning, we must ask whether increased reaction time can honestly be equated with lessened mental abilities. Intelligence tests that demand timed responses generally are unfair to the elderly population.

2.   A second factor that may affect an elderly person's performance on intelligence tests is educational level. Educational level and intellectual performance are more highly equated than are age and intellectual performance. That is, the performance of individuals of similar educational backgrounds, regardless of age, tends to be more alike.

Many tests of intelligence are strongly weighted with items that draw on information obtained within formal learning situations. The older the person, the less formal and less recent has been their education.

3.   A third factor that may affect intellectual performance is the degree of test-taking sophistication. Within our society, the degree of test sophistication—refined techniques—tends to be a function of age. Older people often have had less formal education than have younger people.

They have had less exposure to testing situations, and they lack familiarity with the demands of the procedures of standardized testing.

4.   In old age, individuals who have chronic physical disabilities, particularly those resulting from strokes or any condition involving a progressive reduction of blood to the brain, will usually exhibit a marked decrease in intellectual sharpness.

5.   In addition to health, social conditions may operate to hasten intellectual decline. If a person:

1. becomes isolated from other people,
2. has little opportunity for meaningful friendships,
3. becomes generally separated from everyday social activities,

in all probability, mental abilities will show evidence of decline. Older people who remain in the mainstream of life, who continue to pursue and initiate normal social contacts, and who remain personally involved with other people are less likely to experience intellectual decline. The previous statement is equally true when applied to most human beings regardless of age.

MYTH 9:   Most older people are lonely and isolated.

Some people age sixty-five and older do not, for whatever reason, choose to make personal contacts. Some men and women come to feel personally devalued, unworthy, too shattered, too old to have friends. They drift into social backwaters almost on purpose. Such behavior is unnecessary and potentially disastrous. Old age is a time for the shifting of gears, a reversal of direction, into the mainstream of life.

> Nearly 5 million people have no telephone or other communicative contact with the outside world. We cannot underestimate the disruptive effects of loneliness and anxiety on the physical and mental health of the isolated person.

The results of a number of studies suggest that for most elderly people, the opposite is true (Blenkner 1967, 105). The public has a major misconception about the aged that centers on isolation and feelings of personal loneliness.

FIGURE 10.4

> Twelve percent of those sixty-five and older felt that "loneliness" was a very serious problem for them personally.
>
> Sixty percent of the general public considered "loneliness" to be a very serious problem for most people sixty-five and older.
>
> (Dean 1962)

In the same study, 66 percent of the sixty-five-and-older population stated that they never, or very rarely ever, were lonely or experienced feelings of loneliness.

The elderly do not see themselves as lonely for a number of reasons. Remember that frequent contact between elderly people and members of their immediate family is the rule rather than an exception within our society. Contrary to the beliefs of some people, it is unusual for an older person to be abandoned by family members, to be forgotten, ignored, and rarely, if ever, visited.

In addition to family, friends are of significant importance in helping the elderly ward off loneliness. According to a Harris study (1974, 105), approximately 50 percent of the surveyed older population said they spent a "lot of time" socializing with friends. Only 5 percent of the sixty-five-and-older population perceived "not enough friends" as a serious problem.

In addition to family and friends, volunteer organizations, social clubs, church or synagogue groups, and community activities are instrumental in preventing loneliness or isolation in old age (Hausknecht 1962).

> MYTH 10:   As people become older, they are likely to become
>   more religious.

Religion is such a pervasive and universal phenomenon that every society from earliest times has had some system of religious beliefs and practices.

The Neanderthal burial sites dating back more than 100,000 years reveal that the departed were supplied with tools for the afterlife. Though made of stone and certainly not as elaborate as those of King Tut, they attest to the presence of a form of religion even then.

When King Tutankhamun's tomb was discovered in the 1920s, the world was awed by the magnificent 3,300-year-old treasures that it contained. Among the gilt and gold objects were amulets to protect the king in his travels through the underworld, as well as tools to do any labor the gods might assign him.

Old age has characteristically been associated with religion in many primitive societies. The elderly were peculiarly qualified to perform a leading role in the religious life of preliterate people for three reasons:

1. Because they have lived so long, older people had the opportunity to accumulate a vast knowledge of religious affairs and practices.
2. Since it had been generally accepted that they would soon be spirits themselves, they were the logical go-between in this world to the next.
3. Survival to a great age was uncommon enough to seem unnatural or even supernatural.

The tendency to visualize deities or religious figures as old people occurs throughout history. Even the word *priest* comes from a Greek word *presbyteros,* meaning elder.

When compared with the present younger generations, we find that older people were more religious in their youth, received more religious training as they grew up, and have continued on a religious path established during the early or formative years of their lives (Baldzar and Palmore 1976).

Differences in religious expression appear to be generational rather than age-related.

MYTH 11:   Old age is generally a time of serenity.

In contrast to previous myths, which view the elderly in a negative light, the myth of serenity portrays old age as a kind of adult fairyland. Now, at last, comes a time of peace and serenity, when people can relax and enjoy the fruits of their labors after the storms of active life are over.

Novels, magazine stories, television, and advertising slogans keep this myth before the public eye. Younger generations cherish visions of carefree, cookie-baking grandmothers and fishing grandfathers.

However, with increased public awareness of the problems many elderly people in our society face, the myth of the golden years and serenity of old age is fast losing ground. The adult fairyland is quickly giving way to a more realistic assessment of the realities many members of the older population endure, such as poverty, fear of crime, lack of transportation, grief, physical disease, bodily decline, dramatic changes in life-style, loss of social power, and decline in status.

No other age group faces and endures stresses and traumas comparable to those faced and endured by the elderly. Such stresses are internal and external, physical and psychological, social and economic. Many stresses the elderly face can be lessened through effective social intervention, although at times this may prove an extremely difficult and even impossible undertaking.

Within the United States, the aged make up about 11 percent of the population, yet 25 percent of all suicides are committed by individuals who are sixty-five years and over (Resnik and Cantor 1970). By itself, this statistic should effectively do away with the myth of serenity in old age.

The elderly are expected, even required, by society to be a shining example of all the virtues. Above all, they are called on to display serenity; the world states that they do possess it, and this statement allows the world to ignore their unhappiness.

BIOLOGICAL MYTHS ABOUT AGING

Biological myths are no less debilitating than the social and psychological myths. They may, however, be the cause of more physical suffering than would be necessary if the elderly were treated more as persons or patients rather than as old persons or old patients.

> MYTH 12: Retirement has a negative effect on health and in some instances can lead to premature death.

One of the most popular beliefs about retirement is that it has a negative effect on health and in some instances can lead to a premature death. It is generally assumed that the sudden stopping of a pattern of high activity and the shift to a slower pace at retirement contribute to physical decline. Stories are common about people who worked day and night and then several months after retirement, died suddenly.

It is true that the change from an organized and structured work week to a life of enforced idleness is a shock that weighs more heavily on aging workers than all the other pressures resulting from retirement, unless the individuals are properly prepared for this new mode of living. When mandatory retirement was first instituted, there was no preparation of any kind although warning signals for the danger it threatened already existed. During the Depression, it has been observed that the prolonged inactivity of the unemployed workers was more demoralizing— weakening the spirit more—than their resulting poverty.

Although the retirement population does contain a large number of people in poor health, retirement did not cause their health to decline. They retired because they were in poor health. Poor health is the main reason people give for taking early or voluntary retirement.

Regular activity is essential in the life of every individual for the maintenance of the emotional and physical balance that safeguards our health throughout our work life, not just old age.

Freud explained that no other mode of living ties the individual so firmly to the realities of life as does work. Through work, a person becomes an integral—necessary for completeness—part of society. The value of work is made greater by the possibility it offers of expressing one's drives and instincts. Work helps maintain emotional balance without giving rise to guilt feelings.

Many people say that when they retire, all they want to do is do nothing. People who desire such a retirement have usually had hard lives in which they had to do heavy manual labor. No wonder that doing nothing is their dream of freedom. Yet even if they do carry out this dream, they probably will sit on a bench and actively watch the world go by, and not, as a rule, sit in their room isolated from the life around them. After they have done enough nothing, they will gradually begin to participate again actively in social life.

MYTH 13:   Medical problems in the elderly are assumed to be the inevitable consequences of aging.

Persons aged sixty-five and older are subject to more than twice as much disability, have four times the activity limitation, and see physicians 42 percent more often.

(U.S. Senate 1984, 58)

Such figures can start a myth. However, some additional facts, if read as carefully, can dispel the myth.

Eighty-two percent of people sixty-five and older reported no hospitalization in the previous year.

In 1980, the average length of a hospital stay for all ages was 7.3 days.
In 1980, the average length of a hospital stay for those people sixty-five and older was 10.7 days.

(U.S. Senate 1984, 70)

Aging is a natural process. Physical aging is not simultaneous with chronological aging. The myth associated with aging is that of a disease process added on top of natural aging. Life is a progressive experience from birth to death. Aging takes place in all body structures, beginning very early in life but at a very individual rate. Body functions generally slow down but are still adequate to maintain a fruitful life.

Perhaps what is most often mistaken for illness due to old age are the scores of treatable causes of confusion.

> *Example:* A confused older person is brought into a hospital emergency room in the middle of the night. His confusion prompts a casual diagnosis of senility. He is sent home in the care of a relative.

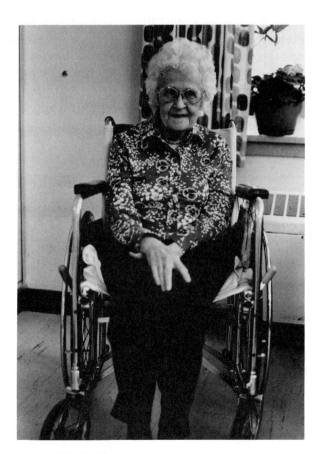

FIGURE 10.5

Instead, this example was of a misdiagnosed infection. Antibiotics could have easily cleared up the infection and the confusion. In this case, origin of the misdiagnosis of senility is not in the elderly patient but in the ageist physician.

Misuse of prescription drugs also creates medical problems that are automatically associated with aging. The size of the problem is suggested by the fact that studies show, on the average, that a person over sixty-five years of age uses at least thirteen prescription drugs a year (American Association of Retired Persons 1984, 9). Drug misuse among the elderly, including taking the wrong dose, drug sharing, and taking drugs that work against one another, each year costs 50,000 lives and 21 billion dollars.

MYTH 14:   Old age is sexless.

Within our society are unfortunate but strong beliefs that sexuality is the exclusive right of youth and that sexual activities, when engaged in by older adults, are inappropriate behaviors. Such beliefs are often accepted by old and young alike and play an important role in determining how older adults are seen by others and how they look at themselves. To believe that our sexuality is lost with the coming of old age is to accept the idea that with advanced age individuals lose a significant portion of their humanity.

> To become sexless is to become less than human!

The myth of lost sexuality in old age is mentally harmful. If older individuals believe that sexual activities are abnormal or impossible, they may unnecessarily become resigned to a life without sexual fulfillment. Moreover, should they continue to engage in sexual activities, they may suffer feelings of guilt, depression, and a loss of self-esteem.

Studies by Masters and Johnson (1966, 1970) found that individuals possess the capacity for sexual fulfillment beyond the eighty-year age level. Four factors that contributed to successful sexual behavior in later maturity were:

1. Physical health.
2. A feeling of psychological well-being.

3. The availability of a willing partner.
4. A history of interest in and enjoyment of sexual activities.

Conversely, factors that contributed to unsuccessful sexual behavior in old age were identified. Among them were:

1. Monotony or boredom with the same partner.
2. Mental or physical fatigue.
3. Fear of failure.
4. Overindulgence in food and drink.

As one examines the variables that contribute to either successful or unsuccessful sexual behavior in later maturity, it becomes obvious that these reasons do not differ much from those that affect successful sexual functioning during adolescence and early and middle adulthood.

> Rustam Mamedor (142 years old) and his wife (116 years old) live in the Caucasus region of the USSR. Their youngest son was born when Rustam was 107 and his wife was 84 years old.

MYTH 15:   If people live long enough, they will become senile.

You can stay mentally young for a lifetime. This is not just a lot of unproven, cotton-candy optimism. More than two decades of studies from the University of California have shattered many negative myths about the aging brain.

First: An aging brain does not necessarily have to be a declining brain.
Second: The brain does not lose thousands of cells daily.
Third: In a stimulating environment, the brain can actually grow in size as we add years.

Testing rats as old as 900 days (the equivalent of 100 to 110 years of age in human beings), it was found that the main ingredients to keeping the brain young are remaining stimulated and having companionship (Ubell 1986).

What have the minds of rats to do with those of human beings? A great deal. Brains are clusters of nerve cells, and nerve cells are nerve cells, no matter whose.

In one study of rats that were almost 100 years old in human terms, part of the groups were placed in large enclosures where they could interact with twelve other rats. This environment was enriched with new toys provided every day.

The other part of the group, fed the same food and water, remained alone in their small, sterile cages. These unstimulated rats without companions moped and aged almost visibly. The others who were curious about their toys, played with them, and seemingly looked forward to the next day's new playthings, did not age visibly.

The stimulated rats measured as having about 6 percent more brain cells and approximately 9 percent less lipofusin-age pigment causing liver spots and aging pigment in the cerebral cortex—the layer of gray matter over most of the brain.

Nerve cells are designed to receive stimuli and will do so at any age. The brain will actually increase in physical size when responding to stimulation and challenge.

Only about 2 to 3 percent of people sixty-five and older develop symptoms associated with senility and are institutionalized for mental illness (Busse and Pfeiffer 1977). The moral about brain power? "Use it and you won't lose it!" Senility, if it were eliminated from the American language, would, by its absence, create a healthier outlook at the process of aging.

MYTH 16:   Older people complain the most about their health.

Hypochondriacs are just as apt to be young people, according to a recent study conducted by federal government aging experts. A nineteen-year follow-up study of 900 men at the National Institute on Aging's Gerontology Research Center found that older people who make excessive and/or exaggerated medical complaints probably have been making them their whole lives.

SUMMARY

Myths, in the minds of people, have the strength of facts but only the reliability of a rumor. The sixteen popular myths discussed in this chapter have been kept alive even though there is little or no basis for them to be believed. The grave danger is that if they are kept alive, they will be on hand negatively to affect the thinking and lives of the next generation. The generation that feeds them as youth must be prepared to digest them as senior citizens.

EXERCISES

1. Select the myth you would like to destroy before you are old enough to become its victim. Research it and present it so convincingly that your audience not only accepts your facts but also becomes active in changing public opinion.
2. List the myths about aging of which you are aware but that were not dealt with in this chapter. Add them to a class list and discuss whether any of them are valid or if they should join the list of sixteen that are not based on fact but on fiction.
3. Interview a minimum of three young children. Ask them what they think getting old will be like. Note carefully what they say and determine how many of their beliefs about aging are based on the myths you have read about and discussed.
4. Consider each of the facts about aging that are universally accepted. Do any of those facts support negative beliefs about aging? Are any of them the reason a particular myth remains so strong in the minds of both young and old? Support your answer with facts.

REVIEW

1. Define myth.
2. Explain its effects on society.
3. Can a nursing home meet all the needs of an elderly person?
4. Are the majority of elderly people ignored or neglected by their family?
5. What are the expectations of the elderly?
6. List the five styles of grandparenting and explain their differences.
7. What is the age phenomenon that is occurring in grandparenthood and great-grandparenthood?
8. Define homogeneous and heterogeneous as they refer to the aging population.
9. Is creativity age-related?
10. Who is more intelligent, a young person or an old person?
11. How differently does society perceive the isolation and loneliness of the elderly in comparison to how they see themselves?
12. Explain the statement, "Religion appears to be generational rather than age-related."
13. Is paid employment essential to the mental and physical health of an individual?
14. List the facts about aging that are universally accepted.

RECOMMENDED READINGS AND REFERENCES

American Association of Retired Persons. *Prescription Drugs: A Survey of Consumer Use, Attitudes, and Behavior.* Washington, D.C., 1984.

Baldzar, D., and E. Palmore. "Religion and Aging in a Longitudinal Panel." *Gerontologist* 16 (1976): 186-89.

Blenkner, Margaret. "Environmental Change and the Aging Individual." *Gerontologist* 7 (1967): 101-105.

Burns, George. *How to Live to Be 100.* New York: New American Library, 1983.

Busse, E. W., and E. Pfeiffer, eds. *Behavior and Adaptation in Later Life.* Boston: Little, Brown and Co., 1977.

Butler, Robert N. *Why Survive?* New York: Harper & Row Publishers, Inc., 1975.

Cutler, S., and R. Kaufman. "Cohort Changes in Political Attitudes." *Public Opinion Quarterly* 39 (1975): 6-7.

Dean, L. "Aging and Decline of Affect." *Journal of Gerontology* 17 (1962): 206-207.

Downs, Hugh. *Thirty Dirty Lies about Old.* Niles, Ill.: Argus Communications, 1979.

Fox, Nancy Littell. "Sex in the Nursing Home? For Lord's Sake, Why Not?" *Registered Nurse,* October 1980, 89-91.

Harris, Louis, and associates. "Widowhood, Morale, and Affiliation." *Journal of Marriage and Family* 36 (1974): 97-106.

Hausknecht, M. *The Joiners.* New York: Bedminster Press, 1962.

Hayes, Helen. *A Gift of Joy.* Philadelphia: J. B. Lippincott Company, 1965.

McKensie, Sheila C. *Aging and Old Age.* Glenview, Ill.: Scott, Foresman & Co., 1980.

Maddox, G., and E. Douglas. "Aging and Individual Differences." *Journal of Gerontology* 29 (1974): 80-81.

Masters, W. H., and V. E. Johnson. *Human Sexual Inadequacy.* Boston: Little, Brown and Co., 1970.

————. *Human Sexual Response.* Boston: Little, Brown and Co., 1966.

Neugarten, B. L., and K. K. Weinstein. "The Changing American Grandparent." *Journal of Marriage and Family* 26 (1964): 266-73.

Reader's Digest. "Quotations," June 1978, 89.

Resnick, H. L. P., and J. M. Cantor. "Suicide and Aging." *Journal of the American Geriatrics Society* 18 (1970): 103-107.

Ubell, Earl. "How Science Is Learning to Understand Your Brain." *Parade Magazine,* February 11, 1986, 3-4.

U.S. Senate Special Committee on Aging. *Aging America: Trends and Projections.* Washington, D.C., 1984.

CHAPTER

11

Reality of Our Aging

Learning Objectives

After studying this chapter, the reader should be able to:

- Look realistically at one's own aging process.
- Prepare for one's own aging with an air of optimism.
- Create changes in society's negative view of aging now so that one's years as an elderly person will be lived in an atmosphere of positive acceptance.
- Establish the personal qualities now that make adaptation to all of life's changes a challenge rather than a crisis.

> If you want to know what you'll be like when you're older, it's as you are *now* and a *whole lot more!*

Preview

There are many ways to view and prepare for one's own aging. When studying gerontology, we look at aging as a group phenomenon. In this chapter, we want to see how the many great events, those unique in terms of personal history, contribute to the individual's aging process. The chapter looks at what makes *our* aging experience subjective and different from anyone else's. For a time, the text sounds like a gerontologist dealing with not simply the fact of growing older but rather the fact of *our* getting older in a special, unique way. Aging is a mystery story, and each one of us is both the author and a character in our own story with a major role to play. "And if you have constructed the world that permits you to live a tranquil, dignified, and enjoyable life, you will be admired not only for a great performance, but for writing a last act that plays so well" (Skinner and Vaughan 1983, 153).

AGING: A PROCESS

> "Birth is only one particular step in a continuum which begins with conception and ends with death. All that is between these two poles is a process of giving birth to one's potentialities, of bringing to life all that is potentially given in the two cells . . . the development of the self is never completed; even under the best conditions only part of man's potentialities is realized. Man always dies before he is fully born."
>
> (Fromm 1947, 91)

Aging is a process. It is a lifelong process. It is a complex, multidimensional process, and each aging person brings to it a unique history.

An excellent example of the unique experiences of aging can be found in a picturelogue following the events in the life of a person who has lived more than 100 years (Figure 11.1). Such a person, in 1875, would have been four years old when the electric light bulb was invented in 1879 and twenty-eight when the Wright brothers flew in 1903. He would

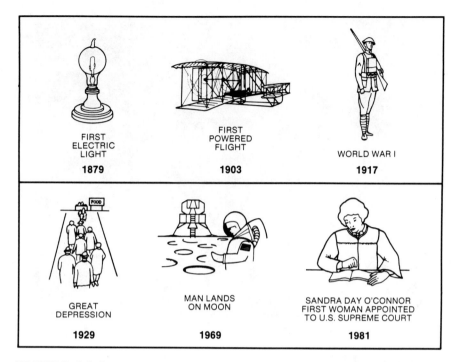

FIGURE 11.1
Historic events during the lifetime of a person who has lived more than 100 years

have been forty-one when the U.S. entered World War I in 1917 and fifty-four when the Great Depression hit in 1929. Although the light bulb was invented when he was four, he would have been forty-seven before he saw an electric light. Incredibly, at age ninety-four, he would have watched the first man land on the moon in 1969.

PERSONAL HISTORY

"Aging is a normal part of life. To not have an interest in it would mean not to have an interest in life itself."
(Rosalynn Carter 1984, 108)

What kind of person were we five, ten, twenty years ago? Where were we then? What took place in that time period that influenced the kind of

FIGURE 11.2

people we are now? Answers to these types of questions can begin to give us insights into the impact of our aging and its effect on our personality.

As in all gerontological studies, we must look at our aging from all aspects:

1. Biologically.
2. Sociologically.
3. Psychologically.
4. Historically.
5. Environmentally.

We must also look at these aspects over that period of five, ten, or twenty years. During that time, there have been positive and negative experiences. Some experiences built self-confidence; some tore it down. There were moments of peak experience and those of boredom. All these experiences had an impact on the person we are today.

Some of those past experiences happened to us, and others we made happen. To whatever degree we are master of our own destiny, we must examine our past experiences as they acted on us and as we reacted to them.

OUR BIOLOGICAL AGING

> "If you are smart and manage to stay healthy, you'll also stay smart, although it may take you longer to demonstrate that fact at sixty-five than it did at twenty-five, and the print in which the questions are written may need to be larger."
>
> (Ward Edwards, as quoted in Comfort 1976, 183)

We look very different now than we did five, ten, twenty years ago. Virtually every aspect of our biology has changed. Cosmetic changes such

FIGURE 11.3
"To put it bluntly, Doc, if our lives depended on your ability to play bridge, none of us'd live to see our old age." (© 1986 by Bill Haas. Used with permission.)

as weight, hair color, shape, and general appearance have changed. Even such things as diet, sleep patterns, physical health, and stamina may have changed.

OUR SOCIOLOGICAL AGING

Our age change has also brought about a different response from society. Age brings about different positions, status, and expectations in our society. We may no longer be a child, a teen, an employee, dependent, single, or the responsibility of someone else. Rather, we may now be employed and in a position of being responsible for other people. Our whole basis of emotional support may have changed. Other people may now expect different behavior patterns from us, and we may, in fact, expect them of ourselves.

Our life experiences have consciously or unconsciously brought about our socialization. Through this socialization process, we have learned the attitudes, values, beliefs, knowledge, and skills that have allowed us to become an accepted member of society. The socialization of people twenty years ago was quite different than it is today. The socialization of our parents may have meant living without telephones, televisions, airplanes, automobiles, running water, or electricity. They certainly did not get a computer for Christmas!

Socialization began in our childhood and is a never-ending process. The degree of our socialization is age-related. As we age, we are being socialized to new positions with new role expectations. Age roles differ from culture to culture and decade to decade. Even in our retirement and old age, society will expect age-related behavior. Our response to society's expectations and to our own will determine how well we have adjusted to our own aging.

OUR PSYCHOLOGICAL AGING

> "Youth is the time of getting, middle age of improving and old age of spending; a negligent youth is usually attended by an ignorant middle age and both by an empty old age."
>
> (Anne Bradstreet as quoted in Comfort 1976, 179)

FIGURE 11.4

Regardless of our present age, we are unique and can be fully understood only in the context of that uniqueness. What can we list as the five adjectives that best describe us right now? Will the following adjectives describe us when we are old?:

1. Obstinate.
2. Skeptical.
3. Forgetful.
4. Wise.
5. Patient.

Do We Change?

Will the fact that we are getting older bring about these personality changes in us? Perhaps the question stated in a more general way is, "Do old people get obstinate, or do obstinate people get old?" Obviously, personality is a lifelong process. There are age-related changes that happen at *all* ages. Also, to separate the changes in personality that come from social, biological, or environmental factors is nearly impossible. To determine what psychological changes occur as a result of aging has been a subject of intense research.

Do We Have Anything in Common?

Even though each individual brings a personal uniqueness into the aging process, there also are common features with regard to aging among all human beings. Six general findings concerning the old and retired are (Kalish 1975):

1. They appear to be somewhat more cautious and less impulsive.
2. They appear to be more rigid and less flexible.
3. They are more often depressed.
4. They have greater ego strength.
5. They have fewer fixed defenses.
6. They are more open and trusting.

It is not difficult to find another dozen studies that will give conflicting statements. Researchers would perhaps unanimously agree with the following statements:

1. There are no age-related characteristics that can be applied to every elderly person.
2. Even though aging is universal, the manner in which aging affects the individual is not.

OUR AGING HISTORICALLY

What was the world doing five, ten, or twenty years ago? Where and who experienced war, famine, peace, and scandal? Who and what entered the world of politics, technology, and ecology? The world at large has changed and taken on many new forms. What of our personal world? We may be at a new address, in touch with new friends, or have started a new career. What of our losses: family, friends, jobs, and material things?

These same forces bring about age-related changes at any time in one's life cycle. They differ according to the time in our life when they occur. Our world and the world in general will still be at work creating changes when we are twenty, forty, seventy-five, and one hundred. Will we be a geriactivist: a person who even when sixty-five and older will actively work to make changes that will make aging an even more positive experience for ourselves and for future generations?

OUR AGING ENVIRONMENTALLY

What and whom we surround ourselves with are matters of choice. Early in our life, we found meaningful activities or relationships that compensated for whatever changes we were required to make. That ability to adjust is not confined to the under sixty-five crowd. That capability is not lost with aging as is any other personality characteristic cultivated throughout life. In fact, once we have reached retirement age, even society allows us to indulge in fancies it may have frowned on earlier, such as taking it easy or spending a forty-hour week encouraging our rose bushes to produce. Research has shown that people, as they age, continue to follow the patterns of activity that have brought them satisfaction in the past. Younger people and older people choose the combinations of activities that offer them the most ego-involvement and are consistent with their long-established value patterns.

> For age is opportunity no less
> Than youth itself, though in another dress,
> And as the evening twilight fades away
> The sky is filled with stars, invisible by day.
> (Henry Wadsworth Longfellow from "Morituri Salutamus")

AGING: OUR ATTITUDE

> If what the future holds closely resembles what we wished it held, then our aging is but a reflection of our attitudes toward aging and old age.

How does our attitude compare with the simple lessons that follow?

LESSON 1: Aging has no effect on us as a person.

When we are old, we will feel no different and be no different from what we are now. What has changed is the amount of accumulated experience. While aging, our appearance will change. We may gradually encounter more physical problems. When we do, these will affect us only as physical problems affect a person of any age. An aged person is simply a person who has lived longer than a young person.

FIGURE 11.5
(From **Geriatrics: A Study of Maturity,** *4th ed., by*
Esther Caldwell and Barbara R. Hegner, copyright ©
1986 by Delmar Publishers Inc.)

> Senator Edward Kennedy adds: "I believe that individuals who have met the challenges of making a living for themselves and their families, who have raised their children and helped their neighbors and who have observed and participated in the many activities of citizenship are deserving of our care and our respect. They have the rich experience, deep perspective and thoughtful vision of the future that America must listen to, and treasure. These elderly citizens possess an important part of our heritage, our culture, and our collective wisdom."
>
> (Senator Edward Kennedy, letter to author, February 25, 1985)

LESSON 2:   Oldness is a political and social institution.

Oldness is based on a system that excludes people from useful work after a set number of years. This institution is supported by a collection of devastating myths. These untruths are used falsely to label the old as weak-minded and incompetent. This, in turn, makes society feel justified in forcing the old out of the work force. The unemployed elderly are made to appear weak-minded and incompetent because they are not involved in gainful employment, which is the vicious circle that keeps the myths alive.

LESSON 3:   Retirement is another name for unjust dismissal.

This forced unemployment must be prepared for and handled psychologically and economically exactly as we would prepare for any job dismissal. It is a fact that unemployment could be a realistic happening.

FIGURE 11.6
Senator Edward M. Kennedy

FIGURE 11.7

LESSON 4:   Old age is automatic membership in an underprivi-
leged minority.

This fact is difficult to accept, but it is a fact nonetheless. If this is
going to cease being a fact, then one cannot wait to get old before taking
action to change it. The remedies may be those available to any other
minority: organizing, protesting, and refusal to believe that this is how it
has to be. The best time to start changing that fact is now.

> "Old age is honored only on condition that it defends itself,
> maintains its rights, is subservient to no one, and to its last breath rules
> over its own domain."
>
> (Cicero, as quoted in Fischer 1978, 15)

LESSON 5:   At a set age, you will be deprived of nearly one-half
your income.

We will be poorer than we think at a time when we need more than
we do now. Being poor will also come at a time when we are no longer

able, through employment, to increase that income. Not only will this prove to be an economic hardship, but a psychological one as well. We will have become accustomed to that higher level of income. Financial planning is just as important as planning for any other facet of aging.

LESSON 6: Do not anticipate illness or inability as a natural fact of aging.

Youth does not have a lock on zest for life. Our memory, desire for activity, capacity for relationships, and our sexuality are ours to have and keep. They are treasures and should be treated as such. Do not plan on losing them or giving them away. Should we lose them, it will be for the same reason that people of any other age do—illness.

LESSON 7: Science still has many solutions to offer.

An increase in longevity and cures for major killers of the body and mind are offerings science will continue to make. Science holds the key for giving us life not only in greater quantities but also with greater quality. It is not likely that aging will ever be abolished or reversed, but it is not impractical to believe that it will be slowed. How soon this will happen depends on society's investment in the sciences and on individual prudence.

LESSON 8: Society gives us the title of *old,* which we all too willingly accept.

Society bestows the title of *old* to its members and then defines the title in negative terms. Society does this to an ever increasing percentage of its population (20 percent by the year 2000). Perhaps when society's numbers of old get large enough, they will, as a group, refuse to accept that new title and insist on keeping the one they had bestowed on them at birth—*people* or *persons.* When this happens, there will be a significant change in their treatment as well.

"Many people start experiencing themselves as old when certain institutional arrangements, such as mandatory retirement, place them outside the circle of those who identify themselves primarily with what they do, have, or can acquire."

(Nouwen and Gaffney 1974, 30)

LESSON 9:   Aging is not a radical change.

Aging is a gradual, imperceptible change. We will not become a different person. A sixty-fifth birthday is like any other of the sixty-four we had—it is a social reason for a party. Our physical, social, and psychological needs do not change. If there are changes, it is because we choose to let them be so.

> "I see people who, the minute they get to be sixty-five, start rehearsing to be old. They start taking little steps, they practice grunting when they sit down and grunting when they get up, they drop food on themselves, they take little naps when you're talking to them, and by the time they get to be seventy they've made it—they're a hit—they're now old!"
>
> (Burns 1983, 131)

LESSON 10:   An old person needs four things:
1. Dignity.
2. Money.
3. Useful work.
4. Medical services.

These are the things we have always needed. They are also things to which everyone has a right. No title can deny anyone the dignity these bring. We must begin now to see that we get them and begin now to ensure that they cannot be taken away.

FEAR OF THE UNKNOWN

An accusing finger cannot be fairly pointed at us for wanting to keep distance between ourselves and the idea of becoming old. Nor can we be blamed for not spending time trying to understand aging when society has placed it before us in a negative light. Try as we may, we cannot project ourselves into the future, neither our own or anyone else's. We can separate human development into phases and come to understand those we have been through. Childhood, for example, we can understand because there are some situations that we have all shared. As a result, we can at least put ourselves in someone else's shoes. These types of common

FIGURE 11.8

experiences form a basis for much of our communication. If we could not share these common life experiences, life would be much like what Shylock expresses in Shakespeare's *The Merchant of Venice:*

> Hath not a Jew eyes? Hath not a Jew hands, organs, dimensions, senses, affection, passions, fed with the same food, hurt with the same weapons, subject to the same diseases, healed by the same means, warmed and cooled by the winter and summer, as a Christian is? If you prick us, do we not bleed? If you tickle us, do we not laugh? If you poison us, do we not die? And if you wrong us, shall we not revenge?
>
> (Act III, scene 1)

Substituting the words *aged* for *Jew* and *the rest of the population* for *Christian* may, better than any other way, express the present-day position of the aged (Knopf 1975, 6). If we can understand all the phases of human development, then we can put ourselves into their shoes and walk an understanding mile.

FIGURE 11.9
Senator Rudy Boschwitz

The Future: Always a Mystery?

To project into the future is still an impossibility. We have never gone from old to young so that we could use that experience to prepare for our own aging. Neither can we compare being young with being old. Each experience is unique, and comparisons are futile. Our plans for the future, at best, are made up of hopes and dreams, many of which cannot or will not be realized.

> "No one can decide for anyone else how his or her aging shall or should be. It belongs to the greatness of men and women that the meaning of their existence escapes the power of calculations and predictions."
>
> (Nouwen and Gaffney 1974, 86)

Young and Old, Together

How, then, do the young come to understand the old and their own aging? How do we put the myths to rest forever and view aging in a realistic manner without aversion or fear? History holds an answer. Let the old live among us, unsegregated, so that we may communicate with them, share their aging with them. If we can economically prepare for our aging by listening to a banker, physically prepare for our aging by listening to a nutritionist, can we not psychologically prepare for aging by listening and living with old people? We have used technological science to try to solve the problems of overpopulation, food shortages, energy crises, inflation, environmental pollution, and the threat of nuclear war. Now, we need to take the time to use human science to solve the problems of fear; isolation; indifference; human need for love, conversation, touch, and renewal of the belief that life includes the whole human life span.

> "Most elderly people have a great deal to contribute to society. My own father, for example, who lived to be 95, continued working until he was 90, so I'm familiar with the contributions people can make even after others urge them to 'slow down!' Also, besides the work that they do, the elderly make a unique contribution to society simply by their presence. Aging is a process of both losing some of the strengths of youth and gaining some strengths that only come with age—such as wisdom, understanding, and historical perspective. I hope we never lose our perspective on the contributions of the elderly and our respect and appreciation for them."
> (Senator Rudy Boschwitz, letter to author, February 28, 1985)

WHO ARE THE AGED?

They are the educated and they are the simple,
They are wealthy and they are on welfare,
They are part of life and they are isolated,
They are well and they are desperately ill,
They are productive and they are dependent,
They are warm and they are mean.   (Smith 1973, xi)

And this author hastens to add:

They are *them* and they will be *us!*

FIGURE 11.10

SUMMARY

One lesson to be learned from studying the lives of other people is that every age has something special to offer. If we long to be older and more experienced, if we crave eternal youth or look back to the good old days, then we fail to live in the present, our present, and to use it to the fullest.

We must take a close look at our own aging and the aging of others. There is a call for American people to look for new answers to solve society's perplexities. We must ask new questions because our old questions receive the same old answers. Age is the crowning culmination of life—the golden years. We and society should look on it with honor, respect, and perhaps even awe. If the elderly themselves look on aging in that light but society does not, then the problem is with society, not with the elderly. The truth is that we are society and we will someday be the elderly.

EXERCISES

1. Select a symbol for your youth and what you believe will be an appropriate symbol for your old age. Write an explanation of why you have chosen each symbol to represent those two periods of your life.
2. List your three greatest fears of aging and three things you most look forward to when you get old. For each of the six items listed, do some solution thinking; list ways to prevent the negatives and ensure the positives.
3. Determine what you believe to be society's most urgent needs in order to deal positively with the growing population of the elderly. If you were the president of the United States, what federal laws would you propose to ensure every American of a fulfilling life after age sixty-five?
4. Beginning with your year of birth, indicate your age at the time of important historic events that have happened up to the present.

Year	Your Age	Event

REVIEW

1. What is meant by the statement, "Aging is a process"?
2. List the five facets from which we must view our own aging. Describe each facet.
3. What does the socialization process give us?
4. Does old age bring about basic personality changes?
5. Define geriactivist.
6. Recall the ten concepts against which you can test your attitude toward your own aging.
7. How do myths play a role in ageism?
8. List the four needs of an elderly person.

9. What was Shylock's contemporary message to society in Shakespeare's play *The Merchant of Venice?*
10. Can we foresee our own aging future?

RECOMMENDED READINGS AND REFERENCES

Burns, George. *How to Live to Be 100.* New York: New American Library, 1983.

Carter, Rosalynn. *First Lady from Plains.* Thorndike, Me.: Thorndike Press, 1984.

Comfort, Alexander. *A Good Age.* New York: Crown Publishers, Inc., 1976.

Fischer, David H. *Growing Old in America.* New York: Oxford University Press, 1978.

Fromm, Erich. *Man for Himself.* New York: Rinehart and Company, 1947.

Kalish, Richard A. *Late Adulthood: Perspectives of Human Development.* Monterey, Calif.: Brooks/Cole, 1975.

Knopf, Olga. *The Facts and Fallacies of Growing Old.* New York: Viking Press, 1975.

Monk, Abraham. *The Age of Aging.* Buffalo, N.Y.: Prometheus Books, 1979.

Nouwen, Henri J. M., and Walter J. Gaffney. *Aging, the Fulfillment of Life.* Garden City, N.Y.: Image Books, 1974.

Rose, Helen. *Begin to Live.* New York: St. Martin's Press, 1979.

Skinner, B. B., and M. E. Vaughan. *Enjoy Old Age.* New York: Warner Books, 1983.

Smith, Bert Kruger. *Aging in America.* Boston: Beacon Press, 1973.

Smith, Richard Knox. *49 and Holding.* New York: The Two Continents Publishing Group, 1975.

CHAPTER
12

Careers in Gerontology

Learning Objectives

After studying this chapter, the reader should be able to:

- Realize the variety of occupations available to anyone interested in the field of gerontology.
- Determine the qualifications required for different gerontological careers.
- Decide if any one of the careers is of specific personal interest.
- Write to a variety of sources to obtain additional information.

Preview

The increase in the elderly population has placed great pressure on American society to expand and improve services to people in this age group. Of particular importance are services that help people deal with the stresses that so often accompany aging.

This chapter provides a brief description, including educational requirements, of career occupations in the field of aging. These particular occupations, as researched by the U.S. Department of Labor and the U.S. Department of Health and Human Services, are representative of many that have been expanded to assist the elderly. The numbers in parentheses at the end of each occupational description correspond to the organizations listed at the end of this chapter, which the reader may find useful.

THE CHANGING NEEDS OF THE ELDERLY PERSON

Being old can mean dwindling finances, unfamiliar legal or financial situations, different housing needs, and fewer close contacts as contemporaries move away or die. By the time people reach their late seventies or eighties, illness or infirmity almost inevitably becomes a problem. Most people eventually need some kind of help, which may range from the informal assistance of neighbors who take turns staying with a newly bereaved widow, to organized programs of health and social services, complete with facilities, equipment, and staff.

VARIETY OF SERVICES

More than one million people work with the aged. Many work in nursing homes. Others work in senior centers, social service agencies, home health programs, nutrition projects, legal aid offices, public housing projects, or retirement communities. The concerns of elderly people are important to the people administering such government programs as Social Security, Supplemental Security Income, veterans benefits, and Medicare. State employment offices have older worker specialists, and a growing number of community agencies have employment counselors who specialize in helping older people find employment. Some people plan and coordinate services for the elderly within a particular city, county, or state.

Multidisciplinary Services

This concern with older people extends to other fields. Educators teach courses on aging; researchers in the biomedical and behavioral sciences examine the causes and manifestations of aging; medical doctors deal with the effects of aging and minimizing its consequences; demographers, economists, political scientists, and other men and women study the effects of an aging population on society.

Volunteerism

Another significant way in which people can work with elderly people is through volunteer programs. Volunteering their time has been a good way for many people to become acquainted with the cares and concerns of older people. Volunteers are often indispensable in providing some social services to the elderly. Many older people are able to maintain their independence in their own homes or apartments because volunteers are available for friendly visits, daily telephone reassurance calls, and shop-

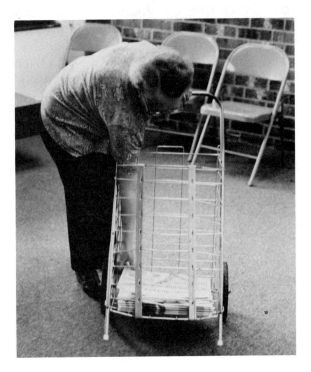

FIGURE 12.1

ping services. Meals-on-Wheels programs run by volunteers deliver nutritious meals to many older people. Transportation has become a major problem for many senior citizens. Volunteers drive them to church, to clinics and doctor's appointments, to stores for shopping, and to recreational events.

NURSES

Nurses, both male and female, provide the largest component of services needed in the delivery of health care to the elderly person. Nurses work in hospitals, nursing homes, home health programs, physicians' offices, clinics, and private duty settings. Nurses who work in this field can be registered nurses, nurse practitioners, or licensed practical nurses.

Registered Nurse (R.N.)

R.N.'s not only care for sick patients, but also promote the physical, mental, and social well-being of people in general. In the care of the aged, they work in various settings, including long-term care, clinics, and visiting nurse agencies, where they apply their knowledge and skill to cope with problems common to aging.

Nurses can train in three ways: a four-year bachelor's degree, or a two-to-three-year hospital diploma program. Associate and diploma graduates are educated to provide traditional technical nursing in health facilities. Their skills include administering medication and treatment prescribed by physicians, monitoring patients' progress, and assisting with intravenous feedings and blood transfusions.

Nurses with the Bachelor of Arts degree are prepared for additional professional roles that may require independent judgment. They may provide such services as health screenings directly to individuals, families, or communities. Health education, counseling, supervision, and administration are among their additional roles.

Geriatric Nurse (G.N.)

G.N.'s are registered nurses who specialize in providing nursing care to older people. This job includes assessing the needs of the elderly person and planning and implementing nursing care to meet the needs. Certification is gained through clinical practice or specialized courses. Graduate programs in geriatric nursing (one to two years) are available. (See 6, 18.)

Nurse Practitioner/Nurse Clinician

These nurses are R.N.'s with special training who provide health services to patients to maintain health, prevent illness, or deal with acute chronic health problems. They can perform physical examinations and diagnostic tests, develop and carry out treatment programs, and counsel patients about their health. In the specialized field of geriatrics, they are mainly concerned with providing maintenance care for the chronically ill.

Some nurse practitioners work independently by opening their own offices or consulting with or referring patients to physicians or other health specialists when necessary. Others work as members of a health team in clinics or other health facilities.

The laws of each state govern what services a nurse practitioner can or cannot perform independently. Training varies widely. Some bachelor's degree programs in registered nursing prepare students to assume roles as nurse practitioners on graduation. Other programs admit registered nurses with training ranging from several months of formal education and clinical experience to a master's degree (See 6, 18.)

Licensed Practical Nurse (L.P.N.)

L.P.N.'s work under the supervision of registered nurses or physicians. They give routine bedside nursing care to patients and assist registered nurses with patients who are more seriously ill. They usually provide specialized care for the elderly in nursing homes.

Generally, training involves a one-year program at a state-approved school of practical nursing. Many programs prefer or require a high school diploma or equivalent. Some other programs admit students with two years of high school or less. (See 15, 17.)

REGISTERED DIETITIAN (R.D.)

Registered dietitians provide nutritional care and dietary counseling. Most of them work in hospitals or doctors' offices; some have private practices. R.D.'s complete a bachelor's degree and an internship (or an

FIGURE 12.2
(From Geriatrics: A Study of Maturity, *4th ed., by*
Esther Caldwell and Barbara R. Hegner, copyright ©
1986 by Delmar Publishers Inc.)

approved, coordinated undergraduate program) and also pass an examination. Medicare generally will not pay for a dietitian's services. However, it does reimburse hospitals and skilled nursing facilities for a portion of dietitians' salaries. (See 6, 11.)

HOMEMAKER HOME HEALTH AIDE

Many elderly people can avoid institutionalization with only a little additional help in their own home. A homemaker home health aide with training in personal care and home maintenance can provide such assistance. The trained aide under the supervision of a county health nurse can perform minimal personal care duties and all of the household chores, such as meal preparation, laundry, and house cleaning. Some states require the completion of sixty hours in vocational training. (See 4, 13.)

PHYSICAL THERAPIST (P.T.)

P.T.'s work with people who have been physically disabled by illness or accident or who were born with a handicap. Some therapists specialize in the care of elderly people with such disabilities as arthritis, loss of limbs, or paralysis. Upon a physician's referral, therapists evaluate the extent of disability and plan a treatment program. Treatment may include exercises to improve muscle strength and coordination, or the application of hot and cold therapy, hydrotherapy, or electrical stimulus to relieve pain or to change the patient's condition.

Physical therapists complete a four-year bachelor's degree in physical therapy. College graduates with degrees in other areas can train in one-to-two-year programs leading to a certificate or a master's degree. (See 8.)

OCCUPATIONAL THERAPIST (O.T.)

O.T.'s help people who have physical, emotional, or developmental disabilities to overcome, correct, or adjust to their particular problem. Therapists may help someone who has become physically disabled relearn such daily living skills as dressing, cooking, and using transportation. They help elderly people adapt to changes resulting from disability or chronic illness.

Therapists complete a four-year bachelor's degree in occupational therapy. College graduates with degrees in other areas can train through a two-year master's degree. (See 7.)

ADMINISTRATORS

Nursing home administrators manage nursing homes and coordinate all necessary services. These persons must establish and maintain close association with civic groups and community health and welfare agencies. Nursing home administrators also work as planners and consultants or as directors of governmental regulatory agencies, neighborhood clinics, and health associations.

Educational requirements for the initial license and its renewal vary greatly among the states. The trend is toward requiring a bachelor's degree. A one-to-two-year master's degree in hospital or health services administration, public health, or public administration is usually required for upper-level management positions in large facilities. Most administrators must be licensed. (See 2, 3, 11.)

PHARMACISTS

Pharmacists are knowledgeable about the chemical makeup and correct use of medicines—their names, ingredients, possible side effects, and uses in the treatment of medical problems. Pharmacists have legal authority to dispense drugs according to formal instructions issued by physicians, surgeons, dentists, or podiatrists. They can also provide information on nonprescription products sold in pharmacies.

Pharmacists must complete five or six years of college, fulfill a practical experience requirement, and pass a state licensure examination to practice. (See 4.)

PSYCHOLOGISTS

Trained psychologists are concerned with the treatment of people with mental and emotional disorders. Psychology is also a research profession. In the field of gerontology, psychologists study the process of aging and the problems of the aged. Psychologists provide counseling and therapy for older people who must cope with stress, depression, and loneliness resulting from the loss of spouse or friends or jobs and income, of health and independence, and of social status and self-esteem.

Education varies. Some positions require a special one-to-two-year master's degree; others almost always require a three-to-four-year Ph.D. degree. (See 9, 14.)

SOCIAL WORKERS

Social workers help elderly people deal with social problems and institutions. They work with individuals, groups, and communities. In a medical setting, they help patients and their families handle problems related to physical or mental illness and disability. Working in the community, social workers assist residents in finding employment or housing and in initiating community projects. The social worker frequently provides the link between an older person and the complex and often confusing array of services designed to provide help.

Specific four-year bachelor's degree programs prepare students for this career. A two-year master's degree is generally required for advanced and specialized social work. College graduates with degrees in other areas can qualify as social workers by completing the master's degree. (See 12, 16.)

SPEECH-LANGUAGE PATHOLOGISTS

Speech-language pathologists are concerned with speech and language problems. Audiologists are interested in hearing disorders. Some specialists work in both areas. They test and evaluate patients, and they plan therapy to restore as much normal function as possible. Many speech-

FIGURE 12.3

language pathologists work with stroke victims, people who have dementia, patients with diseases of the nervous system, and people who have had their vocal cords removed. Many audiologists work with older people whose hearing may be failing. They recommend hearing aids when needed and sometimes dispense them.

Speech-language pathologists and audiologists have at least a master's degree. Most of them are licensed by the state in which they practice. Medicare generally will cover the services of both. (See 4.)

RECREATION WORKERS

Recreational directors provide creative outlets through recreational activities to fill some of the physical and emotional needs that contribute to the overall well-being of the elderly person. A four-year bachelor's degree in recreation is considered minimum preparation. A one-to-two-year master's degree may be required for many positions. (See 4, 19.)

LIBRARIANS

Local librarians make information available to people. They select and organize books and other materials, make them accessible, and assist in their use. They provide special materials and services to culturally and educationally deprived persons. Librarians provide the elderly and handicapped with such special needs as large print books, books by mail, talking books for the blind, and bookcarts for nursing homes.

A one-year master's degree in library science is usually considered minimum preparation. Doctoral programs in library science also are available. (See 5, 20.)

ARCHITECTS

Architects design a wide variety of structures, such as houses, churches, hospitals, airports, and office buildings, incorporating the physical, psychological, and social needs of clients. Architects express their concern for the elderly by designing facilities to permit the old to be as mobile and physically independent as possible.

There are two educational programs in architecture: a five-year program leading to a bachelor of architecture degree and a six-year curriculum leading to a master of architecture degree. (See 10.)

Keep in mind that this list covers only a few of the many occupations in which people work with the elderly. Information about other employment opportunities can be obtained from the various state agencies on aging. These organizations, as listed, correspond with the numbers provided in parentheses at the end of each occupational description.

ORGANIZATIONS

1. Administration on Aging
   Public Inquiries and Public Distribution Division, Room 4146
   330 Independence Avenue, N.W.
   Washington, DC 20201
2. American Association of Homes for the Aging
   1050 17th Street, N.W.
   Washington, DC 20036
3. American College of Nursing Home Administrators
   4650 East-West Highway
   Washington, DC 20014
4. American Health Care Association
   1200 15th Street, N.W.
   Washington, DC 20005
5. American Library Association
   50 East Huron Street
   Chicago, IL 60611
6. American Nurses' Association
   Careers Program
   2420 Pershing Road
   Kansas City, MO 63119
7. American Occupational Therapy Association
   6000 Executive Blvd., Suite 200
   Rockville, MD 20852
8. American Physical Therapy Association
   1156 15th Street, N.W.
   Washington, DC 20005
9. American Psychological Association
   1200 17th Street, N.W.
   Washington, DC 20036

10. The Association of Collegiate Schools of Architecture, Inc.
    1735 New York Avenue
    Washington, DC 20036
11. Association of University Programs in Health Administration
    1755 Massachusetts Avenue, N.W.
    Washington, DC 20036
12. Council on Social Work Education
    345 East 46th Street
    New York, NY 10017
13. Minnesota State Dept. of Vocational Ed.
    Suite 400
    Capitol Square
    550 Cedar Street
    St. Paul, MN 55101
14. National Association of Mental Health
    1800 North Kent St., Rosslyn Station
    Arlington, VA 22209
15. National Association for Practical Nurse Education and Services
    122 East 42nd Street
    New York, NY 10017
16. National Association of Social Workers
    1425 H Street, N.W.
    Washington, DC 20005
17. National Federation of Licensed Practical Nurses
    250 West 57th Street, Suite 323
    New York, NY 10019
18. National League for Nursing
    10 Columbus Circle
    New York, NY 10019
19. National Recreation and Park Association
    1601 North Kent
    Arlington, VA 22209
20. Special Libraries Association
    235 Park Avenue S.
    New York, NY 10003

RECOMMENDED READINGS AND REFERENCES

Working with Older People. U.S. Department of Labor, Bureau of Labor Statistics, Washington, D.C.
Age Pages. U.S. Department of Health and Human Services, Washington, D.C.

INDEX

Nursing homes, see *Long-term care*
Nutrition, 73, 208-10

Occupational therapists, profession of, 327
Organ transplants, 188
Our aging, 302

PEKKANEN, 268, 270
Peridontal disease, 209
Personal history, 303-4
Personality
  change, 134
  defended, 128
  disorganized, 130
  family and, 130-31
  mature, 127-28
  passive-dependent, 128, 129
Pharmacist, profession of, 328
Physical change and loss
  chronic and acute conditions, 199-202
  illness and function capacity, 112-13
Physical therapist, profession of, 327
Politics, 79-81
Population
  aging, 63-64
  developed versus developing, 64
  geographic location, 65-68
  growth, 62-63
Preretirement, also see *Retirement,* 248-51
Professional guidance, 168-69
Psychological aging, 14
Psychologists, 328

QUITELET, LAMBERT A., 8

RAMSDEN, 268
Recreational directors, profession of, 330
Rejuvenescent theory, 6-7
Religion
  death, 228-29
  myths, 291-92

Remarriage at retirement, 102
Research in gerontology, 8-9
RESNIK AND CANTOR, 292-93
Retirement, see *Preretirement*
  activity theory, 95-96
  ages, 264-65
  attitudes, 251
  definition, 248
  disengagement theory, 94-95
  economics, 268-69
  environmental adjustment theory, 96-98
  forced, 94, 109
  marriage at, 102
  modern concept, 257-59
  social breakdown syndrome, 98
  "Who I Am" versus "What I Do," 246
  work force, 247, 255-56
RILEY, 229
Role confusion, 104-5
Role preparation, 107
RUSSELL, 41

Sandwich generation, 114
SANTROCK, 133
SCHNEIDER, EDWARD, 9
SCHWARTZ, 57, 78, 96, 139
Self-fulfilling prophecies, 27
SELYE, 156
Senescence, defined, 184
Senility, 36, 39, 42, 148-49
Sex roles, 105-6
Sexual behavior in old age, 149, 296-97
SHEEKAN, 211-12
SIMPSON, 223, 227
Single-organ theory, 188
SKINNER, 302
SMITH, 317
Social breakdown syndrome, 98
Social changes on future aging, 115-17
Social environment, no deposit-no return generation, 23
Social interaction, 100
Social role, loss of, 94-95, 104-5